USER'S MANUAL
FOR THE GENERAL INQUIRER

760

A Companion Volume to

The General Inquirer: A Computer Approach to Content Analysis

by

Philip J. Stone, Dexter C. Dunphy, Marshall S. Smith, Daniel M. Ogilvie
with associates

USER'S MANUAL
FOR THE GENERAL INQUIRER

Philip J. Stone
and
Cambridge Computer Associates, Inc.,
John Kirsch, *Technical Editor*

The M.I.T. Press
Massachusetts Institute of Technology
Cambridge, Massachusetts, and London, England

The computer programs documented in this manual have been thoroughly tested and have worked satisfactorily in many runs. However, no guarantee as to the functioning of the programs or the accuracy of related materials is expressed or implied. Please report any errors in the programs or this manual to Cambridge Computer Associates, Inc., 380 Putnam Avenue, Cambridge, Mass. 02139.

Set in IBM Contemporary
and printed and bound in the United States of America
by Wm. J. Keller Inc.

Library of Congress Catalog Card Number: 68-14447

Preface

The purpose of this manual is to provide technical specifications of the computer programs in the General Inquirer content analysis system and detailed instructions for using those programs. With this limited end in view, the manual is intended to serve as a companion volume to an earlier work, *The General Inquirer.*[1] In that work, the issues of designing content analysis research and constructing dictionary categories for content analysis are treated at length and illustrated by reports of studies conducted with the General Inquirer system in various research fields. This manual will become of importance to an investigator when he has already made the fundamental decisions of research design and needs technical information to supplement the general description of the system given in *The General Inquirer.*

The manual is divided into four major parts and a series of appendices. Part One comprises an introduction to the system and specifications for preparing dictionary and text data. In Part Two are described the primary programs for assigning tags to text and performing operations of listing, counting, and retrieval on tagged text. In Part Three, the secondary programs for processing tag scores are described. Part Four is devoted to two types of secondary programs to facilitate the development of dictionary categories–one for generating a key-word-in-context index of a sample of text, the other for displaying a dictionary in a special "cross-sorted" format. In Appendix One are presented all formats in which the various programs record data on magnetic tapes for subsequent processing within the system. The formats of punched cards that are read or generated by more than one program in the

[1] Stone, Philip J., Dexter C. Dunphy, Marshall S. Smith, Daniel M. Ogilvie, with associates, *The General Inquirer: A Computer Approach to Content Analysis* (Cambridge, Mass.: The M.I.T. Press, 1966).

system are specified in Appendix Two. Appendix Three describes standardized error routines that the 1401 programs follow in attempting to process a damaged or defective input tape. Finally, in Appendix Four are described procedures for implementing optional sentence summary routines as part of the program TAGGING.

In Parts Two, Three, and Four, one chapter is devoted to each program, and each chapter is divided into four sections.[2] An initial "operational summary" of the program presents machine requirements, schematics of card decks and tapes, and concise instructions for operating the computer. Then follows an introduction that describes the function of the program and its relation to other programs in the system. In the third section of the chapter, input and output specifications of the program are given in detail. Miscellaneous technical considerations, including the response of the program to possible error conditions, are relegated to a concluding section.

The General Inquirer system was originated by Philip J. Stone and developed for research purposes over the last six years by him and his colleagues at Harvard University–in particular, Dexter C. Dunphy, Marshall S. Smith, and Daniel M. Ogilvie. The bulk of General Inquirer research was supported by grants from the National Institute of Mental Health and the National Science Foundation (NIMH USPH M-4169, NSF GS-178 and GS-1253).

Major contributions to the ideas and strategies that constitute the system were made by: Robert F. Bales, Harvard University; Benjamin N. Colby, Museum of New Mexico; Donald Davis, Harvard University; Bruce Frisbie, University of Chicago; Donald H. Goldhamer, University of Chicago; Aram Grayson, Stanford University; J. Zvi Namenwirth, Yale University; George Psathas, Washington University; and Erik J. Steiner, Yale University. A most important recent contribution was made by Mr. Goldhamer, who in connection with his own research at Chicago rewrote the entire tagging program in highly optimized IBM 7094 FAP code. Mr. Goldhamer's version, though functionally equivalent to the previous tagging program, offered such great advantages of speed and flexibility that we postponed publication of this manual several months in order to be able to document it in our Chapter 4. We very much appreciate Mr. Goldhamer's taking the addi-

[2] In the case of Chapter 4, TAGGING, there are some departures from the organizational scheme described here.

tional time and effort to carefully describe his program, and his coming to Cambridge to work with us on details.[3]

The General Inquirer was originally developed at Harvard for the IBM 7090/94 and IBM 1401/1410 series computers. The most recent versions of the programs for these machines[4] are documented in this manual. However, some social scientists at other universities have taken the initiative to rewrite the system for the computers to which they have most immediate access. Thus, a team at Washington University in St. Louis, including George Psathas, Dennis Arp, and J. Philip Miller, has recently been funded to develop General Inquirer programs for the IBM System/360. While initial efforts have focused on the tagging procedures, it is intended eventually to integrate both the current 7094 and 1401 procedures on the System/360. At the University of Pennsylvania, George Miller and his associates have developed a system for the IBM 7040 that is explicitly modeled on the General Inquirer, although it departs in formats and stages of processing at a number of points. This system is called PENNINK (for "Pennsylvania Inquirer") and has been documented by their computation center. At Stanford University, Ole Holsti, Horace Enea, and Quan Lee have developed and refined a "direct tables," one-step version of the General Inquirer for analyses in which few tag categories but many who-to-whom relationships are to be examined.

While it is pleasing to see these other versions of the General Inquirer being developed for different computers and research purposes, it would be impractical for us to try to keep these other versions updated in our own files or to describe them in this manual. We would like to direct people to whatever version of the system best suits their needs and resources, but we cannot be responsible for any version except the one documented here. This excludes not only the Washington, Pennsylvania, and Stanford versions just mentioned but also the earlier versions of programs developed at Harvard. In this regard, if a person intends to use the system and knows that some version of the original Harvard General Inquirer is stored at his institution but has not been used for some time, he is strongly advised to obtain the programs

[3] Mr. Goldhamer's work was supported in part by the Computation Center of the University of Chicago.

[4] Our current TAGGING program (Chapter 4), though written for the 7094, has also been used successfully on various models of the IBM System/360. (See §4.7 with note 10 for detailed requirements.) Similarly, all the other programs (Chapters 5-17), though written for the 1401, can readily be used on a System/360 that has the 1401-compatibility feature.

documented here rather than attempting to use the stored programs. (Procedures for obtaining the most recent version of the Harvard system are described near the end of this preface.)

The authors of the programs documented in this manual are:

TAGGING (Chapter 4): Written by Donald H. Goldhamer, conforming to the formats and procedures originated by Stone, and following the design of a number of routines developed for an earlier version by Horace Enea.

TEXT-TAG LIST (Chapter 5): Outlined by Stone; programmed and developed by Aram Grayson.

TAG TALLY (Chapter 6): Outlined by Stone; programmed by Robert McCarthy. Extensively revised by Donald Davis to fit into an 8K IBM 1401 without repeated overlay.

RETRIEVAL (Chapter 7): Outlined by Stone; programmed by Aram Grayson, who added major conceptual features. Again expanded (with summary tables) by Victor D. Oppenheimer of Cambridge Computer Associates.

SUMMARY PUNCH (Chapter 8): Designed and programmed by Donald Davis.

TRANSPOSE (Chapter 9): Sort logic designed by Stone; program designed and developed by Donald Davis.

GRAPH (Chapter 10): First programmed on an IBM 407 board by Stone. The current IBM 1401 program was written by Marshall S. Smith. Scale factors and other additions were made by Donald Davis.

SORTED TRANSPOSE (Chapter 11): Designed and programmed by Donald Davis.

MEANS-DEVIATIONS (Chapter 12): Designed and programmed by Donald Davis.

KWIC RECORDS (Chapter 13): Designed and programmed by Victor D. Oppenheimer of Cambridge Computer Associates.

KWIC BLOCKS (Chapter 14): Programmed by Marshall S. Smith and Donald Davis.

KWIC PRINT-STATISTICS (Chapter 15): Outlined by Marshall S. Smith; programmed by Donald Davis.

CROSS-SORT RECORDS (Chapter 16): Outlined by Stone; designed and programmed by Anthony M. Marotto and John L. Sweeney of Cambridge Computer Associates.

CROSS-SORT LIST (Chapter 17): Designed and programmed by Anthony M. Marotto and John L. Sweeney of Cambridge Computer Associates.

In the course of preparing this manual, the staff of Cambridge Computer Associates reviewed all the programs just listed with the exception of Mr. Goldhamer's version of TAGGING. A number of the IBM 1401 programs were changed so that the error routines would be standardized.

Earlier versions of the primary programs (Chapter 4-7) may be important to a particular user because they are written in a language available on his computer or conform to the memory specifications of his IBM 1401. Though these earlier versions are still available upon special request, they have not to our knowledge been used for at least a year and are *not* documented in this manual. The earlier versions include:

COMIT Versions of TAGGING (Chapter 4): Programmed by Stone in COMIT I and COMIT II for the IBM 7090/94. The COMIT I version is without contextual (idiom) routines. The COMIT II version has contextual routines that are quite different from those documented here (§ §2.10-2.12). The output of the COMIT II version is in largely the same format as described in Chapter 18. Text input format in both cases is for the most part as described in Chapter 3.

BAGLOL Version of TAGGING (Chapter 4): Programmed for the IBM 7090/94 by Horace Enea in Stanford University's dialect of Burroughs Algol (BALGOL). This version matches most of the input and output formats described in this manual but omits certain control card options described in Chapter 4. The program has both contextual routines and sentence-summary procedures. See further §4.7.

MAD-FAP Version of TAGGING (Chapter 4): Programmed by Erik J. Steiner for the IBM 7090/94, with major processing routines written in MAD and a supervisor and input-output routines written in FAP. This version conforms to the input and output formats described in this manual but omits certain control-card options described in Chapter 4. Contextual routines have been implemented but at this writing have not been fully debugged. The program contains a number of special routines to accommodate the IBM 7090-7040 direct-coupled computer at Yale.

AUTOCODER Version of TAGGING (Chapter 4): Programmed by J. Philip Miller at Washington University for an IBM 1401/60 with IBM 1311 disk.[5] This version conforms to the input and output formats described in this manual. Inasmuch as the current IBM 7094 program is more than 100 times faster than this disk look-up program, the use of the latter can be justified only if a 7094 is unavailable.

4K Version of TEXT-TAG LIST (Chapter 5): This version for an IBM 1401 with a 4000-character memory ("4K") differs from the current 8K version mainly in that it cannot process extremely long sentences.

4K Version of TAG TALLY (Chapter 6): This version for an IBM 1401 with 4K memory differs from the current 8K version in requiring three tape drives (but only two if tape output is not needed).

4K Version of RETRIEVAL (Chapter 7): This version for an IBM 1401 with 4K memory can process all retrieval specifications described in Chapter 7 but unlike the current 8K version does not produce tables of retrieval scores.

Specifications of the General Inquirer programs for a time-shared computer are not given in this manual, since they draw on a resource that is not widely available. However, the same "tree-building" strategy which these programs facilitate can be replicated on the IBM 1401 by the current TAG TALLY and RETRIEVAL programs.[6] This alternative has come to be preferred to the use of the time-shared programs themselves, partly because of the high speed of printers with the now available IBM 1401.

Cambridge Computer Associates[7] distributes, at the cost for materials, mailing, and handling, copies of all the programs documented in this book and is prepared to modify programs to meet special needs or to rewrite them for other computers. Some content analysis dictionaries which have been developed in General Inquirer studies and for which adequate documentation exists are also distributed by Cambridge

[5] For a general description of this program, see Stone *et al., The General Inquirer, op. cit.*, pp. 72-73; for detailed documentation, write to The Social Science Institute, Washington University, St. Louis, Missouri 63130, or to Cambridge Computer Associates (note 7).

[6] The time-shared programs, the "tree-building" strategies, and the special use of TAG TALLY and RETRIEVAL to implement those strategies are described in Stone *et al., op. cit.*, pp. 119-132.

[7] 380 Putnam Avenue, Cambridge, Mass. 02139.

Computer Associates. The programs and dictionaries, as well as the texts analyzed in most past studies, are also available from the Inter-University Consortium for Political Research, University of Michigan.

This manual was prepared to Stone's specifications by the systems analysts and technical editors of Cambridge Computer Associates. The systems analysis was conducted by Cary D. Wyman, Anthony M. Marotto, and Stephen N. Mills under the supervision of Victor D. Oppenheimer. The manual was organized and written by John Kirsch. Kirsch's final draft was checked for technical accuracy by several CCA analysts, notably John L. Sweeney, and was revised by Stone and his colleagues, Dunphy and Smith.

It is a great pleasure to thank Miss Virginia V. Estabrook of Cambridge Computer Associates for the skill and patience with which she typed the three manuscript drafts of this book.

Department of Social Relations
Harvard University
Philip J. Stone

Cambridge Computer Associates, Inc.
February 1967
John Kirsch

Contents

CONTENTS

CONTENTS

APPENDIX FOUR: SENTENCE-SUMMARY PROCEDURES

List of Figures

List of Tables

PART ONE

INTRODUCTION

CHAPTER 1

System Narrative

It is assumed that the reader of this manual is familiar with the description of content analysis, the suggested procedures for dictionary construction and research design, and the rationale for the computer programs given in *The General Inquirer.*[1] In this chapter, the sequence of processing within the system of programs is briefly reviewed (§ § 1.2-1.6); some key variables that reappear in more than one program are identified (§ § 1.7-1.9); and the running times of the programs are specified (§ 1.10). The preparation of dictionary and text input is described from a technical viewpoint in Chapters 2 and 3. The subsequent chapters in the manual present the programs one by one.

An outline of the entire system, without the time-shared procedures but including the major dictionary preparation procedures, is given in Figure 1.A. We begin our discussion with the tagging procedure represented at the top left of this diagram. Aids to dictionary construction—that is, the key-word-in-context and the cross-sort programs[2] —are introduced at the end of Chapter 2 (§ § 2.13-2.16) and treated in detail in Chapters 13-17.

BASIC PROGRAM OPERATIONS

§1.1. Design of the System

Perhaps the most important consideration affecting the design of the General Inquirer system was the need to facilitate a high degree of

[1] Stone, Philip J., Dexter C. Dunphy, Marshall S. Smith, Daniel M. Ogilvie, with associates, *The General Inquirer: A Computer Approach to Content Analysis* (Cambridge, Mass.: The M. I. T. Press, 1966), pp. 3-277.

[2] *Ibid.*, pp. 91, 152-167.

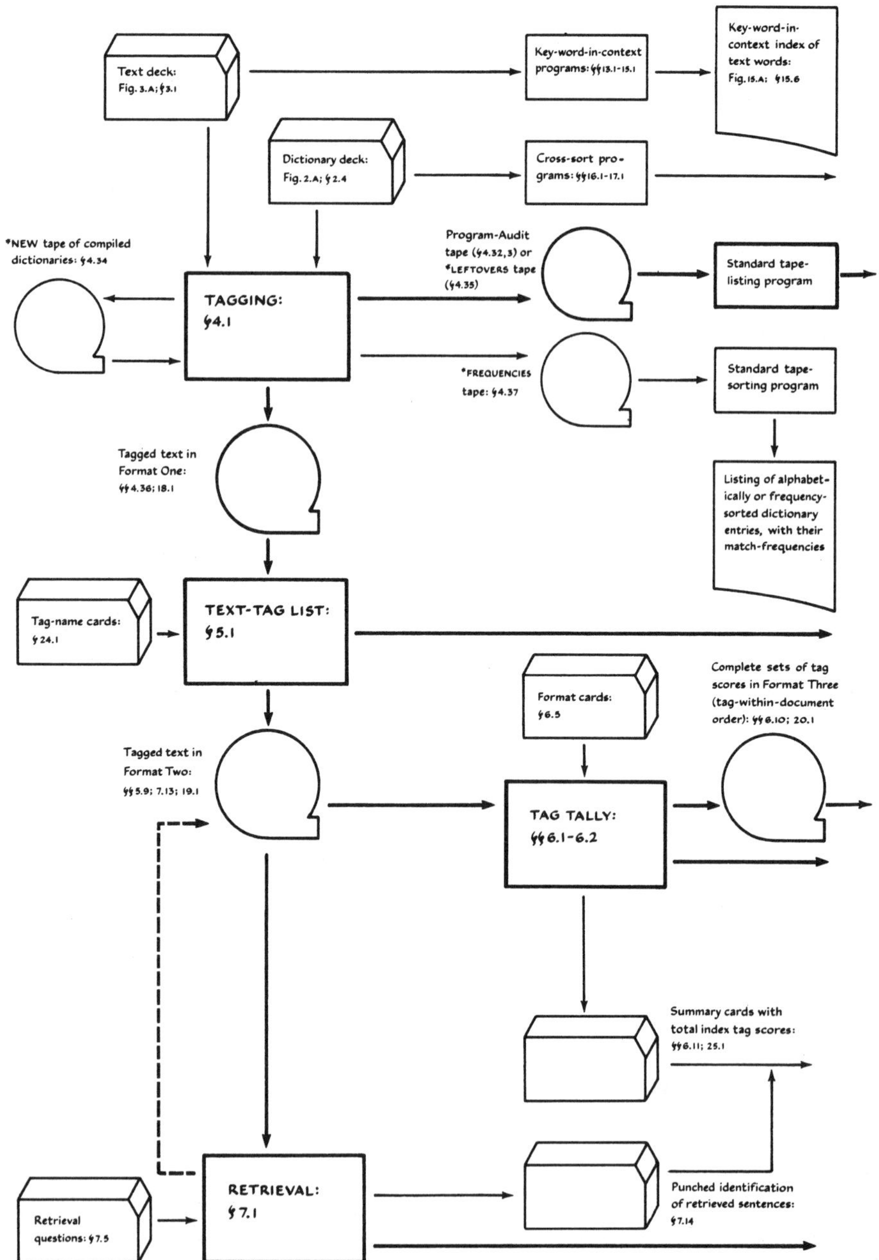

FIGURE 1.A. *Flow of data in the General Inquirer System. Broken lines indicate feedback or second application of a program. Listings in column to right of center are*

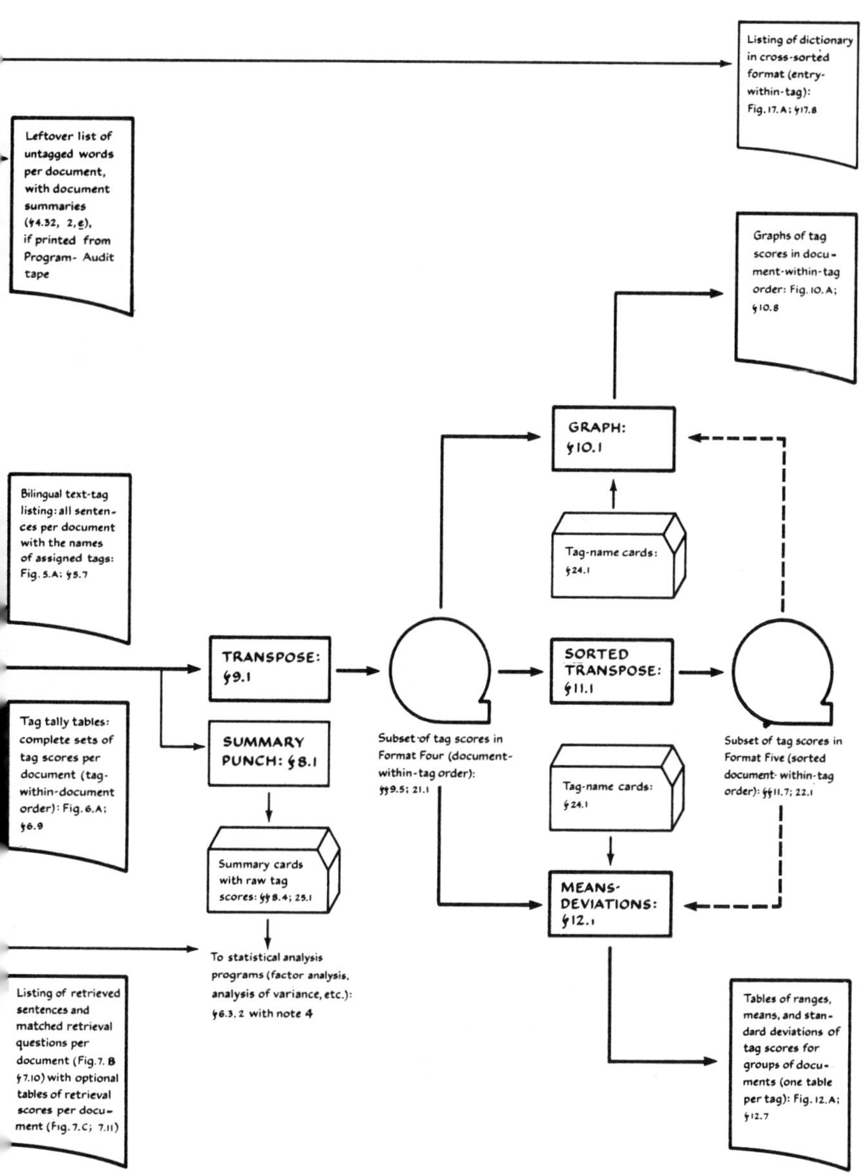

organized by document. Listings in column at extreme right are organized by dictionary tag.

interaction between the investigator and the automated content analysis procedures. Two closely related strategies were adopted in order to achieve this goal. First, it was decided to program as much of the system as possible for a relatively small and hence widely accessible machine–specifically, the IBM 1401. (TAGGING is the only program represented in Figure 1.A that requires a large-scale machine, the IBM 7094.) Second, it was decided to implement each major processing function as a separate program. This second strategy was a concomitant of the use of a small machine, the storage restrictions of which limit the amount of processing that can be done in a single run. But it was also felt that many small programs would both maximize the possibility of intervention by the investigator at crucial stages in the data flow and give him the choice of bypassing processing functions that he did not need.

It is anticipated that in future implementations of the General Inquirer system this same goal of providing the investigator with a fully interactive processing environment can be more directly achieved by the use of remote console inquiry and random-access storage devices.

§1.2. TAGGING and TEXT-TAG LIST

Throughout the tagging operation (§ 4.2), an entire content analysis dictionary is stored in the memory unit of the computer. The stored dictionary consists of a list of entries (words), each entry followed by an instruction consisting of one or more tags and optional contextual specifications. Each tag is a number between 1 and 99 that identifies a content analysis category. When a word in the sentence that the computer is currently reading matches–that is, is identical to–a dictionary entry, the tag or tags by which that word was defined are assigned to the sentence. Words not found in the dictionary are written on a tape in a "leftover" list. When all the words in a sentence have been looked up in this way, the sentence is recorded on magnetic tape with the "string" of tags (if any) that has been assigned to it. Then processing of the next sentence begins.

The TAGGING program can ignore any specified suffix (and/or prefix) of a text word in order to match the root of that word to a dictionary entry. In the present version of TAGGING, a suffix-"removal" routine of this type is implemented for the most common English suffixes (§ 2.8.1; Table 2.A). This routine has had the advantage of reducing by a factor of two or three the number of dictionary entries necessary for adequate analysis of text. Relatively simple changes in the program would be necessary to modify or remove the present routine or to introduce a similar routine for prefixes (§ 4.47).

Contextual specifications within a dictionary instruction can test for preceding words within sentences rather than only individual words (§ § 2.10-2.12). If, for example, "boat" were an entry and had been given this type of definition, the definition might instruct TAGGING to examine a certain number of words[3] immediately preceding every occurrence of "boat," and to assign tag 13 to "miss the boat," tag 54 to "rock the boat," but tag 26 to "boat" if not occurring in one of these specified contexts.

Another tagging option tests for specified co-occurrences among the tags assigned to a sentence after all words in it have been looked up but before the sentence and its tags are written on tape (§ 4.5). If one of the specified co-occurrences is found, tags can be added, deleted, or changed.[4] The basic routines necessary for such "sentence summary" procedures are part of TAGGING. The investigator may make use of these routines in designing his own test specifications. These specifications may be implemented in a compiler-level programming language such as FORTRAN and then incorporated into TAGGING. See further § 27.1.

At any point in a TAGGING run, the investigator may request counts of how many times each entry in the dictionary has been matched (§ 4.23). This information can be written on the *FREQUENCIES tape, as indicated in Figure 1.A and can later be sorted to have the frequencies of entry usage printed in ascending or descending frequency order, in alphabetical order, or in "cross-sort" order.

TEXT-TAG LIST (§ 5.1) is a program for displaying the tagged text generated by TAGGING in a "bilingual" format (Figure 5.A) in which each sentence is juxtaposed with the names of the tags that had been assigned to it.

As is indicated in Figure 1.A, TEXT-TAG LIST also produces a tape of tagged text in the format in which it is to be processed by

[3] The tags assigned to the specified number of preceding words may be tested (§ 2.12) instead of, or in addition to, those words themselves.

[4] For an example of the application of sentence and document summary test procedures, see Stone *et al.*, *op. cit.*, pp. 191-206.

both TAG TALLY and RETRIEVAL. The differences between the two tagged-text tape formats are illustrated by Figure 1.C and explained in § § 1.8-1.8.5.

§ 1.3. TAG TALLY: Counting Tag Assignments

TAG TALLY (§ 6.1) counts the number of times each tag had been assigned to each document (§ 1.9) of text. The raw score that is computed can be either the number of times each tag was assigned (word-count raw score) or, if the investigator prefers, the number of sentences in which tag assignment occurred (sentence-count raw score). An index score is also computed for the assignment of each tag to each document. This index score expresses either the sentence-count or word-count raw score as a percentage of the total number of either sentences or words,[5] respectively, in the document. Since index scores indicate relative frequency of tag assignments, they facilitate comparisons among documents of varying length.

The program can simultaneously record one set of tag scores per document in a printed table (Figure 6.A), on magnetic tape (§ 6.10), and/or (in summary form only) on punched cards (§ 6.11). See Figure 1.A.

The set of tag scores for a document (whether sentence-count or word-count) can include four subtotals of the raw score for each tag and four of the index score (§ 6.2). The primary purpose of these subtotals is to allow differentiation among the assignments of one and the same tag to words in different syntactic positions ("subject," "verb," "object," "unclassified"). Basic options of dictionary preparation (§ 2.9) and text editing (§ 3.12) determine the eventual use of the subtotal scores.

§ 1.4. RETRIEVAL: Testing for Co-occurrences of Text Words, Assigned Tags, and/or Identification Codes

RETRIEVAL (§ 7.1) permits the investigator to specify with great flexibility those characteristics of tagged sentences that may be of particular interest to him and to find ("retrieve") and count all sentences exhibiting the specified characteristics. The investigator's retrieval specifications—or retrieval "questions" (§ 7.5), as they shall be called—may be in terms of the presence or absence of any combina-

[5] See § 1.8.1 on the divisor used in calculating word-count index scores.

tion of the following: one or more consecutive characters in the text of the sentence (that is, a part of a word, a word, or a phrase); one or more tags that have been assigned to the sentence; and one or more consecutive characters in the sentence identification code (§ 1.8.3). For example, a retrieval question might specify a co-occurrence that includes: the presence of tag 48 and the word "father," the absence of tag 32, and the presence of the characters X3 in positions 12 and 13 of the identification code. Each retrieved sentence can be recorded in any of several output media (Figure 1.A)–a printed listing (§ 7.10; Figure 7.B), four tapes (§ 7.13), or (in summary form only) a punched card (§ 7.14).

The total number of matching sentences for each retrieval question and the total number of matching sentences recorded in each output medium can be tabulated at the end of each input document (§ 7.11; Table 7.A) and for any number of consecutive documents.

§ 1.5. Transposing, Sorting, Displaying, and Punching Tag Scores

The five secondary programs for processing TAG TALLY data stem, in Figure 1.A, from the output tape generated by that program in Format Three. That tape contains one complete set of either word-count or sentence-count tag scores for each text document (§ 1.9). The tag scores are organized in tag-within-document order. The complete set of scores for each document consists of ten scores for each tag in the dictionary–two total scores (raw and index) and eight subtotal scores (four raw and four index). All of the secondary programs except SUMMARY PUNCH process any one of the ten types of scores for all the documents whose scores are recorded on the TAG TALLY output tape.

TRANSPOSE (§ 9.1) selects from the tape in Format Three all scores in one of the ten subsets (as specified by the investigator) and copies them onto another tape (Format Four) in *document-within-tag order.* By this it is meant that all scores for the assignment of one and the same tag to different documents are grouped together in the sequence in which those documents had been processed by TAG TALLY. This transposition operation is illustrated in Figure 1.B.

Once the scores have been transposed from document order to tag order and are recorded on a tape in Format Four, they can be displayed by two programs. GRAPH (§ 10.1) prints bar graphs representing the scores for the assignment of each tag to all documents. In applying

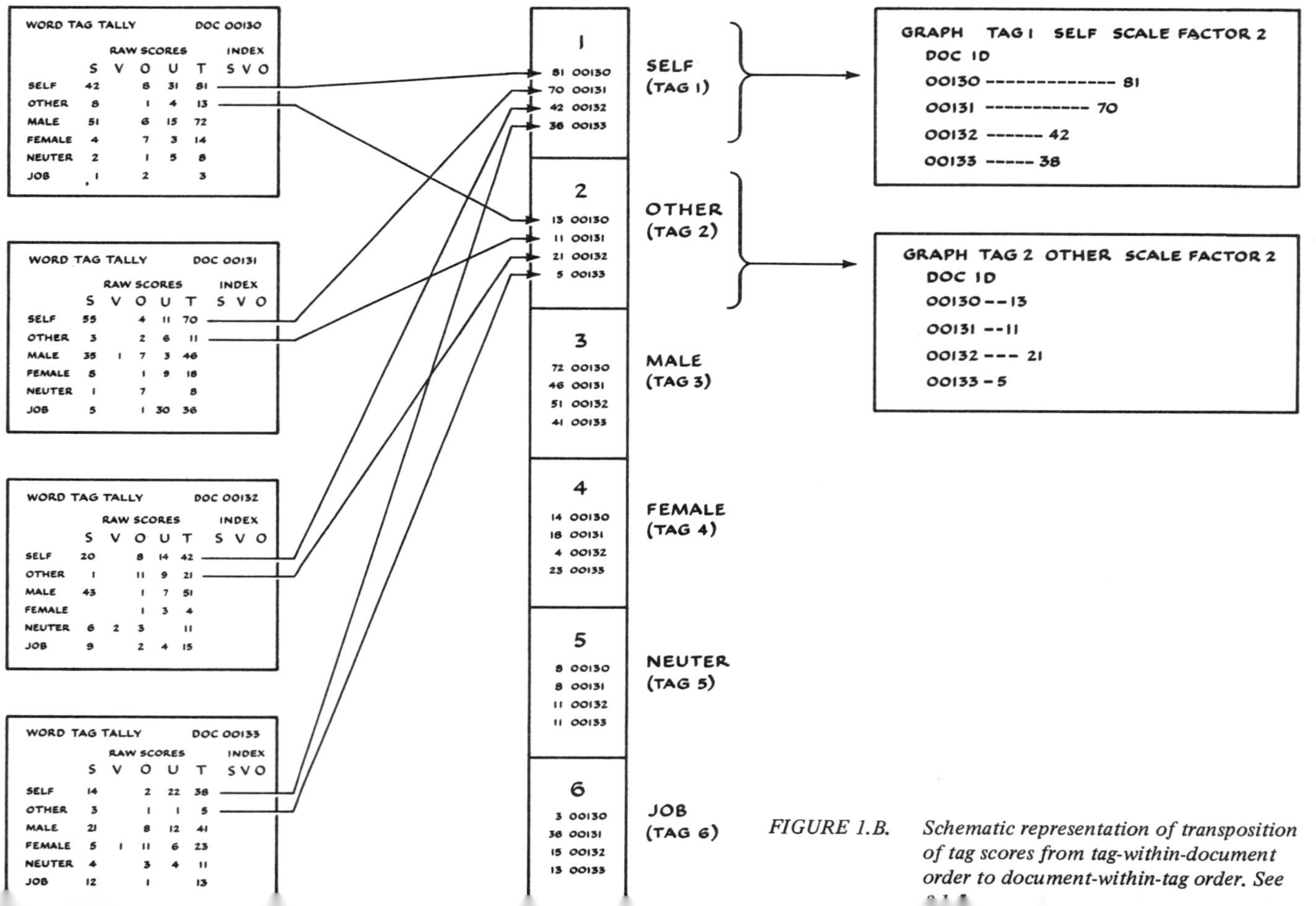

FIGURE 1.B. *Schematic representation of transposition of tag scores from tag-within-document order to document-within-tag order. See*

MEANS-DEVIATIONS (§ 12.1) to the scores, the investigator can define groups of consecutive documents. MEANS-DEVIATIONS generates a separate table for each tag; and each table displays the highest score, lowest score, arithmetic mean, and standard deviation for each group of documents.

Note in Figure 1.A that the display programs GRAPH and MEANS-DEVIATIONS can process not only a TRANSPOSE output tape in Format Four but also a SORTED TRANSPOSE (§ 11.1) output tape in Format Five. The only difference between these two formats is that in Format Four the sequence of scores for different documents within each tag is the same sequence in which the tagged documents had been processed by TAG TALLY, whereas in Format Five the scores within each tag are resequenced in accord with sorting specifications given by the investigator (§ § 11.5-11.6) and based upon information in document-identification codes (§ 1.8.3).

SUMMARY PUNCH (§ 8.1) can generate punched cards (§ § 8.4; 25.1) of any or all of the five subsets of *raw* scores. The punched-card format for frequency counts has been designed in such a way that these cards can readily be used as input to standard programs for performing analysis of variance, factor analysis, and other statistical analyses.

§ 1.6. Feedback: Secondary Retrievals and Tag Tallies

As indicated in Figure 1.A, RETRIEVAL can record retrieved sentences in the very format that both it and TAG TALLY require for input. This source of feedback can be used in two ways. First, RETRIEVAL can be applied iteratively, and thus with increasing selectivity, to smaller and smaller samples of the original body of tagged text. Second, TAG TALLY and all the secondary programs that stem from it can be applied in turn to each successive subset of retrieved sentences. These procedures facilitate attempts to discriminate the effects of co-occurrences in great detail.

It should be noted that any file of sentences generated by RETRIEVAL (§ 7.13) and subsequently processed by TAG TALLY is a subset of one (or more) of the document files (§ 1.9) originally created by TAGGING.

§ 1.7. Dictionary Entries and Text Words

An individual text word cannot be tagged unless it is spelled and keypunched in exactly the same way as is a dictionary entry (§ 2.8). However, because of suffix "removal" (§ 2.8.1), in many cases the uninflected form of a text word rather than the entire word will constitute a unit of data during the tagging operation. Although the order in which a sentence's tags are printed in the text-tag listing (Figure 5.A) corresponds to the order of the words and idioms which had been tagged, that listing does not specifically indicate which tags had been assigned to which words.

§ 1.8. Sentence Records

Although TAGGING separately "looks up" each text word in the stored dictionary, it both reads text input, and writes tagged-text output, sentence by sentence. TAGGING recognizes as a sentence all words between one "sentence delimiter" or "clause delimiter" and the next sentence or clause delimiter. The sentence delimiters are the keypunched equivalents of a period or question mark (Table 3.A). The clause delimiters (Table 3.A) are certain other keypunched characters that can be inserted by the editor between the clauses of compound or complex sentences (§ 3.11). Thus, the use of clause delimiters is a means of controlling sentence length.

TAGGING writes each sentence and the string of tags that has been assigned to it on an output tape in Format One (§ 18.1). The storage unit in which each tagged sentence is written on that tape will be termed a "sentence record" (Figure 1.C). This unit, in which other data besides the text and tag string of a sentence are written, is somewhat rearranged when TEXT-TAG LIST transcribes TAGGING's tape in Format One onto a tape in Format Two (§ 19.1). In view of the importance of the sentence record in subsequent processing, it may be useful to summarize the source of each item of data which this type of record may contain, how each item is incorporated into the record by TAGGING, and how each item may be used by TEXT-TAG LIST, TAG TALLY, and RETRIEVAL.

§ *1.8.1. Word-Count Field.* The number of words in the sentence is counted by TAGGING and written at the beginning of the record.

TEXT-TAG LIST and RETRIEVAL print the word count for each

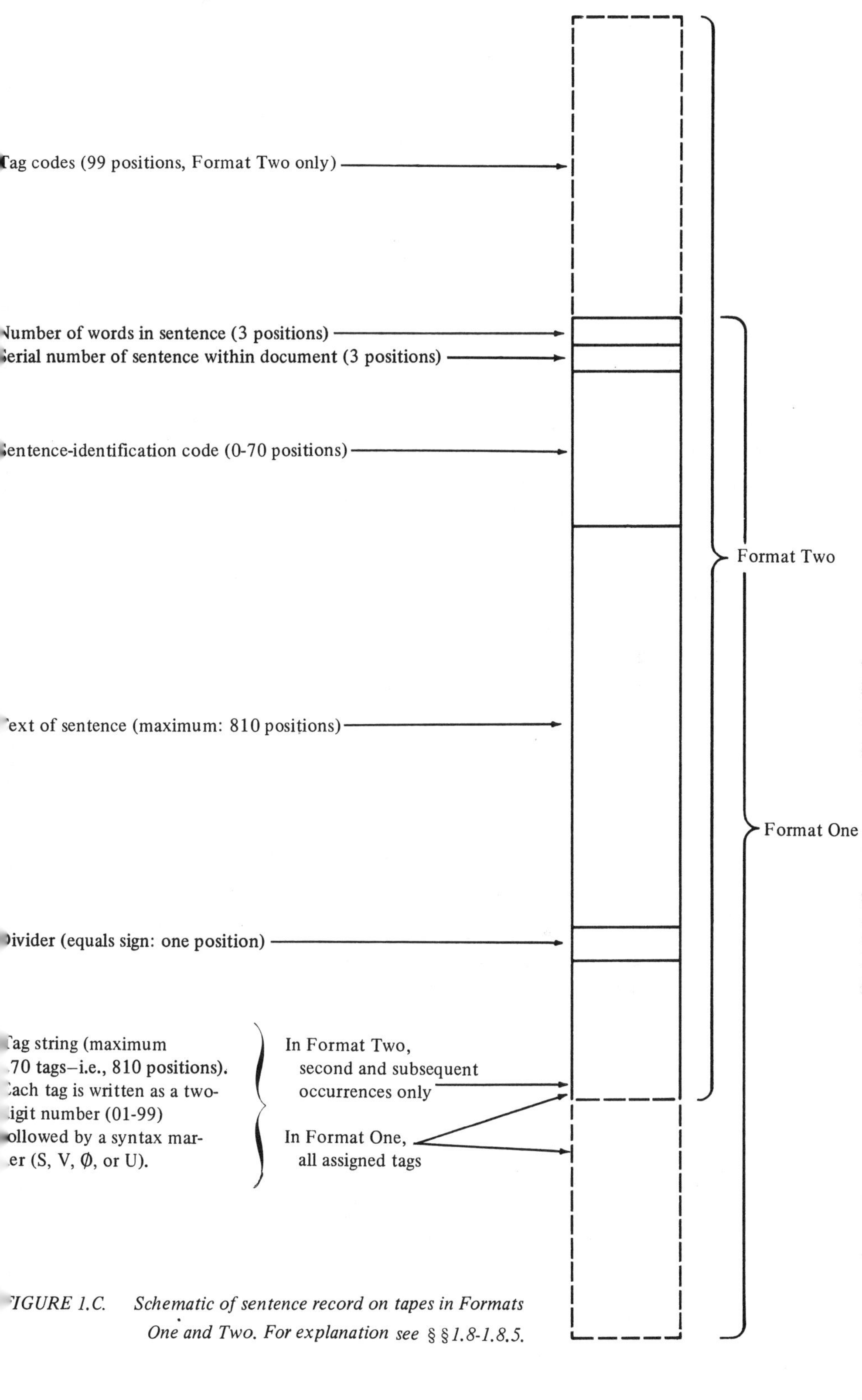

FIGURE 1.C. *Schematic of sentence record on tapes in Formats One and Two. For explanation see §§1.8-1.8.5.*

sentence above the text of the sentence (Figures 5.A, 7.B).

TAG TALLY, if instructed to compute word-count index scores, sums up the word counts in all the sentence records of a document (§ 1.9), prints the total at the top of the TAG TALLY table (Figure 6.A), and uses this total as a divisor in computing word-count index scores (§ § 6.1-6.2).

§ *1.8.2. Sentence-Serial-Number Field.* TAGGING assigns a serial (ordinal) number to each sentence within a document (§ 1.9) and writes this number in the second field of the sentence record. The serial number is printed by TEXT-TAG LIST and RETRIEVAL above the text of the sentence (Figures 5.A, 7.C). When listings of these two programs are compared, sentence serial numbers facilitate relating any particular retrieved sentence to the sequence of sentences from which it was removed by RETRIEVAL.

§ *1.8.3. Sentence-Identification-Code Field.* The third field of a sentence record as written by TAGGING may be an optional sentence-identification code created by the investigator and consisting of as many as 70 characters. These codes are keypunched on the data cards along with the text, and they may be used for any purposes the investigator chooses. These keypunching procedures are described in detail in § 3.8.

The identification code of the first sentence in a document should not be omitted because TAG TALLY and the five programs that stem from it use that code as a document-identification code. See further § 1.9.

A sentence-identification code, if supplied by the investigator, is printed by TEXT-TAG LIST and RETRIEVAL above the text of the sentence (Figures 5.A, 7.B). TAGGING can be instructed to use code information as a criterion both for automatically dividing the text into documents (§ 4.24), and for assigning "sentence summary" tags (§ § 4.5; 27.10.2). RETRIEVAL can be instructed to use code information as a criterion for retrieving sentences (§ § 1.4; 7.5.3).

§ *1.8.4. Text Field.* TAGGING deletes unnecessary blanks between words (§ 3.3), hyphens used to connect the parts of a word keypunched on two text cards (§ 3.3.2), and all subscripts, which the investigator has the option of inserting into the text of any sentence (§ § 3.10; 3.12). However, deletion of subscripts can also be suppressed by means of a control-card option (§ 4.25). If, after all necessary deletions have been made, the text of the sentence exceeds 810 characters in length, it will be divided among two or more sentence records (§ 4.32.5, no.19).

TEXT-TAG LIST prints the text of a sentence on the left side of its "bilingual" listing (Figure 5.A); RETRIEVAL prints the sentence across the page (Figure 7.B). RETRIEVAL can scan the words in the text field of a sentence record in order to determine whether the sentence satisfies a retrieval criterion (§ § 1.4; 7.5.2).

§ *1.8.5. Tag-String Field (and Tag-Code Field in Format Two).* The string of tags that TAGGING has assigned to the words and idioms in the sentence (§ 1.2) is written in the last field of the sentence record. To each tag is appended a syntax marker (S, V, Ø, or U), which, if the text had been edited for syntax (§ 3.12.1), will indicate the syntactic position of the word or idiom to which the tag had been assigned (§ 2.9). The maximum length of this field is 810 characters. Thus, if more than 270 tags can be assigned to a sentence, TAGGING creates an extra sentence record to accommodate the additional tags (§ 4.32.5, no. 19).

Using a set of tag-name cards, TEXT-TAG LIST prints the name of each tag in the tag-string field opposite the text of the sentence (Figure 5.A). In transcribing the sentence records created by TAGGING onto a tape in Format Two, TEXT-TAG LIST also adds at the beginning of each record a tag-code field of 99 positions (Figure 1.C). In this new field, TEXT-TAG LIST writes codes (§ 19.5) that indicate whether each of the 99 possible tags appears at least once in the input tag-string field, and which syntax marker(s) are appended to the instance(s) of any tag that does appear there at least once. The first occurrence of each tag in any syntactic position(s) is thus indicated in the output tag-code field. The first occurrences so accounted for are deleted by TEXT-TAG LIST from the output tag string. Thus in Format Two, the tag-string field at the end of each sentence record lists only second, third, and higher occurrences.

The purpose of creating the tag-code fields is to reduce the time needed by TAG TALLY and RETRIEVAL when searching for the presence or absence of assigned tags. Thus, when sentence-count tag scores are requested (§ 1.3), TAG TALLY consults only the tag codes in the first 99 positions of the Format Two sentence record. Similarly, RETRIEVAL need only consult these code positions in order to determine whether a sentence satisfies the tag specification(s) of a retrieval question (§ 7.5.1).

The tag-string field at the end of the sentence record is consulted only by TAG TALLY when word-count scores are requested.

§ 1.9. Documents

A document in General Inquirer processing is a subdivision of the text consisting of a series of sentences. The text can be divided into documents by the insertion of either end-document cards (§ 3.5) into the text deck or *AUTODOC control cards (§ 4.24) into TAGGING's general input deck.

When TAGGING encounters either type of end-of-document condition, it writes an end-of-file mark (§ 18.5) after a sentence record (§ 1.8) on the tape in Format One. Thus the tagged text is divided into a series of document files, each consisting of a series of sentence records. These document file units are kept intact when the tape of tagged text is transcribed by TEXT-TAG LIST from Format One to Format Two. Thus, the document file remains a major unit of input for TAG TALLY and RETRIEVAL when these programs are applied to the text for the first time. However, the document files created by TAGGING are broken down by RETRIEVAL into files each of which consists of a subset of the sentences in one or more of the original files (§ 7.13).

TAGGING's "leftover" list of untagged words (§ § 4.32.3; 4.35), TEXT-TAG LIST's "bilingual" listing (Figure 5.A; § 5.7), TAG TALLY's tables of tag scores (Figure 6.A; § 6.9), and RETRIEVAL's listing of retrieved sentences (Figure 7.B; § 7.10) are represented in Figure 1.A in a column just to the right of center, and are all organized by document. That is, the words, sentences, or scores displayed in each listing are grouped according to the document from which they originate or to which they refer. This facilitates comparisons among the four types of listings.

Specifically, the parallel organization of these listings is indicated by means of document-identification codes and document serial numbers. Document-identification codes are the most important and consistent means of labeling. This code is the sentence-identification-code field (§ 1.8.3) of the first sentence record in each document file of tagged text (Format One or Format Two). The document code invariably appears immediately above the first sentence of each document in a text-tag listing and at the top of the tag tally table for each document. It is also printed in part or in whole by GRAPH (Figure 10.A) next to the bar graph of the tag score for a document and can be used by

SORTED TRANSPOSE (§ 11.1) as a basis for resequencing the document-within-tag scores from the order in which documents were originally processed by TAGGING. These various uses of document-identification codes should be anticipated when they are first created and assigned during text editing (§ 3.6).

Document serial numbers are printed at the top of each page of a text-tag listing, tag tally table, and retrieval listing. These serial numbers indicate the ordinal position on the input tape of the document file from which the listing is generated.

PROGRAM-RUNNING TIMES

§ 1.10. Program-Running Times

The speed of TAGGING (§ 4.1) will depend upon the size of the dictionary, the number of conditional tests that are part of dictionary instructions (§ § 2.10-2.12), and, especially, the elaborateness of the sentence summary procedures, if any (§ § 4.5; 27.1). The speed also depends on the type of tape drives used on the machine and the extent to which the most frequently matched entries are put at the head of the dictionary. The present version of TAGGING for the IBM 7094 should usually process more than 20,000 text words per minute and should fall below 10,000 words per minute only if extremely elaborate sentence summary procedures are used. See further § 4.39.

The speed of the 1401 programs (§ § 5.1-17.1) depends very much on the type of equipment used by the 1401. The crucial factors are the type of tape unit, the type of printer, and the presence of a printer buffering feature.

In most cases, TEXT-TAG LIST (§ 5.1) will proceed at printer speed (if the machine has buffered print equipment), with an occasional print cycle being missed for tape movement. If a 600 line-per-minute buffered printer is used, printing will take place at an average of over 500 lines per minute.

TAG TALLY (§ 6.1) operates in two phases—counting tags and then transmitting the counts to various output devices. The counting phase proceeds at about 300 sentences per minute if IBM 7330 tape units are used, and at about 500 sentences per minute if IBM 729, Model V, tape units are used. Printing of the tables (Figure 6.A) proceeds at about printer speed. Punching seven output cards per document (§ 6.11) takes about two seconds. Writing the scores for a document on an output tape (§ 6.10) takes about two or three seconds.

The speed of RETRIEVAL (§ 7.1) greatly depends on the number and type of retrieval questions asked (§ 7.5). If only a few tags are specified in these questions, the input tape will be searched as fast as it can be read by the tape unit. In this case, it makes a great difference what kind of tape unit is used. Questions containing text specifications can be particularly slow, as discussed in § 7.5.6.

The speed of TRANSPOSE (§ 9.1) and SORTED TRANSPOSE (§ 11.1) again depends very much on that of the tape units. Tape speed is especially crucial in TRANSPOSE operations in which many passes over an intermediate data tape prove necessary (§ § 9.6; 9.7.2). Unless a lot of information is to be rearranged, these programs can usually finish their work in one or two minutes.

The speed of GRAPH (§ 10.1) and MEANS-DEVIATIONS (§ 12.1) is dependent upon that of the printer in use. GRAPH will usually operate at printer speed, occasionally missing a cycle for tape movement or reading title cards.

The speed of the key-word-in-context programs (§ § 13.1-15.1) is discussed in § 13.2.1.

CHAPTER 2

Preparation, Processing, and Revision of a Content Analysis Dictionary[1]

INTRODUCTION

§2.1. Terminology

A General Inquirer dictionary may contain as many as 4000 to 8000 *entries.* Each entry (§2.8) is a word associated with an *instruction* as to how any occurrence of that word in the text to be analyzed should be classified among as many as 99 different *tag* categories.[2] The instruction may be *unconditional* (§2.9); that is, any time the word occurs in the text, all tags specified in the instruction will be assigned. However, at the investigator's option, an instruction may be *conditional* (§§2.10-2.12); in this case, the given context of the word can be examined in order to determine which of two or more sets of tags specified in the instruction should be assigned.

The execution of dictionary instructions is carried out by TAGGING (§4.1). In looking up text words in the dictionary, TAGGING is capable of ignoring suffixes (and prefixes) so that a match may be made on the word root alone (§2.8.1).

[1] Stone, Philip J., Dexter C. Dunphy, Marshall S. Smith, Daniel M. Ogilvie, with associates, *The General Inquirer: A Computer Approach to Content Analysis* (Cambridge, Mass.: The M. I. T. Press, 1966), pp. 85-91, 134-206.

[2] A version of the General Inquirer other than the one documented in this manual can accommodate a maximum of 297 categories. This expansion is obtained at the cost of processing of syntax specifications (§§2.9; 3.12.1).

A General Inquirer dictionary may be constructed for any language that can be transliterated or encoded in the roman alphabet or a combination of the roman alphabet and decimal digits. One existing General Inquirer dictionary is in the Mexican Indian language, Tzotzil.

§2.2. Scope of This Chapter

The information in this chapter is presented for an investigator who either is developing his own special dictionary or wishes to revise for his own purposes a previously developed dictionary. All sections of this chapter are potentially relevant to either of these endeavors.

In the second major section of this chapter (§ § 2.4-2.12), the formats of dictionary entries and instructions are specified, and the ways in which TAGGING processes the several types of formats are described.

In the next section of this chapter (§ § 2.13-2.14), the usefulness of the KWIC programs (Chapters 13-15) for the task of developing a content analysis dictionary is briefly explained.

In the last section of this chapter (§ § 2.15-2.21), various aids are described for appraising the effectiveness of a dictionary in relation to a given body of text. Also included in this section is an explanation of technical restrictions on the size of a dictionary.

§2.3. Distribution of Existing Dictionaries

Most of the 17 General Inquirer dictionaries listed on pages 140-141 of *The General Inquirer* are available for distribution to research projects.[3]

ENTRIES AND INSTRUCTIONS: FORMATS AND PROCESSING

§2.4. The Dictionary Deck

A dictionary must initially be keypunched onto standard 80-column cards in the formats described in §2.5. Each dictionary card typically consists of an entry word followed by an instruction to TAGGING (§4.2) as to how to assign tags to any text sentence in which the entry is found. The resultant series of dictionary cards—that is, the dictionary deck—can then be submitted for processing by TAGGING or CROSS-SORT RECORDS (§ §2.16; 16.1).

[3] See Preface, notes 7 and 8.

TAGGING automatically compiles—that is, translates into compact codes—the dictionary before beginning to apply it to the text (§ 4.3). After compilation but before, during, or after application of the dictionary to the text, TAGGING also can rapidly implement any revisions of the dictionary that the investigator may have specified on a separate set of dictionary cards (§ 4.4). The cards on which such revisions are specified should also be keypunched in the formats specified in § 2.5.

A dictionary deck contains two kinds of entries: "regular" and "special." Most of our concern is with "regular" entries, which direct the assignment of tags to text. "Special" dictionary entries are for the purposes of presetting certain features of the program. The special entries are in turn divided into two kinds: "required" and "optional." The required ordering of these different kinds of dictionary entries is illustrated in Figure 2.A. The regular entries need *not* be arranged in alphabetic order. However, if they are in alphabetic order, this order will be maintained in *FREQUENCIES transcriptions generated by TAGGING (§ § 2.17; 4.23).

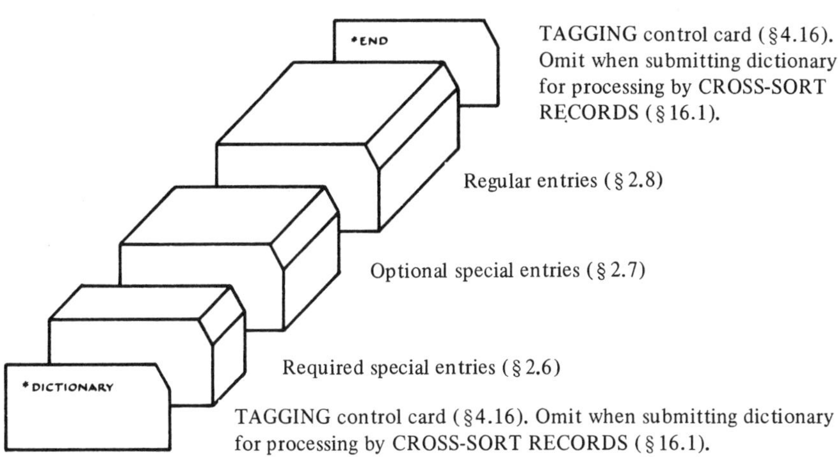

FIGURE 2.A. Schematic of dictionary deck. See § 2.4.

§ 2.5. Dictionary Cards

§ *2.5.1. General Format.* The general format of a dictionary card is described in this section. Note carefully that with one exception blanks are not permitted between the first character of an entry and the last character of its instruction.

Card Columns	*Contents*
1 to n	Entry. A special entry, whether required (§ 2.6) or optional (§ 2.7), consists only of a period in column 1, followed immediately by an alphabetic character. A regular entry consists of one or more alphanumeric[4] characters, which should be keypunched starting in column 1, and which may be punctuated by one or more hyphens or apostrophes (§ 2.8). No blanks may occur between the first character of the entry in column 1 and the last character of the entry in column n. The entry must be no longer than 39 characters if CROSS-SORT RECORDS (§ 16.1) is to be used.
n+1	= [equals sign]
n+2 to 72	Instruction (and, after the first blank column, comments, which TAGGING will ignore). If columns 1 to n contain a required special entry, its instruction should be one of the tags between 101 and 110 (§ 2.6). If columns 1 to n contain an optional special entry, its instruction should be of the unconditional type (§ 2.9). If columns 1 to n contain a regular entry, its instruction may be of either the unconditional or the conditional (§ 2.10) type. The operator N may also be used as the instruction of a regular entry (§ 2.8.2). In any instruction, each tag, syntax marker, or idiom expression should be separated by a comma from the next tag, marker, or expression. One column after the last character of the instruction must be blank,

[4] The alphanumeric characters are the 26 capital letters of the roman alphabet and the ten decimal digits.

	but all columns remaining between this necessary blank and column 72 (or 80) may be used for comments that TAGGING and CROSS-SORT RECORDS will ignore. See § 2.5.3.
73 to 80	Ignored by programs, but can be used for comments. See § 2.5.3.

§ *2.5.2. Instruction Continued onto Second Card or Ending in Column 72.* An instruction that does not end in or before column 72 of the card on which its entry has been punched should be continued in column 1 of the next card. Similarly, if the instruction does not end in or before column 72 of that second card, it may be continued in columns 1-72 of as many additional cards as necessary. (See § 2.11 with note 9 for an example of a definition that requires continuation on several cards.) Note that in all cases column 72 must be nonblank if the next card contains a continuation. If the dictionary is to be processed by CROSS-SORT RECORDS (§ 16.1), not more than 20 continuation cards may be used for a single entry.

If the very last character of an instruction falls in column 72 (either of the card on which its entry has been punched or of a card onto which the instruction has been continued), the next card in the dictionary deck should be blank in column 1, but it may contain comments or a serial number in columns 2 to 80 (§ 2.5.3).

§ *2.5.3. Comments before Column 72 and Use of Columns 73-80.* Since all columns after the first blank on a dictionary card and columns 73-80 of all dictionary cards are ignored by the programs, these columns may be used for comments, such as the names of the tags in the instruction or for card serial numbers or other information which will permit the cards to be sorted automatically or manually at any time.

§2.6. Required Special Entries

Columns 1-6 of each of the first five cards in the dictionary deck for TAGGING must contain the following special entries[5] and instructions:

.S=101
.V=102

[5] The grapheme Ø is used instead of the letter O when the latter might be confused with the digit zero. Keypunch operators should be told of this convention.

.Ø=103
.U=104
.N=110

Column 7 on each of these five cards must be blank. Columns 8-80 may contain comments or card-identifying information (§ 2.5.3).

These cards satisfy certain technical requirements of TAGGING (§ 4.45, NTPRET). The "control" tags in the definitions of these required special entries are the only tags over 99 that may appear anywhere in the dictionary deck.

§2.7. Optional Special Entries and Comparability of Results of Different Studies

Twenty alphabetic characters other than those specified as the required special entries (§ 2.6) may be used as alphabetic subscripts when the text is edited (§ 3.10). Each character so used should be included in the dictionary as a special entry, together with an instruction, in the format specified in § 2.5.

To a text sentence in which a word has been given an alphabetic subscript, TAGGING assigns any tags specified by the special entry for that subscript in the dictionary.

Comparability among the results of various studies in which the same dictionary is used with different groups of optional special entries can be controlled, if all optional special entries are defined with tags which are not used to define regular entries.

§2.8. Regular Entries

Any of the following characters or combinations of characters will, if keypunched as the first character of a dictionary card and if not interrupted by blank columns, be correctly processed by TAGGING (§ 4.1) and CROSS-SORT RECORDS (§ 16.1) as a regular dictionary entry:

1. One or more alphabetic characters—for example, I or MAGIC
2. One or more numeric characters—for example, 3 or 1966
3. Any combination of alphanumeric characters—for example, 99TH
4. Any combination of alphanumeric characters punctuated by one or more hyphens or apostrophes (Table 3.A, column II) or equivalent punches (Table 3.A, column III)—for example, FLEA-BITTEN, SISTER-IN-LAW, 4-F, LET'S, O'CLOCK, BULL'S-EYE, WILL-O'-THE-WISP, CAT-O'-NINE-TAILS

Each regular entry should be keypunched with its instruction on a dictionary card in the format specified in § 2.5. Note that no entry may be longer than 39 characters if CROSS-SORT RECORDS (§ 16.1) is to be used.

§ *2.8.1. TAGGING's Suffix-"Removal" Capability.* TAGGING can in many cases assign tags as a result of encountering a text word that differs from an entry with respect to the common suffixes listed in Table 2.A. That is, TAGGING can "remove" the suffix from the text word in order to attempt to match the resultant uninflected form with a dictionary entry and then assign the tags in the instruction for that entry.

*Table 2.A. Suffixes "Removed" by Tagging from Text Words**

Single Suffix	*Suffix Plus S*	*Doubled Letter Plus Suffix*	*Doubled Letter Plus Suffix Plus S*	*Regular Grammatical Forms*	*Examples ("Removable" Suffixes Italicized)*
S				Plural nouns	POT*S*
				3rd person singular verbs	BUILD*S* INSIST*S*
				Possessive pronouns	HER*S* YOUR*S*
'S				Possessive nouns	GOD'*S*
ED		*-ED*		Past participles	ACT*ED* STOP*PED*
				Adjectives from nouns	MONEY*ED* GIFT*ED*
ING	*INGS*	*-ING*	*-INGS*	Present participles Gerunds	DO*ING* PLAN*NING* BEGIN*NINGS*
ION	*IONS*		*-IONS*	Nouns of condition, action, etc.	CONNECT*ION* INSTRUCT*IONS*
E	*ES*		*-ES*	Plural nouns	CHURCH*ES*
				3rd person singular verbs	GO*ES* TEACH*ES*
LY (either alone or preceded by any of above)				Adverbs	COLD*LY* CHARM*INGLY* CONTENT*EDLY*

*For explanation, see § 2.8.1 and § 2.10.3. A hyphen in the third or fourth column stands for the second instance of a doubled letter—for example, the second n in planned.

For example, if PERFECT appears as a regular entry in the dictionary, the tag(s) defining it may be assigned to any of the following words encountered in the text (the "removable" suffixes are *italicized*):

PERFECT
PERFECT*S*
PERFECT*ED*

PERFECT*ING*
PERFECT*ION*
PERFECT*IONS*
PERFECT*LY*

Similarly, TAGGING can "remove" from a text word both a doubled letter that is followed by a common suffix and that suffix itself. For example, if STOP appears as a regular entry in the dictionary, the tag(s) defining it may be assigned to any of the following words encountered in the text (the "removable" suffixes are *italicized):*

STOP
STOP*S*
STOP*PED*
STOP*PING*

Routines for prefix and suffix "removal" can be easily changed to fit the purposes of the investigator. In this section, we describe the routines used with the Harvard III Psychosociological Dictionary. Some other existing General Inquirer dictionaries for English text require the use of somewhat different procedures. The procedures described here do not include prefix "removal," a feature that is more useful, for example, in analyzing German text. Procedures for changing this routine are noted in § 4.47.

Not counting all possible combinations with LY, there are 15 suffixes and combinations of suffixes which TAGGING, in its current form, can "remove" from an inflected text word, in order to attempt to match it to a regular dictionary entry (Table 2.A). As a result of this automatic suffix-"removal" procedure, the number of regular dictionary entries that are necessary for adequate analysis of text can be reduced by a factor of two or three. Note in Table 2.A that the grammatical forms created by the addition of the "removable" suffixes to uninflected words include the most frequent inflected forms in English–that is, all inflected forms of regular nouns and verbs and all adverbs regularly formed from adjectives by the addition of LY.

If the investigator wishes to *prevent* TAGGING from matching an inflected form of a word to the uninflected form, the inflected form should be separately entered in the dictionary. For example, if PASS is defined in a regular entry but PASSION is not, the latter will be tagged as the equivalent of the former; that is, TAGGING will look up the complete word, as encountered in the text, before any prefix or suffix "removal" is attempted. If a match is made, a test for possible "removal" of suffixes (or prefixes) is not performed. If a match is not made, the present procedures make all possible "removals" before the word is looked up a second time. Thus, if PASSIONS is not also a separate entry in the dictionary, it will be reduced to PASS, without any regard for whether PASSION appears as an entry. (An alternative procedure, which is not implemented in the current version of TAGGING, would be to look up progressively shorter forms of the word until a match was found in the dictionary. For example, the text word BEGINNINGS could be looked up first as BEGINNINGS, next as BEGINNING, then as BEGINN, and finally as BEGIN, although the look-up procedure would, presumably, stop as soon as any one of these shortened forms was matched exactly to a dictionary entry.)

The inclusion of E, which is no longer a true English suffix, among the suffixes "removable" by TAGGING (Table 2.A) makes possible another type of economy in the number of regular entries necessary for adequate analysis of text. Hundreds of important and regular English verbs (for example, accuse, complete, live, surprise) have an uninflected form (the first principal part) ending in silent e. This silent e is dropped in the spelling of the present participle (accusing, completing), but retained in the spelling of the past participle (accused, etc.). Neither participle could be successfully matched by TAGGING to a correctly spelled uninflected entry (accuse), but both could be matched if the entry were spelled without the final silent e (accus). For example, having removed ING from CONFUSING (or ED from CONFUSED), TAGGING would be *unable* to match the resultant CONFUS to a regular entry spelled CONFUSE. However, if the regular entry were spelled CONFUS to begin with, then the tags defining that entry would be assigned—in accordance with the normal suffix-"removal" procedures (Table 2.A)—to any of the following words encountered in the text (the "removable" suffixes are *italicized)*:

CONFUS*E*
CONFUS*ES*
CONFUS*ED*
CONFUS*EDLY*
CONFUS*ING*
CONFUS*INGLY*
CONFUS*ION*
CONFUS*IONS*

In general, then, the regular entry for a verb whose uninflected form (first principal part) ends in silent e may be spelled and keypunched without that final e.

Exceptions to this rule should obviously be made in cases in which a verb entry, if spelled without its final e would look exactly like a different word that might be encountered in the text. For example, even if the noun "hat" were not entered in the dictionary but the verb "hate" were entered as HAT, the text words HATE, HATES, HATED, HATING would be correctly tagged but the text words HAT and HATS would also be tagged—and, of course, incorrectly. In this case, in order merely to prevent the nouns HAT and HATS (when encountered in the text) from being considered forms of the verb "hate," there would have to be a separate dictionary entry for all of the basic forms of the verb "hate":

HATE
HATES
HATED
HATING

On the other hand, if both the verb "hate" and the noun "hat" were to be defined in the dictionary and tagged in the text, there would have to be five separate entries, as follows:

HAT
HATE
HATES
HATED
HATING

With these five entries in the dictionary, TAGGING's suffix-"removal" procedure would correctly match the text word HATS to the entry HAT.

There are other possible sources of difficulty with the suffix-"removal" procedures that are implemented in TAGGING for use with the Harvard III Dictionary. These difficulties result from the treatment of doubled letters and of ED. The procedures will reduce inflected words whose uninflected forms normally end with a doubled letter—for instance, KILLING or FILLING—to a "root" without a double letter, such as KIL or FIL. This problem can be handled by specifying both the uninflected form and the "root"—for instance, both KILL and KIL—as separate entries in the dictionary. Similarly, the "removal" of ED can cause such difficulties as matching both WEED and WE, as text words, to the regular entry WE. ED "removal" combined with ING "removal" can, for example, reduce RED and RING to the same "root," R, unless the full forms of both words are specified as separate entries.

The instances of incorrect suffix "removal," while amusing, are in fact quite limited in number. Most of them have been eliminated, in the case of the Harvard III Dictionary, by the necessary additional entries. In developing his own suffix-"removal" procedures, the investigator should bear in mind the inconsistencies which can result from consistent application of spelling rules.

§ 2.8.2. Regular Entries for Excluding Text Words from TAGGING's Leftover List. After the suffix-"removal" procedure has been applied, any text word that still does not match a dictionary entry is recorded by TAGGING in a "leftover" list (§ § 4.32.3; 4.35). This list will be easier to use for dictionary revision (§ 2.18) if it is not crowded with frequently occurring words that are irrelevant to the analysis at hand, such as relative and demonstrative pronouns, prepositions, and conjunctions. Note that each such word would be recorded in the leftover list once for each of its occurrences in the text.

In order to prevent any word from being recorded on the leftover list, the word may be entered in the dictionary as a regular entry (§ 2.8) with an instruction consisting only of the operator N. This is the only function of the operator N. For example, a dictionary card with

WAS=N

would prevent all instances in the text of the word WAS from being recorded in the leftover list.

The suffix-"removal" procedures (§ 2.8.1) are also applied to text words that are inflected forms of regular entries using the instruction N. For example, all instances in the text of both BE and BEING would be excluded from the leftover list by the dictionary card

BE=N

On the other hand, instances in the text of BEING but not of BE would be excluded by

BEING=N

The operator N may also be used as the sole unparenthesized element in a conditional instruction (§ 2.10.4).

§2.9. Unconditional Instructions and Processing of Syntax Markers

An unconditional instruction is one that consists of one or more tags. Each tag must be a one- or two-digit integer from 1 to 99 that identifies a content-analysis category in which an entry has been classified. The instruction must be keypunched after the entry in the format described in § 2.5.1. When TAGGING encounters a text word that is matched to a regular entry (§ 2.8) defined by an unconditional instruction, all tags in the instruction are assigned to the sentence in which that text word has occurred. Similarly, the tags specified in the definition of an optional special entry (§ 2.7) are invariably assigned to any text sentence in which TAGGING encounters an alphabetic subscript identical to the character in the special entry dictionary card. The tags defining a given entry are assigned to a sentence as many times as a text word or an alphabetic subscript matching that entry is encountered in the sentence.

In no case may a blank column occur between the first and last characters of an unconditional instruction. On instructions which end in column 72 or which must be continued onto a second card, see § 2.5.2.

An unconditional instruction may, but need not, contain as many syntax markers as the number of tags specified in the definition. On the processing of syntax markers in unconditional instructions, see later. Whether of an optional special entry or of a regular entry, an unconditional instruction may consist of any of the combinations of tags and syntax markers illustrated in the list that follows:

1. *One tag.* Examples:

    .D=88
    PREVENT=9

2. *Two or more tags.* Each tag must be separated from the next by a comma. The tags need not be in any particular numerical order. Examples:

    .Y=89,90
    DISCOVER=42,8,76

3. *One or more tags modified by one or more syntax marker(s).* The syntax markers are the alphabetic characters S, V, Ø,[6] and U. Each tag or syntax marker must be separated from the next tag or marker by a comma. Each syntax marker in an unconditional instruction modifies any tags following it until another marker is specified in that same instruction. (On the sense in which a marker "modifies" a tag, see the next paragraph.) To take an improbable example, in

[6]On the grapheme Ø, see § 2.6, note 5.

COST=12,S,13,8,V,33

tag 12 is unmodified, tags 13 and 8 are modified by S, and tag 33 is modified by V. Two syntax markers should not be specified consecutively (that is, without at least one tag–with its comma–between them). A syntax marker should not be the last specification in an instruction. Any one tag or any one of the four markers may, but need not, be specified more than once in a single unconditional instruction.

If one of the syntax markers S, V, Ø, or U modifies a tag specified in an unconditional instruction (§ 2.9,*3*), that particular marker will, except under one condition, be appended to the tag whenever the latter is assigned to a sentence by TAGGING. The exception is when the text word that matches the dictionary entry is followed by a numeric subscript (§ 3.12.1) that corresponds to a syntax marker other than the marker that modifies the tag to be assigned. In other words, the syntax marker corresponding to a numeric subscript supersedes the syntax marker modifying a tag in a dictionary instruction whenever that tag is assigned to a numerically subscripted text word. If a numeric subscript does not follow the word to be tagged and the tag to be assigned is not modified in a dictionary instruction by a syntax marker, then TAGGING will append the marker U to that tag when the latter is assigned.

Thus, TAGGING never assigns a tag without appending to it one of the four syntax markers, and the priorities that govern which particular marker is to be appended to any assigned tag may be summarized as follows:

1. *Highest priority:* the syntax marker (only S, V, or Ø) which is controlled by the numeric subscript, if any, which may have been inserted after the text word during editing (§ § 3.12.1-3.12.3).
2. *Second priority:* the syntax marker (S, V, Ø, or U), if any, which in the dictionary instruction modifies the tag to be assigned.
3. *Lowest priority:* in the absence of both (1) and (2), the syntax marker U.

§2.10. Conditional Instructions

A conditional instruction is one which includes at least one conditional expression (§ 2.10.1). A conditional instruction may be applied to any regular entry (§ 2.8) but not to a required or optional special entry (§ § 2.6-2.7).

§*2.10.1. Types of Conditional Expressions.* A conditional expression refers to a specified number of words immediately preceding the text word which has matched the regular entry. There are two types of conditional expressions. A word test (§ 2.11) instructs TAGGING (§ 4.2) to determine whether one or more particular words are present among a specified number of words preceding the text word that has matched the regular entry. A tag test (§ 2.12) instructs TAGGING to determine whether one particular tag has already been assigned to any of a specified number of words preceding the text word that has matched the regular entry.

If a tag test is satisfied, tags previously assigned to the word in which the tag was found are erased. If a word test is satisfied, only tags previously assigned to text words that are quoted in the conditional expression are erased. In other words, in both types of tests, tags previously assigned to words other than those constituting the expression are maintained.

§*2.10.2. Composition and Keypunching of Conditional Instructions.* A conditional instruction may consist of any number of either or both types of conditional expressions and may also contain any number of unparenthesized tags. Each expression must be separately enclosed within a pair of parentheses. The following illustrate some entries with conditional instructions prepared in a correct format:

ENDS=(W,2,ODDS AND,32)
ARM=(W,2,TWIST,11),(T,4,36,82),(W,2,UP IN,52)
BOAT=49,32,(W,3,IN THE SAME,41),18,S,39,(W,2,MISS THE,Ø,59)
BOAT=(W,3,IN THE SAME,41),(W,2,MISS THE,Ø,59),49, 32,18,S,39

In these examples, the character W at the beginning of a parenthesized expression indicates a word test (§ 2.11). It is followed by a number indicating how many previous words are to be examined. The words to be looked for are then specified in the order they are to be found and are followed by the tags to be assigned if they (the specified words) are found. Note that the number of words to be examined may be more than the number of words specified in the test. The extra words thus allowed for in the text may appear before, after, or among the words specified in the test.

The character T at the beginning of a parenthesized expression indicates a tag test (§ 2.12). The first number following the T is the number of previous words to be examined. The second number is the tag to be tested. The remaining numbers (and letters) up to the right parenthesis are the tags (and syntax markers) to be assigned if the tag is found.

The tag test is not the only procedure available for testing tag contingencies during the actual tagging operation (§ 4.2). Other more elaborate procedures are described in § 4.5 and Appendix Four (§ 27.1).

All tests in an instruction that contains more than one conditional expression are evaluated by TAGGING in the order in which the expressions had been keypunched, until one of the tests is satisfied. If one of the tests is satisfied, the tags specified in that expression are assigned and any subsequent expressions in the instruction are ignored. Therefore, in the possibility that a single group of text words might satisfy more than one test in the same instruction, care should be taken in deciding which one is to have priority.[7] Aside from this consideration, there is no restriction on the order in which conditional expressions should be keypunched within a conditional instruction.

If *no* test in the conditional instruction is satisfied and if unparenthesized tags are included in the instruction, *all* the unparenthesized tags will be assigned (regardless of where the unparenthesized tags are keypunched in relation to the conditional expressions). Thus, in either of the last two examples, if BOAT were not found in the phrase IN THE SAME BOAT or MISS THE BOAT, tags 49U, 32U, 18U, and 39S would be assigned. See further § 2.10.5.

TAGGING treats syntax markers in conditional instructions in the same way as syntax markers in unconditional instructions (§ 2.9). However, a syntax marker in a conditional instruction modifies only the tags that follow it *and precede the next left or right parenthesis.*

§ *2.10.3. Suffix "Removal" in Conditional Expressions.* If a conditional expression is a word test (§ 2.11), the specified words can be matched by the appearance of the words in the text exactly as spelled, or—in many but not all cases—by inflected word forms in the

[7] The possibility of such redundancy among two or more word-test expressions (§ 2.11) in a single instruction is rather slight if all of the tests must be satisfied within no more than five or six words preceding the text word that has matched the regular entry. The possibility of such redundancy among two or more tag-test expressions (§ 2.12), or between a word-test and a tag-test expression, is probably somewhat greater and rises sharply with the number of words preceding the matched text word within which any one tag test may be satisfied. See further § 2.11 with note 11.

text that are handled by the suffix-"removal" procedures (§ 2.8.1). The match depends on whether the inflected form of the word is a separate entry in the dictionary.

If the root or uninflected form of a word is specified in a word test and an inflected form of that word does not appear as a regular entry in the dictionary, then any regularly inflected form of the word will satisfy the test. For example, the word-test expression in the instruction BOAT=49,32,(W,2,ROCK,V,37) would be satisfied by the text phrases "rock the boat," "rock*s* the boat," "rock*ing* the boat," and "rock*ed* the boat," unless "rock*s*," "rock*ing*," or "rock*ed*" were separate entries in the dictionary.

If some inflected form of a word is specified in a test, only that form can satisfy the test. For example, the word-test expression in the instruction BOAT=49,32,(W,2,ROCKS,V,37) could only be satisfied by "rock*s* the boat," "rock*s* our boat," or the like, but not by "rock the boat," "rock*ing* the boat," "rock*ed* the boat," etc.[8]

§ 2.10.4. The Operator N in Conditional Instructions. The operator N (§ 2.8.2) may be specified as the only unparenthesized element in an instruction that includes one or more conditional expressions. When

[8]Word-test conditional expressions can perhaps be best explained by reference to the way TAGGING compiles the dictionary and later performs the tests. While the dictionary is being compiled by the program (§ 4.3), all words quoted in word-test expressions are compared with the regular entries (§ 2.8) in the dictionary. If such a word is found to be a regular entry, the storage address of that entry replaces the word itself in the word test. If the word is not an entry in the dictionary, an entry is automatically *created* for it, and the storage address of this created entry replaces the actual word in the word test. Because it has been found that those words quoted in conditional expressions tend also to be included by users as regular entries in their dictionaries, the storage of addresses rather than of actual words makes possible considerable economies in the storage space required by conditional expressions.

Now while the program is looking up the words in a sentence, going from the first word to the last, the dictionary address of each word that has been looked up is stored in a special list. If an inflected dictionary entry is matched, the address of that entry is stored in the special list. If there is no inflected entry and the program "removed" the suffix(es) of the text word in order to match it to an uninflected entry, then the address of that uninflected entry is added to the special list. If no match whatsoever can be found, the text word is made a temporary dictionary "entry" and the address of this temporary entry is put on the special list.

In performing a word test, the program searches back in the special list for an "address" that matches the one that was stored in the conditional expression when the dictionary was compiled. The search begins the number of addresses back specified by the parameter δ in the expression (§ 2.11). The search continues until a match is made or until the last assigned address is reached without a match having been made. If two or more words are quoted in the word test, the test can be satisfied if the addresses of those words appear in the list in the same order (though not necessarily one immediately after the other) as they appear in the stored expression.

so specified, N functions conditionally: It excludes from the leftover list (§ § 4.32.3; 4.35) a text word that has matched the regular entry but has failed to satisfy any test in the instruction. For example, if an occurrence in the text of the word BOAT failed to satisfy either test in the instruction BOAT=(W,3,IN THE SAME,41),(W,2,MISS THE,59), N, the N would prevent that occurrence of BOAT from being recorded in the leftover list. But if N had not been specified, an occurrence of BOAT that failed to satisfy either test would be recorded in the leftover list.

§ *2.10.5. Optional Retention of Unparenthesized Tags.* If the first tag specified for assignment in a conditional expression (§ § 2.11-2.12) is preceded by a plus sign (+), all unparenthesized tags keypunched to the left of that expression will be assigned in addition to the tags within the expression whenever the test is successful. For example, the instruction BOAT=(W,3,IN THE SAME,Ø,41),S,49,32,(W,2,MISS THE,+59,63) would cause only tag 41Ø to be assigned to an occurrence in the text of IN THE SAME BOAT, yet would cause not only tags 59U and 63U but also tags 49S and 32S to be assigned to an occurrence of MISS THE BOAT.

§ 2.11. Format and Examples of Word Tests

A word-test conditional expression should be keypunched in the general format (W,δ,*word or words*,τ) where the enclosing parentheses indicate to TAGGING (§ 4.2) the beginning and end of the expression; the character W instructs TAGGING that the expression is to be of the word-test type; δ is any one- or two-digit integer specifying how many words preceding every occurrence in the text of the regular entry are to be tested; *word or words* is the actual word or words whose presence is to be tested for among the δ words preceding every occurrence in the text of the regular entry; and τ is any number of tags (which may be modified by syntax markers) that TAGGING is to assign to any sentence satisfying the test. A syntax marker in τ modifies all tags that follow it in τ until another syntax marker is specified. In order to instruct TAGGING to retain unparenthesized tags (§ 2.10.5), τ may be preceded by the character +. Each of the first three specifications within the parenthesized expression—that is, W,τ,*word or words,*—must be separated by a comma from the next specification, and each tag or syntax marker in τ must be separated by a comma from the next tag or marker. The last tag in τ must be immediately followed by the right parenthesis with which the expression ends. Thus, the only blank columns that may occur within the parenthesized expression are among ,*word or words*,—that is, among the words whose presence is to be tested for (if more than one word is to be tested for). Unless the right parenthesis with which the expression ends happens to be the very last character of the entire instruction, that right parenthesis must be immediately followed by a comma.

If the δ words preceding a given occurrence in the text of the regular entry are not all in the same sentence as the entry, the test of the expression begins with the beginning of the sentence.

Table 2.B presents various phrases containing the noun ARM, a tentative classification of these phrases into content analysis categories, the tags by which these categories might be identified, and sample word-test conditional expressions that would instruct TAGGING to search for the presence of the various phrases and to assign tags appropriate to each. A conditional instruction in which all these

*Table 2.B. Phrases Containing ARM as a Noun and Corresponding Word-Test Conditional Expressions**

Phrases	*Names of Content Analysis Categories*	*Tags*	*Word-Test Conditional Expressions*
ARM (not in idiomatic phrase)	Body Part	9	
TWIST SOMEONE'S ARM	Control	11	(W,2,TWIST,11)
WITH OPEN ARMS	Pleasure	24	(W,3,WITH OPEN,24,25)
	Sign-Accept	25	
ARM IN ARM	Sex Theme	37	(W,2,ARM IN,37)
BABE IN ARMS	Neuter Role	43	(W,2,BABE IN,43,44,45,46)
	Lower Status	44	
	Follow	45	
	Affection	46	
UP IN ARMS	Arousal	52	(W,2,UP IN,52)
UNDER ARMS	Military	68	(W,1,UNDER,68,69)
	Sign-Strong	69	
BEAR ARMS	Military	68	(W,1,BEAR,68,69)
	Sign-Strong	69	
LAY DOWN ARMS	Military	68	(W,3,LAY DOWN,68,73)
	Sign-Weak	73	

*The names of the categories in Table 2.B—though not the tag numbers that are used to identify them nor the conditional expressions in which these tags are used—have been taken from the Harvard III Psychosociological Dictionary. See Stone *et al., op. cit.,* 170-186. See also §2.11 of this book.

expressions are specified would have to be keypunched within columns 1-72 of three dictionary cards as follows:[9]

ARM=(W,2,TWIST,11),(W,3,WITH OPEN,24,25),(W,2,ARM IN,37),(W,2,BABE IN,43,
44,45,46),(W,2UP IN,52),(W,1,UNDER,68,69),(W,1,BEAR,68,69),(W,3,LAYDO
WN,68,73),9

All expressions in this instruction would be applied by TAGGING to all instances in the text either of the word ARM or of inflected forms thereof (§ 2.10.3). Thus WITH OPEN ARMS can be specified in the same definition as TWIST SOMEONE'S ARM. Instances of ARM or of regularly inflected forms thereof that satisfy none of the word tests in the instruction would be assigned the unparenthesized tag 9 (Body Part).

The first word-test expression (W,2,TWIST,11) instructs TAGGING to test for an occurrence of TWIST (or an inflected form thereof) within the two words preceding any text occurrence of the regular entry ARM (or of an inflected form thereof). Thus, this test could be satisfied by the text phrases

TWIST ARM
TWIST OUR ARMS
TWISTING SOMEONE'S ARM
TWISTED HIS ARM

provided that the inflected forms of TWIST are not separately defined in the dictionary. But the text phrase TWISTED AND BROKE HIS ARM would not satisfy this test. Since the conditional expression quotes only *one* word, TWIST, but specifies that the test is to be performed upon *two* words, any one word may, but need not, intervene between TWIST and ARM. If this were satisfied, any tags that might already have been assigned to TWIST would be erased and tag 11 would be assigned to the sentence. However, tags previously assigned to a text word not explicitly cited in the test—for instance, OUR, SOMEONE'S, or HIS in the examples just given—would not be erased (§ 2.10.1). Since tag 11, as specified to the conditional expression, is not modified by a syntax marker, TAGGING will append the marker U to the assigned tag 11 (§ 2.9). But if the test were satisfied by a numerically subscripted (§ 3.12.1) occurrence of ARM—such as TWISTING/3 MY ARM/5—the marker controlled by the numeric subscript of the text word that matched the regular entry (but never

[9] See § 2.5.2, and note that a comma falls in column 1 of the second card and that the word DOWN has to be divided between the second and third cards. Continuation of the instruction from one card to the next requires no special spacing or punctuation.

a marker controlled by the subscript of any preceding word in the text phrase) would be appended to assigned tag 11. In the last example, the marker which TAGGING would append to assigned tag 11 would therefore be Ø, the marker controlled by /5, the subscript of ARM (Table 3.B).

The next word-test expression in the instruction–(W,3,WITH OPEN,24,25)–tests for the occurrence of WITH OPEN within *three* words preceding any text occurrence of ARM–or in this case, obviously, of ARMS. When, as in this conditional expression, the presence of more than one word is to be tested for, all the words quoted in the conditional expression must occur sequentially (though not necessarily consecutively) in any text phrase satisfying the test. Thus, each of the text phrases WITH OPEN ARMS, WITH OPEN WELCOMING ARMS, WITH OPENED WELCOMING ARMS, or WITH WIDE OPEN ARMS could satisfy the test in this expression.

The third word-test expression in the instruction–(W,2,ARM IN,37)–illustrates a test in which the number of words to be tested for–that is, ARM IN–equals the number of word positions in which they must be found–that is, 2. Thus, unlike both (W,2,TWIST,11) and (W,3,WITH OPEN,24,25), the test in this expression would be satisfied only[10] by ARM IN ARM.

If this phrase occurred in the text sentence THEY WERE WALKING ARM IN ARM, the first occurrence of ARM would fail to satisfy *all* tests in the instruction and would therefore be assigned the unparenthesized tag 9 (§ 2.10.2). Then, when the instruction came to be applied to the second occurrence of ARM, the assigned tag 9 would be erased and tag 37 would be assigned instead. Similarly, in the sentence THEY LAY DOWN ARM IN ARM, the first occurrence of ARM, with two of its three preceding words, would satisfy another test in the instruction–(W,3,LAY DOWN,68,73)–but the tags assigned as a result of this test–68 (Military) and 73 (Sign-Weak)–would be removed once TAGGING came to apply the instruction to the second occurrence of ARM, and determined that this second occurrence, with *its* two preceding words, satisfied the test in (W,2,ARM IN,37). Thus, only tag 37 would, in the end, be assigned to this sentence. In general, then, if any word or words in the text are shared between

[10]We assume that the probability of an occurrence of any inflected version of ARM IN ARM–for instance, ARMS IN ARMS–is negligible, although such inflected versions of the phrase would also satisfy the test.

two or more phrases each of which satisfies a different conditional expression (whether or not the expressions are specified in a single instruction), the net result of the co-occurrence will be the assignment *only* of the tags specified in the expression satisfied by the phrase which ends *last* in the text.[11]

§2.12. Format and Examples of Tag Tests

A tag-test conditional expression should be keypunched in the general format (T,δ,θ,τ) where the enclosing parentheses indicate to TAGGING (§ 4.2) the beginning and end of the expression; the character T instructs TAGGING that the expression is to be of the tag-test type; δ is, as in a word-test expression (§ 2.11), any one- or two-digit integer specifying how many words preceding every occurrence in the text of the regular entry are to be tested; θ is one tag (not modified by a syntax marker) whose previous assignment to any of those δ words is to be tested for; and τ is, as in a word-test expression, one or more tags (which may be modified by syntax markers) which TAGGING is to assign to any sentence that satisfies the test. The tag θ, whose previous assignment is to be tested for, may appear again as one of the tags in τ. Any tag in the expression may also appear as an unparenthesized element of the instruction (§ 2.10.2). A syntax marker in τ modifies all tags which follow it in τ until another syntax marker is specified. Each of the first three specifications within the parenthesized expression—T,δ,θ—must be immediately followed by a comma, and each tag or syntax marker in τ must be separated by a comma from the next tag or marker. The tag τ may be preceded by the character + in order to instruct TAGGING to retain unparenthesized tags (§ 2.10.5). The last tag in τ must be immediately followed by the right parenthesis with which the expression ends. Thus, no blanks may occur anywhere within a tag-test expression. Unless the right

[11] Another special situation is "nested" idioms, each of which satisfies a different conditional expression. Consider the instructions

```
LOV=(W,1,EVER,88),23
BOAT=(W,3,ROCK,6),41
```

as applied to the text sentence DON'T ROCK THE EVER LOVING BOAT. First, EVER LOVING would satisfy the test in the first instruction, which would cause the assignment of tag 88. Tag 6 would be assigned when the second instruction is applied to BOAT. This would happen despite the fact that ROCK in this sentence is the fourth, not the third, word before BOAT. Thus, one idiom that is wholly "nested" within another in the text counts as only a single word when TAGGING starts scanning back from the last word in the surrounding idiom.

parenthesis with which the expression ends happens to be the very last character of the entire instruction, that right parenthesis must be immediately followed by a comma.

If the δ words preceding a given occurrence in the text of a regular entry are not all in the same sentence as the entry, the test starts with the beginning of the sentence.

Assume that we want to test whether the word ARM in the text is preceded by the assignment of any of these tags:

Male Role	(tag) 67
Military	68
Large-Group	70

A separate tag-test expression would have to be specified for each of these three tags (θ) whose presence is to be tested for (since, as just stated, θ may consist of only one tag). However, the same tag or group of tags (τ) might be specified for assignment in each of the three tests. Assume that the tags to be assigned (τ) if any one of the tests is satisfied are:

Sign-Strong	(tag) 69
Attack	71
Danger Theme	72

The three tag-test expressions to be added to the instruction (§ 2.11) for the regular entry ARM would then be as follows:

(τ,4,67,69,71,72), (τ,4,68,69,71,72), (τ,4,70,69,71,72)

USE OF KWIC PROGRAMS FOR DICTIONARY CONSTRUCTION[12]

§2.13. KWIC Index and Statistics

The group of KWIC programs (Chapters 13-15) that has been incorporated into the General Inquirer system is designed to produce a keyword-in-context index of a sample of text (§3.1) keypunched in formats that are also acceptable for processing by TAGGING. In such an index, all occurrences in the text of a word, together with several words that preceded and followed each occurrence, are printed alphabetically in a format that permits easy inspection. A sample page of such an index is reproduced in Figure 15.A. Immediately after all the contexts in which one and the same word has appeared in the text have been

[12] See Stone *et al.*, *op. cit.*, pp. 152-167, for full discussion of the application of the KWIC programs to problems of dictionary construction.

displayed in successive lines in the index, the program prints a line containing statistics on the frequency and distribution of that word (§ 15.6).

The frequency and distribution scores for each word are also recorded on a tape (§ 15.7). The information on this tape can then be automatically sorted in order to generate a listing of the words in the text (each word with its scores) in order of decreasing frequency. This frequency-sorted list of the vocabulary of the processed text can be used as a cross reference to, and summary of, the full key-word-in-context index.

§2.14. Application of KWIC Index and Statistics to Dictionary Construction

If a special dictionary is to be constructed for the purpose of content analysis of a particular body of text, it is advisable first to generate a key-word-in-context index and a frequency-sorted vocabulary list of some significant sample of the text. The sorted list may be used to determine which conceptually significant words recur often enough to merit inclusion in the dictionary as regular entries (§ 2.8). The appearance of different meanings for a given word will also indicate what conditional expressions (§ § 2.11; 2.12) should be included in the dictionary instruction for that word.

A general-purpose analysis of word usage based on a KWIC index for half a million words of text is described in *The General Inquirer.*[13] The results of this analysis will be a set of general computer-based procedures for identifying the different senses that words tend to have in the various kinds of data studied by behavioral scientists. When this analysis is completed, the investigator may draw on these general procedures and supplement them, if necessary, with special routines appropriate to the particular texts he is studying.

AIDS FOR DICTIONARY EVALUATION AND REVISION

§2.15. Display of Alphabetically Sorted Dictionary

The regular entries in a dictionary deck (§ 2.4; Figure 2.A) can be alphabetically sorted by card-sorting equipment or standard computer sort programs. An alphabetic listing of the dictionary is virtually

[13] *Ibid.*

obligatory for almost all revision and checking purposes. (It would, for example, be most time-consuming to attempt to confirm the absence of a regular entry from a dictionary for which an alphabetic listing was unavailable.) For future reference, it is also helpful to record in the alphabetic listing all revisions made in the dictionary.

On printing the contents of any dictionary cards, see § 3.2, note 4.

§ 2.16. Display of "Cross-Sorted" Dictionary

Two programs in the General Inquirer system—CROSS-SORT RECORDS (§ 16.1) and CROSS-SORT LIST (§ 17.1)—have been designed for use together in order to generate from a dictionary deck (§ 2.4; Figure 2.A) a printed listing of a dictionary in "cross-sorted" format, as illustrated in Figure 17.A. In such a listing, all entries in the respective instructions of which one and the same tag has been specified are grouped together. Thus, the entire listing consists of as many sections as the number of different tags specified in dictionary instructions; and in the section for a given tag are displayed in alphabetic order all entries that have been defined, wholly or in part, by that tag.

A "cross-sorted" listing thus makes explicit the structure of each content analysis category in the dictionary. Moreover, whether of itself or supplemented by an alphabetic listing of the dictionary (§ 2.15), the "cross-sorted" listing facilitates checking both entries and definitions for inconsistencies, omissions, redundancies, and the like.

§ 2.17. Frequency of Matches Between Entries and Text Words

If a *FREQUENCIES control card (§ 4.23) is used in a TAGGING run, that program records all entries in the dictionary (or, at the investigator's option, a specified subset of entries), together with the number of times each entry had been matched by text words. This list of entries and their match-frequencies can—again, at the investigator's option—be recorded either on a special *FREQUENCIES tape (§ 4.37) or on the Program-Audit tape (§ 4.32.2, d).

The contents of a *FREQUENCIES tape can be sorted and printed twice—first, by numeric order of the frequencies, and then, by alphabetic order of the entries.[14] (However, an alphabetic sorting operation

[14] The program recommended for both these sorting operations is Sort 7 for the IBM 1401. If a 1401 with 1311 Disk is available, and the file to be sorted is small enough to be stored on the disk, then Sort 6 is probably preferable to Sort 7.

will be unnecessary if the entries were in alphabetic order when the dictionary was first used by TAGGING.)

These two listings—that of frequency-sorted entries, and that of alphabetically sorted entries and frequencies—can be useful for eliminating infrequently matched entries from a dictionary, particularly from a dictionary already so large as to almost exceed TAGGING's storage capacity (§ 2.21), but to which new entries must be added.

By means of the listing of frequency-sorted entries, the most frequently matched regular entries can be rearranged so as to precede all other regular entries in the dictionary deck. With regular entries sequenced in the dictionary deck in this way, running time of TAGGING will be slightly lessened when the dictionary is next used to process very large amounts of text (§ 4.39).

§2.18. Dictionary Revision on the Basis of TAGGING's Leftover List

TAGGING records every occurrence of any text word for which it has been unable to find an entry in the dictionary. The resultant "leftover" list displays these untagged words in the order in which they were encountered by TAGGING in the text deck (§ 3.1). The leftover list may, at the investigator's option, be written on either TAGGING's Program-Audit tape (§ 4.32.3) or a special *LEFTOVERS tape (§ 4.35).

As a repertory of words not defined in the dictionary, the leftover list constitutes an important aid in appraising the effectiveness of a dictionary and in making additions to it. The operator N (§ 2.8.2) can be judiciously used to keep unimportant but very frequent words off the leftover list and thus keep the list fairly short. If a *LEFTOVERS tape is generated and is then sorted alphabetically and printed, patterns of recurrence will be easier to detect.

§2.19. Dictionary Revision on the Basis of Text-Tag Listing

The final evidence for judging the quality of tagging is the "bilingual" listing generated by TEXT-TAG LIST (§ 5.1; Figure 5.A): Judged against the investigator's purpose in attempting content analysis, does this printed "tag-translation" represent accurately the content of the text? If not, revisions or additions to the dictionary should be evident.

§ 2.20. Other Data Pertinent to Dictionary Revision

The Program-Audit tape written by TAGGING can contain a great variety of data pertinent to dictionary revision. For complete details, see § 4.32.2 and § 4.32.5.

§2.21. Size of Dictionary

The size of a dictionary is limited by the amount of core[15] that TAGGING allocates for the purpose of storing the dictionary while it is being used by the program to process text. The present version of TAGGING allocates approximately 23,000 machine words of core for this purpose, but this may be varied by any programmer.

The number of entries in a dictionary is not a precise index of its size, since the actual amount of core necessary to store the dictionary will largely depend on the number of characters in each entry and each instruction. It has been found, however, that the present version of TAGGING can readily accommodate dictionaries which have between 4000 and 8000 entries, and in which conditional instructions (§2.10) of some length are frequently specified.

In every run, TAGGING reports how many entries are in the dictionary, how many machine words the dictionary occupied in core, and how many machine words are still available to accommodate additions to the dictionary (§4.32.2,a,f).

[15]Core is the "memory"–that is, the internal storage area–of computers. The core capacity of a "binary" computer is often measured by a unit termed a "machine word." One machine word of the IBM 7094 is a part of core which is sufficient to store six keypunch characters (§2.5.1, note 4). Core capacity of the IBM 7094, for which TAGGING is programmed, is 32,768 machine words.

CHAPTER 3

Editing and Keypunching of Text[1]

INTRODUCTION

§3.1. The Text Deck

The body of text to be studied must be keypunched on consecutive standard 80-column punch cards.[2] The resultant text deck (Figure 3.A) should consist of three types of cards—text cards, title cards, and end-document cards—in formats that are acceptable as input to TAGGING (§4.2).

Before keypunching, the punctuation of the text must be routinely changed and several types of descriptive information or coding may, but in most cases need not, be inserted into the text. The scope of such required and optional editing is outlined in §3.2.

The end of a document is indicated in the text deck by the insertion of an end-document card (§3.5) after the text card containing the end of the last sentence of that document.[3] The title of a given docu-

[1] Stone, Philip J., Dexter C. Dunphy, Marshall S. Smith, Daniel M. Ogilvie, with associates, *The General Inquirer: A Computer Approach to Content Analysis* (Cambridge, Mass.: The M. I. T. Press, 1966), pp. 76-85.

[2] The cost of keypunching text materials approximates that of having them typed. Recently developed visual scanning devices can encode and transcribe specially typewritten text directly onto magnetic tape. For example, the Control Data 915 Page Reader can convert information typed in the standard font of the American Standards Association onto magnetic tape at a speed of about 370 characters per second. The American Standards Association standard font is available in the form of an interchangeable cartridge or "ball" of the kind used on IBM Selectric typewriters.

[3] However, end-document cards can be wholly omitted from the text deck if the investigator exercises an option by which TAGGING can automatically divide the text into documents of equal or variable length (§4.24).

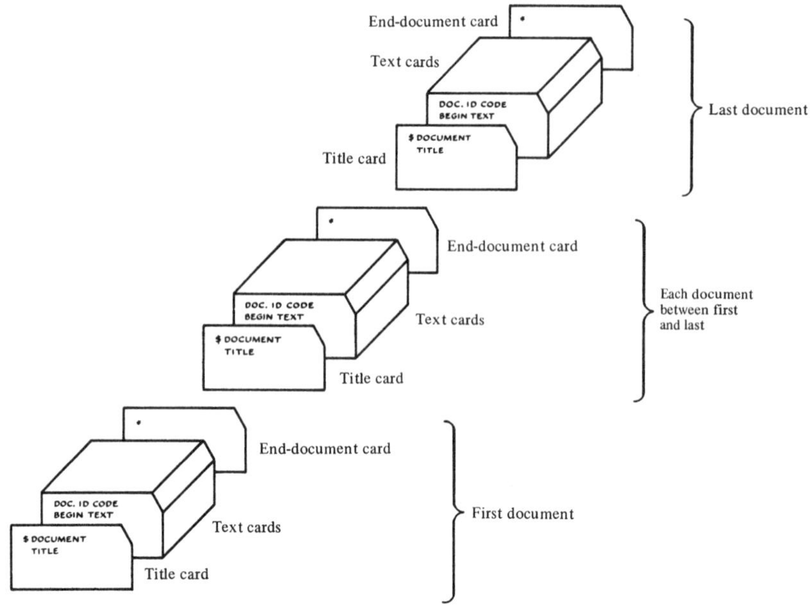

FIGURE 3.A. Schematic of text deck. For explanation see §3.1.

ment should be specified on a title card (§ 3.4) inserted in the text deck immediately before the text card on which the first sentence of the document begins.

With the exception of relatively minor format restrictions that will be noted in the course of this chapter, a text deck ready for processing by TAGGING is also acceptable as input to KWIC RECORDS (§ § 13.1; 13.2.2).

§3.2 Scope of Required and Optional Editing

Aside from specifying title and end-document cards for insertion into the text deck (§ § 3.4-3.5), the required editorial procedures involve assigning a unique document-identification code to each document (§ 3.6) and some punctuation changes (§ 3.7; Table 3.A).

The insertion into the text of various types of descriptive information usually requires considerable editorial preparation and is completely optional. These optional procedures are:

§ 3.8 Assignment of sentence-identification codes to any or all sentences in each document.

§ 3.9 Insertion of descriptors after proper nouns and pronouns.

§ 3.10 Insertion of alphabetic subscripts to be defined in optional special dictionary entries (§ 2.7).

§ 3.11 Insertion of clause delimiters between clauses of compound and complex sentences.

§ 3.12 Insertion of numeric subscripts to differentiate usage of the same word in various syntactic positions.

§ 3.13 Insertion of comments not to be processed by TAGGING.

System considerations pertinent to each of these types of optional editorial insertions are discussed throughout this chapter and are summarized in the description of the tagging operation in § 4.2.

It is advisable to proofread a printed listing of the keypunched text[4] before it is processed by TAGGING. Spelling checks are important since TAGGING cannot correctly assign a tag to a text word which, with the possible exception of its suffix (§ 2.8.1), is spelled differently from a dictionary entry.

CARD FORMATS

§3.3. Text Cards

Once edited according to the conventions described in the rest of this chapter, the text should be transcribed literally onto as many successive 80-column punch cards as necessary. The keypunching of the text can be considered a kind of retyping in which the text is continued from one punch card to the next instead of from line to line on a page. As in typed text, each keypunched word should be separated from the next by at least one blank card column or keypunched mark of punctuation (§ 3.7; Table 3.A). Any number of consecutive blanks may occur anywhere on a text card, since all but the first of consecutive blanks will be automatically deleted by TAGGING (§ 4.2).

TAGGING processes as text only those characters on a text card that follow the first blank card column. This allows for the insertion of a document- or sentence-identification code of up to 70 characters (§ § 3.6; 3.8) before the first blank column on any card. If no code is

[4] The information punched on a deck of cards can be listed, one card per printed line, by various types of EAM devices. A small computer such as the IBM 1401 is often used for this task.

to be assigned to a sentence that ends on the card, column 1 should be blank and the text may begin in column 2.

§ *3.3.1. Sentence Divided Among Successive Text Cards.* A sentence may be continued onto as many successive text cards as necessary. A new sentence may begin on the same card on which the previous sentence ends.

When a sentence is divided among successive text cards, the last character of the last word on each card may fall in any column. That is, the last whole word on a card may be followed by any number of blanks through and including column 80, since, as noted in § 3.3, TAGGING will delete nonsignificant blanks. The continuation on the next card may begin in any column after the necessary first blank.

A sentence longer than 810 characters (not counting nonsignificant blanks and certain hyphens [§ 3.3.2]) will be divided by TAGGING among as many output sentence records as necessary (§ 18.2). See further § 3.11 and § 4.32.5, no. 19.

§ *3.3.2. Word Divided Between Two Text Cards.* If a word is to be divided between two cards, the last character of the first part of the word must be immediately followed on the first card by a hyphen or other word connector (Table 3.A), and the second part of the word should begin after the necessary first blank column (§ 3.3) on the next card. If the hyphen that immediately follows the first part of a divided word falls before column 80, all columns remaining to the right of the hyphen must be blank.

In processing words divided between two cards according to the rules just given, TAGGING (§ 4.2) automatically deletes the hyphen, ignores any blanks that follow it on the first card and unites the two parts of the divided word.

The use of the hyphen as the last character on a card should not be confused with its use in column 1 (§ 3.8) or with its use immediately between two alphanumeric characters on one card. In the latter case, TAGGING considers the hyphen to be part of the normal spelling of a single compound word such as FLEA-BITTEN or ANTI-WAR and does not delete the hyphen.[5]

[5] The elements of a compound word such as FLEA-BITTEN may be divided between two cards by making the first character after the necessary first blank (§ 3.3) on card 2 another hyphen. The hyphen that is the last character on card 1 will be deleted by TAGGING, and the second hyphen (on card 2) will be treated as part of the correct spelling of the word.

§3.4. Title Cards: Format and System Considerations

A title card may be inserted before the first text card of every document.[6] The format of a title card should be:

Card Columns	*Contents*
1	$ [dollar sign]
2-80	Title (any alphanumeric and/or special[7] characters) of the document keypunched in the following text cards.

When TAGGING (§ 4.2) encounters a title card in the text deck, the precise image of that card is transcribed onto the output tape (§ 18.4). Each such title record will subsequently be printed by both TEXT-TAG LIST and RETRIEVAL at the top of every page of sentences (Figures 5.A, 7.B) that followed that title card in the text deck.

If the text deck is to be processed by the KWIC programs as well as by TAGGING, column 3 of title cards should contain a different character for each document (§ 13.2.3).

§3.5. End-Document Cards: Format and System Considerations

An end-document card in the format specified in this section should be inserted immediately after the last text card of *every* document in the text deck, unless automatic documenting (§ 4.24) is used exclusively.

Card Columns	*Contents*
1	* [asterisk]
2,8	Blank.
3-7,9-80	Ignored.

When TAGGING (§ 4.2) encounters an end-document card in the text deck, it writes an end-of-file mark on the output tape and a document summary on the Program-Audit tape (§4.32.2,e). Each document is identified and serially numbered in the printed output of TEXT-TAG LIST (Figure 5.A) and RETRIEVAL (Figure 7.B). TAG TALLY recognizes each end-of-file mark as the delimiter of a document for which a separate set of tag scores is to be computed and tabulated (Figure 6.A).

If the investigator exercises TAGGING's *AUTODOC option

[6] Title cards may also be inserted anywhere else in the text deck.

[7] The 11 special characters other than blank that may be used in General Inquirer processing are those listed in Table 3.A, column II, or their equivalents in Table 3.A, column III. On the alphanumeric characters, see § 2.5.1 note 4.

Table 3.A. Summary of Punctuation Conven

I	II	III	IV	V
	Keypunch Character On IBM 24 or 26 with:			
Unedited Punctuation Marks	Keyboard Arrangements H	Other Keyboard Arrangements	Punch	Printed IBM 1403 BCD Print H
Period or exclamation mark	.	.	12-8-3	.
Question mark	$	$	11-8-3	$
Open or close quotation marks	,,	,,	0-8-3 twice†	,,
Left parenthesis	(	%	0-8-4	(
Right parenthesis	)	¤ or <	12-8-4	)
Comma, semicolon, or dash	,	,	0-8-3	,
Apostrophe	'	@ or – or >	8-4	'
Hyphen	–	–	11	–
Any punctuation mark	*	*	11-8-4	*
Any punctuation mark	=	#	8-3	=
Optional Editing				
Proper noun and pronoun descriptors (§3.9)	( )	% ¤ or <	0-8-4 12-8-4	( )
Alphabetic and/or numeric subscripts (§§3.10; 3.12)	/ //	/ or & // or &&	0-1 0-1 twice†	/ //
Clause delimiter (§3.11)	+ ,, ––	+ or && or – @@ or – – or >> –– or //	12 8-4 twice† 11 twice†	+ ,, ––
Unprocessed comments (§3.13)	((	%%	0-8-4 twice†	((

*For explanation see §3.7 with note 9.
†That is, in two consecutive card columns.

ʾther Special Character Usage in Edited Text*

VI ted by 403 with rint Chain A	VII Keypunch Characters As Interpreted by TAGGING (§4.2)	VIII Comments
	Sentence delimiter	Do *not* use periods to indicate abbreviations such as *Mr.*
$	Sentence delimiter	But if in column 1, indicates that the card is a title card (§3.4).
,,	Word delimiter	But asterisk could be used instead of double commas as keypunched representation of quotation marks. Choice of representation is arbitrary.
%	Word delimiter	Precedes parenthetic statement in original text.
¤	Word delimiter	Follows parenthetic statement in original text.
,	Word delimiter	Do not use commas between digits of large numbers such as *300,000.* For semicolon or dash in syntax-edited text, see "Clause delimiter" in column I (below left).
@	Word connecter	Use normally between parts of a possessive or contracted word such as DON'T or JOHN'S.
–	Word connecter. Printed if it is between two alphabetic characters on one card; deleted if it is the last character on card.	Use normally to connect parts of a compound word such as FLEA-BITTEN or ANTI-WAR; otherwise use to connect parts of a word which must be divided between successive cards (§3.3.2), either case, must immediately follow an alphanumeric character (never a blank); in first case only, must precede an alphanumeric character (never a blank).‡
*	Word delimiter	But if in column 1, indicates that the card is an end-document card (§3.5).
≠	Word delimiter	No predefined use on text cards.
%	Word delimiter	Precedes inserted descriptor.
¤	Word delimiter	Follows inserted descriptor.
	Word delimiter. Every character before the next blank is a subscript.	Must be *immediately* followed by at least one alphabetic or numeric subscript; must not be followed by more than one numeric subscript.
/	Word delimiter. Every character before the next blank is a subscript.	Must be *immediately* followed by at least one alphabetic subscript; can also be followed by no more than one numeric subscript.
& @@ --	Sentence delimiter	Use to divide clauses of compound or complex sentence. TAGGING treats each divided clause as though it were a *separate* sentence.
%%	Word delimiter. All words before the next) or ¤ are not to be tagged.	Precedes inserted comment that is not to be processed by TAGGING as part of the text. End of inserted comment indicated by single right parenthesis.

For the special use of a hyphen in column 1 of a text card, see §3.8.

(§ 4.24), single end-document cards are ignored (and may be omitted) and documents of equal or variable length are automatically created on the tape in Format One.

REQUIRED EDITING

§3.6. Document-Identification Codes: Format and System Considerations

An identifying combination of as many as 70 alphanumeric and/or special characters[8] must begin in column 1 of the first text card of each document in the text deck. At least one blank column (§ 3.3) must separate the last character of this document-identification code from the beginning of the text.

The identification code assigned to the first sentence of a document will serve to identify the tag scores for the entire document when these scores are computed by TAG TALLY (§ 6.1) and undergo further processing by five other programs (§ § 1.5; 6.3.2). However, TAGGING (§ 4.2) treats a document-identification code merely as the sentence-identification code of the document's first sentence (§ 3.8).

If the text deck is to be processed by KWIC RECORDS (§ § 13.1; 13.9), only the first 19 characters of the code will be processed.

§3.7. Punctuation Conventions

Marks of punctuation in the text that are not included in the character set of the IBM 24 or 26 Card Punch must be changed to special characters that can be keypunched, as summarized in columns I-IV of Table 3.A.[9] This table also summarizes usage of special characters in optional text editing procedures (§ § 3.8; 3.13).

[8] See note 7. However, the special characters * and $ should *not* be used in the *initial* position (card column 1) of a document- or sentence-identification code; and a hyphen may be used in that position only in order to indicate that the code keypunched on a previous card remains valid for the current card. See further § 3.8.

[9] There are ten possible "combination" keyboard arrangements of an IBM 24 or 26 Card Punch. These arrangements differ *only* in the markings on the keys that cause the punching of the special characters (Table 3.A, columns II-III) but not in the punch–that is, the configuration of holes–that any given key causes to be made in a card column (*ibid.*, column IV). Arrangement H, on which the characters listed in column II appear, is the most suitable for keypunching a General Inquirer text deck. If H is available, column III may be ignored. Though all the punches specified in column IV can also be made by an IBM 29 Card Punch, the characters on the keys of this machine will sometimes differ from those in either column II or III.

OPTIONAL EDITING

§3.8. Sentence-Identification Codes: Format and System Considerations

Any combination of as many as 70 alphanumeric and/or special[10] characters may be assigned to any sentence as its identification code. The code for a sentence must be keypunched beginning in column 1 of a text card. The first blank column (§3.3) on that card indicates the end of the code and the beginning (or resumption from the previous card) of the sentence to which the code applies.

TAGGING (§4.2) will assign to a given sentence the code which is stored in a special buffer[11] in the computer's memory when the end of the sentence is reached. By "assignment" is meant the writing of the code in a field of the tape record for the given sentence (§18.3, positions 7 to n). The contents of this code buffer can change each time the program begins to read a new card in the text deck. If column 1 of the new card is blank, any identification code currently stored in the buffer is erased, and if a sentence happens to end on that card, no identification code can be assigned to it. If, however, column 1 of the new card contains a hyphen, any identification code currently stored in the buffer is maintained and will be assigned to any sentence that happens to end on that card.[12] The third possibility is that of column 1 containing a valid code character—that is, any character except * $—or blank. In this case, the contents of all columns (up to the maximum of 70) before the first blank on the card are immediately recorded in the code buffer (replacing the previously stored code, if any) and will be assigned to any sentence that happens to end on the card.

The use of hyphens in column 1 of text cards permits efficiency in the actual keypunching of codes. For example, if a sentence must be keypunched on two or more text cards (§3.3.1), its code never has to be keypunched on more than one of those cards, provided a hyphen is then punched in column 1 of all subsequent cards containing any part of the sentence.

[10] See notes 7 and 8.

[11] The term "buffer" is used to denote an area in the computer's memory that is used for temporary storage of data which have just been read from an input medium or which, as in the present case, are about to be recorded on an output medium.

[12] Code characters may immediately follow a hyphen in column 1 of a text card, but will be ignored by TAGGING and will not affect the code, if any, currently stored in the code buffer.

Sentence-identification codes are particularly important for studies of text materials in which there is little or no formal continuity from one sentence, or group of sentences to the next. For example, in analyzing sentence-completion tests, it may be necessary to give each sentence a code indicating the characteristics of the respondent and the position of the sentence in the test. Suppose that the respondent's identification number were punched in columns 1-2 of the code, the respondent's sex in column 3, whether he is in the experimental or control group in column 4, and the sentence item he is completing in column 5. If it is assumed only a respondent's completions were punched, then the first six cards of the text deck–including an initial title card (§ 3.4)–would be as follows:

$ GROUP ONE, EXPERIMENTAL GROUP, MALES, 3/17/66
01111 AFTER EATING BREAKFAST.
01112 WALK AWAY MAD.
01113 ASK MY GREAT AUNT MATILDA WHETHER OR NOT
–THERE IS A SANTA CLAUS.
01114 ORDER FISH INSTEAD.

In this example, each sentence completion is started on a new card. But if a completion has to be continued onto a second card, the hyphen with which the continuation card begins indicates that the last keypunched sentence-identification code remains valid.

Sentence-identification codes can be used by TAGGING as criteria both for automatic documenting (§ 4.24) and for assigning "sentence summary" tags (§ § 4.5; 27.10.2). These codes can also be used as retrieval criteria by RETRIEVAL (§ § 7.1; 7.5.3). In editing the text, the investigator should anticipate these important possible uses of sentence-identification codes.

Often a document-identification code (§ 3.6) is to be applied as a sentence-identification code to each sentence in the document. All cards after the first card containing the identification code must then begin with either the entire document identification or a hyphen.

§ 3.9. Proper Noun and Pronoun Descriptors: Format and System Considerations

In order to achieve greater thoroughness and accuracy of tagging, parenthesized descriptors may be inserted into the text after proper nouns and after pronouns whose antecedents, expressed or implied, are significant in the content analysis. For instance, in a study of responses to a survey of attitudes to the arts, the sentence, "I think she is the best one at the Met," might be edited and keypunched as I THINK SHE (SINGER) IS THE BEST ONE AT THE MET (OPERA). The assumption underlying the assignment of descriptors is that the proper noun and the pronoun are not defined entries (§ 2.8) in the dictionary to be used by TAGGING (§ 4.2), whereas the inserted descriptors are or may be defined there. Thus, if the descriptors SINGER and OPERA in the example just given are entries in the dictionary, TAGGING will be able to assign to this sentence tags that in this context are appropriate to SHE and MET, although the latter are not in the dictionary.

The rationale for the insertion of proper noun and (in particular) pronoun descriptors is to enable TAGGING (§ 4.2) to tag implied or oblique references in the text to dictionary categories and thus to enable RETRIEVAL (§ 7.1) to locate and retrieve the greatest number of sentences to which a certain tag had been assigned.

TAGGING (§ 4.2) excludes inserted descriptors from its count of the number of text words in each sentence (§ 18.3) and in each document (§ 4.32.2,e). Thus, the tag scores that can be computed by TAG TALLY on the basis of the total number of words in a document (§ 6.2) are *not* affected by the number of descriptors inserted into the text.

In the case of proper nouns, an alternative, and perhaps simpler, strategy for insuring that they are correctly tagged is the use of alphbetic subscripts (§ 3.10).

§3.10. Alphabetic Subscripts: Format and System Considerations

If a single slash (/) is inserted immediately after a text word and is in turn followed by an alphabetic subscript that constitutes an optional special entry (§ 2.7) in the dictionary, TAGGING (§ 4.2) will look up the subscript but not the text word in the dictionary and will assign the tag(s) of the subscript. For example, if the text word "Buffalo" is keypunched as BUFFALO/C and if C is defined in a special dictionary entry with a tag for cities, then TAGGING will not attempt to determine whether BUFFALO itself is defined in a regular dictionary entry (§ 2.8) but will instead look up the subscript C and assign the tag for cities.

However, if two slashes (//) intervene between the text word and its subscript, TAGGING not only will assign the tag(s) for the subscript but will also attempt to find the text word itself among the regular dictionary entries. In this case, if the text word is defined as a regular entry, the tag(s) in the instruction for that entry will *also* be assigned. For example, BUFFALO//C could be assigned the tags for both cities and animals. But if two slashes and an alphabetic subscript follow a text word that is *not* a regular dictionary entry, TAGGING will record that word, preceded by an asterisk, in the leftover list (§ 4.32.3).[13]

Any number of alphabetic subscripts, whether introduced by one or two slashes, may follow a single text word. In such cases, all tags used to define every subscript character will be assigned.

Alphabetic subscripts have the advantages of not requiring as much keypunching as inserted descriptors (§ 3.9) and of being able to cancel the tags associated with the subscripted text word.

An alternative to editing proper nouns with alphabetic subscripts is to temporarily incorporate the nouns into the dictionary by means of TAGGING's dictionary-editing routines (§ § 4.4; 4.13). However, although this procedure works well for nouns, it does not handle the identification of pronouns.

TAGGING generates an error message (§ 4.32.5, no. 1) for, but otherwise ignores, any alphabetic character used as a subscript in the text but not defined in the dictionary as an optional special entry.

Alphabetic subscripts and the preceding slashes are normally removed form the text by TAGGING (§ 18.3) and will thus not be recorded in the listings and tapes generated by TEXT-TAG LIST (Figure 5.A; § 5.9) and RETRIEVAL (Figure 7.B; § 7.13). However, a TAGGING control card option (§ 4.25) permits retention of subscripts in the tagged output tape. If this option is exercised, the subscripts will be available for use in retrieval operations (§ 7.5.2).

§3.11. Clause Delimiters: Format and System Considerations

The clause delimiters are the following punches (Table 3.A):

+	(12-punch)
,,	(8-4 punches in two consecutive card columns)
@@	(8-4 punches in two consecutive card columns)
——	(11-punches in two consecutive card columns)

[13] A text word followed by *one* slash and an alphabetic subscript will never be recorded in TAGGING's leftover list. This is because the single slash together with the alphabetic subscript prevents the word from being looked up in the dictionary, and a leftover word is by definition one that has been looked up in the dictionary but not found there.

Any one of these clause delimiters may be inserted between two text words. A clause delimiter may, but need not, be immediately preceded or followed by blanks. TAGGING (§ 4.2) treats the words between two clause delimiters, or between a clause delimiter and a sentence delimiter (period or dollar sign), as a separate sentence. That is, TAGGING writes a separate sentence record (§ 18.3) on the tagged text output tape for each group of words between two delimiters.

Clause delimiters are to be inserted between the clauses of compound or complex sentences. TAGGING will process each of the following examples as consisting of two separate sentences:

THE SOLOISTS SANG WELL + BUT THE CHORUS KEPT DROWNING THEM (SOLOISTS) OUT.

WHEN THE PRESIDENT FINISHED HIS ADDRESS, + WAS THERE A RECEPTION FOR THE DIPLOMATIC CORPS$

The use of a clause delimiter may occasionally necessitate insertion of an implicit subject or predicate. Such insertions may be parenthesized. For example:

JOHNSON HAS SENT 500000 SOLDIERS TO FIGHT IN VIETNAM + BUT STILL (JOHNSON) HAS NOT FORMALLY DECLARED WAR.

The division of long sentences into shorter, self-contained units can greatly improve the results of RETRIEVAL's searches for within-sentence tag co-occurrences (§ § 7.1; 7.5.1). That is, if text units are short, the investigator can be more certain that the given tags co-occur within a single thought and do not merely happen to have been assigned to completely different sections of a strung-out sentence.

Use of clause delimiters is especially important if the full syntax-editing capability of the General Inquirer is to be implemented by the insertion of numeric subscripts (§ 3.12).

Note also that TAGGING cannot process as a single unit a sentence longer than 810 characters (§ 4.32.5, no. 19) and that subsequent programs in the system also impose restrictions on sentence length (§ 5.10).

§ 3.12. Numeric Subscripts

§ *3.12.1. Formats.* By the insertion into the text of numeric subscripts, TAGGING (§ 4.2) can be made to recognize syntactic distinctions in the usage of words that are to be tagged. There are six numeric subscripts (Table 3.B), each consisting of a single digit and each to be inserted after a slash (/) when that slash is in turn immediately preceded by the text

*Table 3.B. Syntax Markers Controlled by the Numeric Subscripts**

Syntactic Position in Which Text Word Occurs	*Numeric Subscript Inserted by Editor after Text Word*	*Syntax Marker† Appended by TAGGING to Tag (s) Assigned to Subscripted Text Word*
Subject	1	S
Verb	3	V
Object	5	Ø
Subject of "attributive" clause	8	S
Verb of "attributive" clause	9	V
Object of "attributive" clause	0	Ø

*See § § 3.12.1-3.12.3.
†On the grapheme Ø, see § 2.6, note 5.

word to be subscripted. Only one numeric subscript may be applied to a given text word. In addition to the numeric subscript, one or more alphabetic subscripts (§ 3.10) may, but need not, be applied to a text word. (If both types of subscripts are applied to a single word, the order in which they are keypunched is insignificant.) A numeric subscript may be preceded by a double slash (//) only if the numeric is accompanied by one or more alphabetic subscripts.

As further described in the following sections (§ § 3.12.2-3.12.4), the current use of numeric subscripts is to control the syntax markers to be appended by TAGGING to every tag assigned to a subscripted word (and/or its alphabetic subscripts, if any). Like the suffix-"removal" procedures (§ 2.8.1), the numeric subscript procedures have been designed especially for use with the Harvard III Psychosociological Dictionary.

§ *3.12.2. Noun-Verb and Subject-Object Distinctions.* The first type of distinction that can be made by the insertion of numeric subscripts is whether a word occurs in the text as a noun or a verb, and if a noun, whether it occurs in a "subject" or "object" position.

The noun-verb distinction is for the most part grammatically unambiguous. But the subject-object distinction exhausts only three of five major syntactic possibilities of nouns—subject of a verb, and direct or indirect object of a verb (examples a-d in the list that follows). A predicate nominative, the fourth possibility, is perhaps best classified as an object (example e). But objects of prepositions, the fifth possibility, can be considered as belonging in either the subject or object category, depending on whether the prepositional phrase falls in the subject (example f) or predicate (example g) of the sentence. Most investigators who have used numeric subscripts for syntax editing have tried to identify only the main subject and object of sentences and have left unmarked indirect objects, predicate nominatives, and objects of objects of preposition.

a. LOVE/1 MAKES THE WORLD GO ROUND.
b. I LOVE/3 YOUR MAJESTY ACCORDING TO MY BOND.
c. GREATER LOVE/5 HATH NO MAN + THAN THAT HE SHOULD LAY DOWN HIS LIFE FOR HIS FRIEND.
d. GIVE LOVE/5, NOT THE DEVIL, ITS DUE.
e. THERE'S NO LOVE/5 LOST BETWEEN THEM.
f. A WOMAN IN LOVE/1 IS NOT TO BE SCORNED.
g. IT IS GENERALLY TRUE + THAT ONLY WEAK MEN MARRY FOR LOVE/5.

Numeric subscripts have also been applied in some studies to distinguish between the use of *adjectives* in "subject" and "object" positions—for instance, GREATER/5 in c, as opposed to HIS LOVE/1 WAS GREATER/1 THAN HERS.

§ *3.12.3. Attributive Versus Nonattributive Distinctions.* The other type of distinction that can be made by the insertion of numeric subscripts involves the use of words in "attributive" clauses. The special subscripts used for this purpose are 8, 9, and 0 (Table 3.B). By an "attributive" clause is meant any clause whereby one person specifies that he is reporting the words or thought either of another person or source or of himself. For example:

a. DR JOHNSON/8W AT ALL TIMES INSISTED/9 THAT ONLY WEAK/1 MEN/1 MARRY/3 FOR LOVE.
b. I (FALSTAFF/8C) SHALL TELL/9 THE PRINCE/0 + THAT HONOR/1 IS BUT A WORD.

In processing a sentence into which one or more attributive subscripts had been inserted, TAGGING creates two sentence records rather than one (§ 4.2). In the first of the two records (§ 18.3, record a), only the words to which an attributive subscript had been applied are written in parentheses and are followed by any tags that were then assigned to those words. In the second record (§ 18.3, record b) are written *all* the words in the sentence, but these are followed *only* by those tags assigned to words without a numeric subscript, or words to which nonattributive subscripts had been applied. For example, sentence (a) might be displayed by TEXT-TAG LIST (§ 5.1; Figure 5.A) as follows:

(JOHNSON INSISTED)	WRITER	S	OVERSTATE	V
DR JOHNSON AT ALL TIMES INSISTED THAT	MALE-ROLE	S	SIGN-WEAK	S
ONLY WEAK MEN MARRY FOR LOVE.	SEX-THEME	V	SEX-THEME	U

On the syntax marker U in this example, see § 2.9.

§ *3.12.4. System Considerations.* Inasmuch as the syntax markers controlled by numeric subscripts supersede those specified in dictionary instructions (§ § 2.9; 2.10.2), the tag assigned to a text word may have one syntax marker if the text word had been subscripted but a different marker if the word had not been subscripted. For example, the syntax marker V might be specified in the instruction for the dictionary entry LOVE. This marker would, then, automatically be appended to the tags assigned to text occurrences of LOVE, unless an edited subscript indicated that the word was being used as a noun.

Numeric subscripts and the preceding slashes are normally removed from the text by TAGGING (§ 18.3). However, a TAGGING control card option (§ 4.25) permits retention of subscripts in the tagged text output tape. If this option is exercised, the subscripts will be available for use in retrieval operations (§ 7.5.2).

§ 3.13. Unprocessed Comments

The investigator or editor may insert comments into the text at any point. Two left parentheses should precede the first word of the comment, and one or two right parentheses should follow the last word of the comment. TAGGING (§ 4.2) will transcribe the comment verbatim in the output tape record (§ 18.3) for the sentence in which the comment was encountered. However, no tags will be assigned to the words in the comment, and those words will not be included in the counts of the number of words in the text sentence (§ 18.3) or document (§ 4.32.2,e) in which the comment occurred.

PART TWO

PRIMARY PROGRAMS

CHAPTER 4

Tagging[1]

INTRODUCTION

§4.1. Function

This program assigns tags specified in an input dictionary to a body of input text and records the text, as thus tagged, on an output tape that can be processed by TEXT-TAG LIST (§5.1). During the tagging operation, the program automatically responds to any of the numerous options that may have been elected when the input dictionary was prepared and the text edited (§§2.4-2.12; 3.1-3.13). In the next section (§4.2), the tagging operation is described, and the ways in which it may be affected by these options are reviewed.

TAGGING can be executed on an IBM 7094[2] either under control of a monitor system (§§4.7-4.10) or independently as a self-loading program (§4.11). Execution of the program under control of a monitor system is generally assumed throughout this chapter.

With the exception of options exercised in preparing dictionary and text input, all program options depend on the use of program control cards, as summarized in §4.6 and described in detail in §§4.14-4.26.

Figures 4.C-4.F illustrate the preparation of card decks, tapes, and machine-operator instructions for typical program runs.

§4.2. The Tagging Operation and Supplementary Output

In a tagging operation, the program looks up in the resident dictionary

[1] Stone, Philip J., Dexter C. Dunphy, Marshall S. Smith, Daniel M. Ogilvie, with associates, *The General Inquirer: A Computer Approach to Content Analysis* (Cambridge, Mass.: The M. I. T. Press, 1966), pp. 93-96.

[2] For running TAGGING on an IBM 7090 or System/360, see §4.7. Other technical characteristics of the program are discussed at the end of this chapter. See §4.41 on machine requirements; §4.42 on installing the object program for execution under control of a monitor system; and §§4.44-4.46 on the language and organization of the program.

(§ 4.3) each successive word of the text input (§ 4.12). In so doing, the program attempts to find an exact match between each text word and a regular entry (§ 2.8) in the dictionary.[3] The program considers a text word to be any combination of alphanumeric characters (§ 2.5, note 4) and word connectors (Table 3.A) that had been keypunched in consecutive columns on a text card (§ 3.3) after the obligatory first blank column on that card. A blank column or one of the word, clause, or sentence delimiters specified in Table 3.A indicates the beginning and the end of a word.

If no matching entry can be found in the dictionary but the given text word is inflected with one or more common suffixes, the program can "remove" the suffix(es) in order to attempt to match the uninflected form of the word to a regular dictionary entry (§ § 2.8.1; 2.10.3).[4] If, after this suffix-"removal" procedure has been performed, the text word still cannot be matched, the word is recorded in a "leftover" list of untagged words. Words that are not to be tagged may be purposely excluded from this leftover list (§ 2.8.2).

If a single slash (/) followed by one or more alphabetic subscripts had been inserted after a text word during editing (§ 3.10), TAGGING does not attempt to match the text word itself to a regular dictionary entry but rather compares each alphabetic subscript with optional special entries (§ 2.7) in the dictionary. If one or more matches are found, the program assigns any tags whereby each matching special entry had been defined. If two slashes (//) intervene between a text word and one or more alphabetic subscripts, the subscript character(s) are compared with optional special entries and the text word itself with regular entries. Then the program assigns any tags whereby matching entries of either or both types had been defined. If no match is found for a subscripted text word with which two subscripts had been used, the word itself, preceded by an asterisk, is recorded in the leftover list.

If the entry to which a text word has been matched is followed by an unconditional instruction (§ 2.9), all tags in that instruction are assigned to the sentence in which the word occurs. But if the entry is followed by a conditional instruction (§ 2.10), each conditional expression in the instruction is evaluated in the order in which the expressions had been keypunched until a test specified in one of them is satisfied (§ § 2.10-2.12).

[3]On some technical aspects of the look-up procedure, see § 2.10.3, note 8.

[4]Suffix "removal" is an optional feature of the present version of TAGGING. See § 4.47.

To every tag that it assigns the program appends one of four syntax markers–S, V, Ø, or U–in accordance with the priorities enumerated in § 2.9.

Tagged text is recorded on a tape in Format One (§ 4.36). Following the text of the sentence are written all tags that may have been assigned to words or phrases in the sentence. The tags in this "string" are sequenced in the order in which they had been assigned–that is, in an order corresponding to that of the words in the sentence. Each text sentence is transcribed with its tags onto this output tape as part of a separate physical record. These "sentence records" (§ § 1.8; 18.3) are created in the order in which input text sentences are encountered by the program. All consecutive text words between one sentence delimiter or clause delimiter and the next are considered by the program to constitute a sentence (§ 3.11). A sentence in which one or more attributive numeric subscripts are encountered is always written in two separate records (§ § 3.12.2; 18.3).

TAGGING also writes on the output tape the number of text words in each sentence, the serial number of each sentence, and a sentence-identification code, if such a code had been recorded in a special storage area of the computer's memory by the time the program reached the end of the sentence (§ 3.8).

A final optional step before tagged sentences are written on the output tape may be a search for co-occurrences among the assigned tags. If such "sentence summary" tests (§ 4.5) are executed, their only possible effect on the tagging operation is to add or remove tags to or from the tag string of a sentence.

Upon encountering either an end-document card (§ 3.5) in the text deck after the last text card of the final sentence of a document or an automatic documenting condition (§ 4.24), TAGGING writes an end-of-file mark on the tape in Format One (§ 18.5), and a document summary on the Program-Audit tape (§ 4.32.2, e). Thus, sentence records of all sentences in a text document are grouped together in a separate file (§ 1.9). Title cards (§ 3.4), when encountered in text input, are transcribed literally onto the tape in Format One (§ 18.4).

The program automatically generates a running description of the progress of a run on a Program-Audit tape (§ 4.32). The information recorded on this tape during a tagging operation invariably includes summaries of the volume of all text, dictionary, and dictionary-editing input (§ 4.32.2) and lists of format errors discovered in such input

(§ 4.32.5). The leftover list is also recorded on the Program-Audit tape (§ 4.32.3), unless the investigator explicitly instructs the program to record it on a special *LEFTOVERS tape (§ 4.35).

A completely optional by-product of tagging is a list of dictionary entries with the number of times each entry had been matched by any processed text word. At the investigator's option, this list can include all dictionary entries or only a specified subset of them (§ 4.23) and can be recorded on either the Program-Audit tape (§ 4.32.2, d) or on a special *FREQUENCIES tape (§ 4.37).

§ 4.3. Dictionary Compilation

After a run has begun but before a tagging operation (§ 4.2) can be initiated, the program must load the input dictionary into core.[5] If the input dictionary had been submitted in uncompiled form, the dictionary, while being loaded, is "compiled"[6] under program control. During compilation of a previously uncompiled dictionary, redundant or otherwise erroneous entries are automatically deleted with appropriate error messages (§ 4.32.5, no. 14), and compilation continues. If the uncompiled dictionary is too big to be loaded into the area in core allocated for storing it (§ 2.21), the program run will be terminated immediately (§ 4.32.5, no. 10). A dictionary that has been successfully compiled and loaded and thus is ready for use in a tagging operation will be referred to as the resident dictionary.

In any run TAGGING can transcribe the resident dictionary from core as a file on a special output tape to be referred to as a *NEW tape (§ 4.34). If this option is elected, the resultant tape file may be used as dictionary input in subsequent runs. From that point of view—that is, when considered as input—a *NEW tape file is simply a precompiled dictionary. A precompiled dictionary is read from a *NEW tape file under control of a *LOAD card (§ 4.15); conversely, a resident dictionary is transcribed onto a *NEW tape file under control of a *NEW card (§ 4.19).

[5] The loading process, also to be referred to as the "reading-in" process, involves transfer of information from external storage media such as magnetic tape into the machine's internal storage area—that is, core (§ 2.21, note 15).

[6] The term "compilation" is generally used to describe a translation process by which a computer automatically converts a program from a problem-oriented source language such as FORTRAN into binary machine instructions. The term has here been extended to describe an analogous process by which TAGGING encodes dictionary data from the prescribed punched card formats (§ § 2.5-2.12) into a more compact form known as a "hash list." See § 2.10.3, note 8.

Compilation and transcription of a resident dictionary onto a tape may be the sole purpose of a program run. A run for this purpose alone is advisable in the case of any uncompiled input dictionary, or even a precompiled dictionary to which extensive additions are to be made by means of the dictionary-editing procedures (§ 4.4). If part of the input dictionary or the additions thereto fail to be compiled or loaded in the special run, the conditions that have caused this are recorded on the Program-Audit tape, and measures to correct them can be taken before another run is attempted. Moreover, the frequency counts (§ 4.2) of matches between dictionary entries and text words are set at zero only when a dictionary is first compiled; and it is useful to have such a "cleared" dictionary on a *NEW tape for future runs.

However, a *NEW tape file can also be written in runs during which tagging and/or dictionary editing is to be performed. For example, an extra copy of a *NEW tape file can be generated during a run in which the "original" of the desired copy is also used for tagging.

§4.4. Editing Resident Dictionary

Once an input dictionary has been compiled and loaded (§ 4.3), the resultant resident dictionary can, at the investigator's option, be subjected to three types of revisions: new entries (with their respective instructions) can be added to the resident dictionary; the instructions for entries present in the resident dictionary can be corrected; and entries can, together with their respective instructions, be deleted from the resident dictionary. The revisions themselves are specified on dictionary cards (§ 4.13). There is no restriction on the type or number of revisions that can be made during a single program run, provided only that additions and corrections, if any, do not cause the resident dictionary to overflow its storage area in core (§ § 2.21; 4.32.5, no. 10). (Additions and corrections made with these automatic procedures occupy more of core than would be the case if they were made part of the original dictionary deck.)

Once the dictionary is resident in core, it can be edited at any point in the run—before, during, or after it is used for tagging (§ 4.2) and before or after it is transcribed onto a *NEW tape file (§ 4.3). The sequence of operations is determined merely by the arrangement of data and control cards in the general input deck. If dictionary-editing cards precede a *NEW card (§ 4.19) in the general input deck, any revisions specified on those cards will have been made in the resident dictionary before the latter is transcribed onto the *NEW tape file. This procedure will be termed "permanent editing," since its results become available for future runs. But if dictionary-editing cards follow the *NEW card (or if there is no *NEW card), then the editing of the resident dictionary is temporary, since its sole purpose is to affect a tagging operation that is to be performed in the same run. If in either permanent or temporary editing the editing cards interrupt rather than precede the text in the general input deck, then revisions of the resident dictionary will affect the tagging of only that portion of text which follows the editing cards. Several sets of dictionary-editing cards can interrupt the text at several points in the input deck.

§4.5. Sentence-Summary Procedures

A sentence-summary capability has been designed as a supplementary and purely optional part of the tagging operation (§ 4.2). All sentence-summary tests are performed on each text sentence immediately after all words in the sentence have been processed—that is, looked up in the dictionary—but before the resultant tag string is transcribed onto the tape in Format One (§ 4.36). If this option is elected, the program can test for the co-occurrence of certain tags in the string of tags assigned to a sentence. The program can then add tags to, and/or delete tags from, the string assigned to any sentence satisfying a test. Any number of tests can be performed.[7] For each test, the investigator himself specifies which tags should be tested for, what logical or sequential patterns among the specified tags should satisfy the test, and what tags should be added to, and/or deleted from, the tag string of any sentence satisfying the test. If test specifications are designed in such a way that test results are stored in the computer's memory, it is possible to test across as well as within sentence boundaries (§ 27.12) and thus to detect and summarize patterns of tag co-occurrence in one or more entire text documents.[8]

Procedures for designing sentence-summary tests and incorporating them into the TAGGING source program are described in greater detail in Appendix Four (§ 27.1).

[7] The investigator can also test the values of the major counters in the program (§ 27.10.1), and can write on the Program-Audit tape to indicate exceptional circumstances (§ 27.11).

[8] Across-sentence summaries are described in Stone *et al., op. cit.*, pp. 91-92, in connection with scoring need-achievement. See pp. 203-205 of that work for three examples of need-achievement summary scoring.

§4.6. Use of Control Cards

Loading a dictionary, editing a dictionary, tagging text, recording counts of how many times each dictionary entry has been matched by text words, retaining subscripts, and writing a *NEW tape file are all under the direction of control cards. These cards may appear in the input deck in any order; in general, the order of these cards determines the relative sequence in which the program executes the operations the cards specify. In any run, any type of control card may be used more than once or need not be used at all.

Following is a list of the control card commands, the operations they initiate, and the sections in which each is discussed in detail:

Command	*Operation*
*LOAD (§ 4.15)	A precompiled dictionary is to be loaded into core from a file of a *NEW dictionary tape.
*DICTIONARY (§ 4.16)	The cards that follow are an uncompiled dictionary, which continues until an *END card is reached. The dictionary is to be compiled.
*TAPE (§ § 4.12; 4.17)	Switch input and/or output unit to tape number indicated.
*STOP (§ 4.18)	Stop the program run until START is pushed.
*NEW (§ 4.19)	The resident dictionary is at this point to be transcribed onto a *NEW tape file. (Frequency counts for the entries in the resident dictionary are also transcribed.)
*PATCH (§ 4.20)	The following dictionary cards (until an *END card is reached) will be added to the resident dictionary, or, if already present in the resident dictionary, will be redefined.
*DELETE (§ 4.21)	The following dictionary entries (keypunched with or without instructions) will be deleted from the resident dictionary. The last entry to be deleted is followed by an *END card.
*LEFTOVERS (§ 4.22)	The leftover list is to be recorded hereafter on a special *LEFTOVERS tape

	rather than on the Program-Audit tape, or is to be printed in rows rather than in a single column.
*FREQUENCIES (§ 4.23)	Counts of how many times any or all dictionary entries have been matched by text words are written on either a special *FREQUENCIES tape or on the Program-Audit tape.
*AUTODOC (§ 4.24)	Follow special instructions for dividing tagged text into documents.
*UNEDITED (§ 4.25)	Include slashes and subscripts in tagged text.
*END (§ § 4.16; 4.20; 4.22; 4.23)	The end of an uncompiled dictionary, of dictionary-editing cards or of *FREQUENCIES SINGLE specifications has been reached.
*FINISHED (§ 4.26)	The run is completed.

If input is encountered that is not associated with one of these control cards, it is assumed to be text data and is tagged with the current resident dictionary.

SYSTEM CONSIDERATIONS

§4.7. Introduction: Monitored and Self-Loading Runs

The version of TAGGING described in this chapter can be executed on an IBM 7094 (§ 4.41) either independently as a self-loading program or under control of a monitor system such as FMS or IBSYS (§ 4.42).[9] All special characteristics of a self-loading run are presented in § 4.11. Elsewhere in this chapter, it is assumed that TAGGING will be run under control of a monitor system.

With some loss of efficiency, this same version of TAGGING can be run on various models of the IBM System/360, which, by means of special hardware modifications or special software, can use 7094 programs. On a System/360 capable of "emulating" the 7094, the program

[9] Monitor system control facilitates "batch processing"—that is, virtually uninterrupted execution of a series of unrelated programs. Batch processing is the most efficient, and the most usual, mode of operating a large-scale computer to which many users must have access for a diversity of data-processing purposes.

has run at about half its usual speed of 20,000 text words per minute. On a System/360 capable of "simulating" the 7094, the program has run at about a tenth of its usual speed.[10]

If only an IBM 7090 is available, a version of TAGGING written for that machine in BALGOL must be used instead of the 7094 FAP/MAP version described here. The dictionary and text input formats for the BALGOL version are identical to those for the FAP/MAP version; but control card formats and sentence-summary procedures are slightly different; and the frequency, dictionary-editing, and special leftover-tape options are unavailable. The BALGOL version is slower than the FAP/MAP version.

§4.8. Tape-Assignment Procedures

TAGGING must read all input from, and write all major output on, magnetic tapes. The tape units[11] the program uses for these purposes are listed in Table 4.A. These assignments, which agree with Fortran Monitor System usage (§ 4.42), are part of the program, but must be changed if they are inconsistent with assignments of the monitor system under which TAGGING is to be run.

Tape unit A1 is used only by the monitor system. However, the program also uses this unit in self-loading runs (§ 4.11).

Unit A2 is used for the general input deck (§ 4.9). However, optional input tapes for dictionary input or text input can be read from units A5, A6, A7, A8, A9, and/or A0 (§ 4.12). This option is exercised by the inclusion in the general input deck of one *TAPE control card (§ 4.17) for each optional input tape file to be processed. This card must specify the physical number of the unit on which the special tape will be readied and from which it will, accordingly, be read by the program when the given *TAPE card is encountered in the general input deck on unit A2. When the end-of-file mark at the end of the optional input tape is reached, the program automatically switches

[10] At this writing, only a System/360, Model 65 or Model 67, can, if equipped with the "7094-Compatibility Feature," *emulate* the 7094. A Model 40 or any higher numbered model can, if equipped with at least 256K bytes of core, *simulate* the 7094 by means of IBM's "7090/94 Simulator Program" (IBM Systems Reference Library Form No. C28-6532).

[11] Tape units–and, by extension, the tapes readied on them–will be designated throughout this chapter by "physical" numbers, each of which consists of the letter A or B, followed by one of the ten digits (1-0). Machine operators, and TAGGING itself, use these physical numbers to identify tape units. (A 7094 may be connected with as many as 80 tape units, each with a unique physical number.)

*Table 4.A. Summary of Tape-Assignment Procedures**

I *Tape*	II *Initial Assignment*†	III *Optional Assignment*	IV *Program Control Card for Specifying Optional Reassignment*	V *Machine-Operator Instruction (cf. Table 4.B)*
Monitor system library tape (but in self-loading runs only, input *NEW program tape [§4.11])	A1	None	None	None
Program's (and monitor's) primary input tape (general input deck)	A2	None	None	None
Optional input tapes (§4.12)	None	A5-A0	*TAPE (§4.17)	2 or 3
Input *NEW dictionary tape (§4.3)	A4	A5-A0, B8-B0	*LOAD (§4.15)	1
Output *NEW program or dictionary tape (§4.34)	A4	A5-A0, B8-B0	*NEW (§4.19)	4
Program-Audit tape (also monitor system print tape) (§4.32)	A3	None	None	None
Tape in Format One (§4.36)	B5	B8-B0	*TAPE (§4.17)	6
*LEFTOVERS tape (§4.35)	B6	B8-B0	*LEFTOVERS TAPE (§4.22)	7
*FREQUENCIES tape (§4.37)	B7	A5-A0, B8-B0	*FREQUENCIES TAPE (§4.23)	5

* See §4.8 with note 11.

†In this column, "A5-A0" means "A5, A6, A7, A8, A9, or A0," "B8-B0" means "B8, B9, or B0." In the sections of this chapter dealing with the control cards listed in column IV, "Ax" will sometimes be used to mean any one of the "A5-A0" units, and "Bx" any one of the "B8-B0" units.

back to the primary input tape on unit A2 from the unit designated on the last *TAPE card.

Unit A3 is used by both the program and the monitor. The program records Program-Audit information on the A3 tape; the monitor records its own information on A3 between execution of "batched" programs (§ 4.7, note 9).

The functions assigned to units A1, A2, and A3 are not subject to control card options. (However, as described earlier, by means of the *TAPE control card option the program can transfer temporarily from A2 to an optional input tape on a different unit.) All other units in column II of Table 4.A are merely "initial assignments" in that the control card listed in column IV can instruct the program to use one of the units listed in column III instead of that listed in column II. The initial assignment will be used by the program for reading or writing a certain type of tape (column I) if a reassignment is not specified on the appropriate control card, or until a reassignment is so specified. Once a reassignment has been specified, it remains in effect until a different unit is specified on the same type of control card. Any given type of tape output can be written on as many different tape units as are available for that purpose. The only restriction on these reassignment options is that, in general, no unit should be used for more than one type of input or output during a single program run.

The investigator should ascertain from the computer installation which of the units listed in columns II and III of Table 4.A are available for his use in any run. See further § 4.9.

§4.9. I/O Conversion Procedures and Machine-Operator Instructions

Any program used to transcribe input from cards to tape before a TAGGING run must employ a blocking factor of one. That is, each physical record (§ 9.1, note 2) of a tape submitted as input to TAGGING must contain only a single card image (14 machine words).[12] This applies both to the primary input tape on unit A4 and any optional input tapes. Any program used to list the contents of the Program-Audit tape (§ 4.32) must be able to process unblocked records of variable length that are headed by FMS-convention carriage-control characters. These restrictions apply to both monitored and self-loading (§ 4.11) runs.

[12] On the meaning of the term "machine word" see § 2.21, note 15. Fourteen machine words actually equal 84 characters—that is, an "expanded" card image.

Under assumed monitor system procedures, card input may be submitted for processing as such but will be transcribed onto the A2 tape by the computation center (using an IBM 1401, or similar machine) before the monitored program run. It is in this sense that the general input deck is "on" the tape that is read from unit A2 (Table 4.A). Similarly, after a monitored program run, the computation center normally takes responsibility for printing the contents of the Program-Audit tape written on unit A3.

Output tapes other than the Program-Audit tape usually will not be processed without explicit instructions from the investigator. The computation center should be informed of the blocking and carriage-control restrictions if different conventions are normally followed at the center.

Table 4.B summarizes machine-operator instructions that might have

*Table 4.B. Machine-Operator Instructions for Monitored Runs**

I/O Condition or Operation	*Machine Operator-Instruction*
1. Precompiled dictionary input (§ §4.3; 4.15).	1. Ready input tape (*NEW dictionary tape) on unit A4, or on unit X.
2. Uncompiled dictionary on optional input tape (§4.12).	2. Ready optional input tape (uncompiled dictionary) on unit X (ring out).
3. Text on optional input tape (§4.12).	3. Ready optional input tape (text) on unit X (ring out).
4. Transcribe resident dictionary onto tape (§4.3; 4.19).	4. Ready tape for output (*NEW tape) on unit A4 or on unit X (ring in).
5. Write frequences of dictionary-entry usage on a special tape (§ §4.2; 4.23) rather than on Program Audit tape.	5. Ready tape for output (*FREQUENCIES tape) on unit B7 or on unit X (ring in).
6. Write tagged text (§ §4.2; 4.36).	6. Ready tape for output (tape in Format One) on unit B5 or on unit X (ring in).
7. Write leftover list on a special tape (§ §4.2; 4.22) rather than on Program Audit tape.	7. Ready tape for output (*LEFTOVERS tape) on unit B6 or on unit X (ring in).

*The symbol X in all instructions represents the physical number of a tape unit which is available for optional reassignment (Table 4.A, column III). See further §4.9. On additional instructions for self-loading runs only, see §4.11. The specification "ring out" protects an input tape from being written upon; "ring in" permits output to be written on a tape.

to be issued for a run under monitor system control. These instructions should accompany the general input deck, input tapes, and tapes to receive output (on any units other than A3) when these materials are submitted for computer processing. All instructions presuppose that tapes are labeled in such a way that the operator can recognize which instruction applies to which tape.

Instructions for various typical runs are specified together with the schematics for those runs in Figures 4.C-4.F.

Any instruction may have to be specified more than once for a run. This is most typically the case with instruction 3, since text input will often be submitted on more than one special tape.

§4.10. Monitor System Control Cards

When TAGGING is run under Fortran Monitor System control, any or all of the following monitor control cards may have to be inserted into the general input deck in the designated positions:

	Format				
Name of Card	*Col. 1*	*Col. 2-6*	*Col. 7-9 (or 7-10)*	*Col. 10-80 (or 11-80)*	*Position in Input Deck*
*JOB	*	Blank	JOB	Depends on installation's procedures.	First card in input deck.
*XEQ	*	Blank	XEQ	Blank	First card before TAGGING object program.
*DATA	*	Blank	DATA	Blank	First card after object program (that is, immediately before dictionary and text data).
End-of-file	7-8 punch	Blank	Blank	Blank	After *FINISHED program control card.

For the control cards necessary for IBSYS or other monitor systems, consult the computing center at which the run is to be made.

§4.11. Self-Loading Runs

A *NEW program tape (§4.34)—that is, a *NEW tape that had been generated in response to a *NEW 0 (zero) control card (§4.19)—can subsequently be used as a self-loading program tape. When so used, the tape should be readied on unit A1 and put into operation by pressing the LOAD TAPE key on the 7094 console. A *NEW self-loading program tape can easily be transferred from one machine or system to another.

If a *NEW 0 control card is placed before any dictionary input in the general input deck, the resultant *NEW self-loading program tape will not contain a precompiled dictionary. But if the *NEW 0 card is placed after a dictionary in the general input deck, the *NEW tape will contain a precompiled dictionary in addition to the self-loading program.

A *NEW self-loading program tape may be created during either a run under control of a monitor system or a self-loading run.

SPECIAL INPUT OPTIONS

§4.12. Example of *TAPE Input Option

Figure 4.A partially illustrates a run in which text input is submitted on a combination of decks and optional input tapes. Each optional input tape is "represented" in the general input deck by a *TAPE control card (§4.17). In this example, we have arbitrarily assumed that the entire body of text input occurs in four equal parts of 25 documents each, and that tape inputs (documents 1-25, 51-75) neatly alternate with card inputs (documents 26-50, 76-100). But if the tape on A8 contained documents 26-50, then the *TAPE A8 card which "represents" that

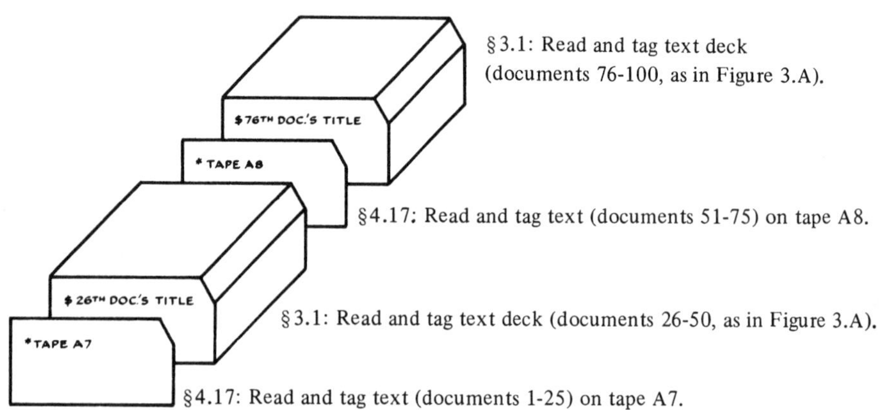

FIGURE 4.A. Schematic of "text" part of input deck. See §4.12.

tape in the general input deck might better be placed immediately after the *TAPE A7 card. This would assure that documents 26-50 would immediately follow documents 1-25 on the output tape in Format One (§ 4.36).

An uncompiled dictionary may also be read either from the general input deck (as in Figure 4.C, schematic I) or from an optional input that is "represented" in the general input deck by a *TAPE control card (as in Figure 4.C, schematic II).

§4.13. Dictionary-Editing Cards

In general, see § 4.4. Optional special entries (§ 2.7) or regular entries (§ 2.8), together with their instructions (§ § 2.9; 2.10), may be added to, or deleted from, a resident dictionary (§ 4.3) by means of dictionary-editing cards placed between appropriate control cards. Similarly, editing cards may be used to replace instructions of optional special entries or of regular entries in the resident dictionary.

Additions or replacements should be keypunched in full dictionary card format (§ § 2.5.1-2.5.3) and should be placed in the general input deck between a *PATCH and an *END control card (§ 4.20). But if an entry, together with its instruction, is to be deleted, only the entry itself, terminated by an equals sign (§ 2.5, columns 1 to n+1), need be specified on a dictionary-editing card, which should be placed in the general input deck between a *DELETE and an *END control card (§ 4.21).

There is no restriction on the number of dictionary-editing cards that may be placed between one *PATCH and the next *END card, or between one *DELETE and the next *END card. There is no restriction on the total number of dictionary-editing cards that may be used in a given run, provided that additions and corrections do not cause the resident dictionary to overflow its storage area in core (§ § 2.21; 4.32.5, no. 10). The program reports the size of the dictionary before and after each editing operation (§ 4.32.2, a-c).

Figure 4.B illustrates a permanent dictionary-editing operation—that is, one in which the edited version of the resident dictionary is transcribed for future use onto a *NEW tape file. Note that tagging of text read from an optional input tape ("represented" by the *TAPE A8 card) is performed after the dictionary has already been edited and transcribed.

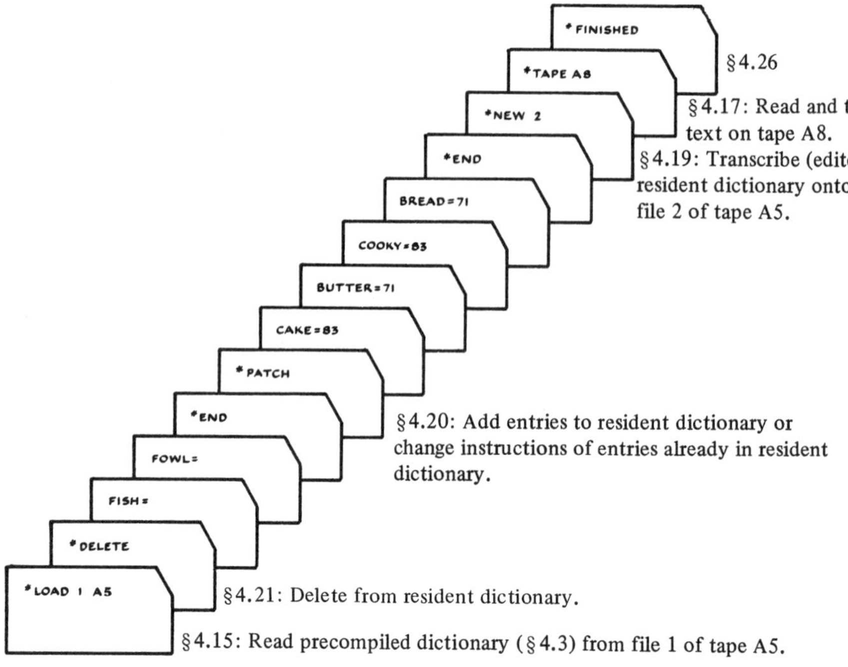

FIGURE 4.B. *Partial schematic of general input deck for dictionary-editing (and tagging) run. See §4.13.*

PROGRAM CONTROL-CARD SPECIFICATIONS

§ 4.14. Program Control Cards

Detailed specifications of the program control-card options summarized in § 4.6 are given in this and following sections (§ § 4.15-4.26).

As soon as encountered in the general input deck, each program control card is automatically recorded in its entirety on the Program-Audit tape (§ 4.32.1) and is also immediately printed out on the on-line printer. Certain control cards also cause data summaries to be recorded on the Program-Audit tape (§ 4.32.2).

All control cards are in the following format: The first word on the card is a control word preceded by an asterisk (*). The control word must immediately follow the asterisk without intervening spaces. Some control words have arguments associated with them. These must follow the control word in correct order, and there must be at least one blank column both before and after each argument. Comments may follow the blank after the last argument (or after the control word itself, if there are no arguments). The asterisk must be the first non-blank character on the control card but need not be in column 1.

§4.15. *LOAD Control Card

This card instructs the program to locate the precompiled dictionary in a specified file on a *NEW dictionary tape on a certain tape unit and then to read that dictionary directly into core. The format of this card should be:

Field	*Contents*
1	*LOAD
2	Blank.
3	One-digit or two-digit filc number (1-99) of the desired precompiled dictionary on the *NEW tape.
4	Blank.
5	Either blank if the *NEW tape is readied on unit A4 (but see the next sentence); or Ax or Bx (Table 4.A, column III) if the *NEW tape is readied on some unit other than A4.

If the *LOAD card does not specify a tape unit and is preceded in the general input deck by any *LOAD card or *NEW card (§ 4.19, field 5) that explicitly specified a tape unit, the program will assume that the last explicit specification of a unit remains valid for the current *LOAD card.

If the file number that *must* be specified in field 3 of any *LOAD card is greater than the number of the last file on the *NEW tape that is to be read, the program run will be terminated immediately (§ 4.32.5, no. 31).

§4.16. *DICTIONARY and *END Control Cards

These cards, which should be used as a set, instruct the program to erase the resident dictionary (if any) and to read and compile an un-compiled dictionary. If, as illustrated in schematic I of Figure 4.C, the uncompiled dictionary is submitted in the form of a dictionary deck (§ 2.4), a *DICTIONARY card must immediately precede and an *END card must immediately follow that deck. If, as illustrated in schematic II of Figure 4.C, the uncompiled dictionary is on an optional input tape (§ 4.12), the *TAPE card that specifies from which unit that tape is to be read must be immediately preceded by a *DICTIONARY card and immediately followed by an *END card (unless these two cards were included on the optional input tape). *DICTIONARY and *END cards do not have any arguments.

§4.17. *TAPE Control Card

This card can be used for either or both of two purposes—first, to signal the program to read an optional input tape (whether uncompiled dictionary or text) from a specified unit on channel A (§ § 4.8; 4.12); second, to signal the program to write tagged text in Format One (§ 4.36) on a B-channel tape unit other than B5 (Table 4.A, column III). The format of this card should be:

Field	*Contents*
1	*TAPE
2	Blank.
3	Either Ax (Table 4.A, column III) to specify the unit from which an optional input tape is to be read; or Bx (Table 4.A, column III) to specify the unit other than B5 on which tagged text is to be written.
4	Blank.
5	Either blank (if Bx is specified in field 2, or if tagged text output is not to be reassigned by this card); or Bx (Table 4.A, column III) to specify the unit other than B5 on which tagged text is to be written.

The physical tape unit number(s) specified in field 3 or 5 must be identical to physical number(s) of the unit(s) on which the operator is instructed (§ 4.9) to ready the optional input tape and/or the tape to receive tagged-text output.

Each optional input tape file submitted for processing must be "represented" in the general input deck by a different *TAPE card.

All text input that follows a *TAPE card with a Bx specification will, when tagged, be written on the B-channel unit specified on that card until a subsequent *TAPE card with a different Bx specification is encountered in the general input deck.

§ 4.18. *STOP Control Card

A *STOP card instructs the program to stop all processing immediately and not to resume until START is pressed on the computer console. Comments on a *STOP card are printed out on-line (§ 4.32.1) to instruct the machine operator what to do when the program halts.

The *STOP option permits more than one optional input tape (§ 4.12) to be read from a single tape unit during a run. In such cases, the *STOP card would precede that *TAPE card (§ 4.17) which "represents" the next special tape to be readied on and read from the given unit Ax (§ 4.8).

§ 4.19. *NEW Control Card

This card has two distinct uses: (a) to transcribe a resident dictionary from core onto a specified file of a specified *NEW dictionary tape (§ 4.34) for later use, and (b) to create a *NEW self-loading program tape for nonmonitor running of the program (§ 4.11). The first use, which is the more common, requires that the file number in field 3 of the *NEW card be from 1 to 99. The second use requires that the file number be zero (0). A *NEW self-loading program tape may also contain any dictionary that was resident in core at the time the tape was created (§ 4.11).

The format of a *NEW card should be:

Field	*Contents*
1	*NEW
2	Blank.
3	Either a one-digit or two-digit file number (1-99) indicating where the resident dictionary is to be written on the *NEW dictionary tape; or zero (0) indicating that a *NEW self-loading program tape is to be written.
4	Blank.
5	Either blank if the *NEW tape to be written upon is readied on unit A4 (but see the next sentence); or Ax or Bx (Table 4.A, column III) if the *NEW tape is readied on some unit other than A4.

If the *NEW card does not specify a tape unit and is preceded in the general input deck by any *LOAD card (§ 4.15, field 5) or any *NEW card that explicitly specified a tape unit, the program will assume that the last explicit specification of a unit remains valid for the current *NEW card. For example, if a *LOAD 1 A5 card preceded a *NEW 2 card, the resident dictionary that had been read from file 1 of the A5 tape will later be transcribed onto that same tape as file 2. If, as in Figure 4.B, dictionary-editing cards (§ 4.13) at some point intervened between the *LOAD 1 A5 card and the *NEW 2 card, the dictionary transcribed as part of file 2 will be an edited version of that read from file 1. In each case, the *NEW tape is automatically rewound after each command is executed.

If the file number specified in field 3 of a *NEW card is greater by more than one than the number of files already on the tape that is supposed to be written upon, the program run will be terminated immediately (§ 4.32.5, no. 31). If the file number is equal to (or less than) the number of files already on the tape, the resident dictionary will be transcribed onto the designated file, but the dictionaries previously stored in that file and any subsequent files will be erased. In short, each dictionary transcribed onto a *NEW dictionary tape automatically becomes the last file on that tape.

§4.20. *PATCH and *END Control Cards

These cards, which should be used as a set, instruct the program to add entries (with their instructions) to the resident dictionary and/or to replace the instructions of entries already present in the resident dictionary. A set of dictionary-editing cards (§ 4.13 with Figure 4.B) that specifies such additions and/or corrections must be immediately preceded by the *PATCH card and immediately followed by the *END card. *PATCH and *END cards have no arguments.

§4.21. *DELETE and *END Control Cards

These cards, which should be used as a set, instruct the program to delete entries (with their instructions) from the resident dictionary. A set of dictionary-editing cards (§ 4.13 with Figure 4.B) that specifies suc deletions must be immediately preceded by the *DELETE card and immediately followed by the *END card. *DELETE and *END cards have no arguments.

§4.22. *LEFTOVERS Control Cards

There are two types of *LEFTOVERS control cards. The purpose of the first type, a *LEFTOVERS TAPE card, is to cause the leftover list generated during a tagging operation (§ 4.2) to be written on a special tape, termed a *LEFTOVERS tape (§ 4.35), rather than on the

Program-Audit tape (§4.32.3). The purpose of the second type, either a *LEFTOVERS ACROSS card or a *LEFTOVERS DOWN card, is merely to alternate the format in which the leftover list is written on the Program-Audit tape. However, any *LEFTOVERS ACROSS or *LEFTOVERS DOWN card that follows a *LEFTOVERS TAPE card in the general input deck will also serve to cancel the preceding *LEFTOVERS TAPE instruction by switching the leftover list from the special tape back to the Program-Audit tape. Any type of *LEFTOVERS card affects the leftover list derived from all text input between that card and the next *LEFTOVERS card, if any. In the absence of a *LEFTOVERS card, or until the first *LEFTOVERS card of any type is encountered in the general input deck, the program automatically records the leftover list on the Program-Audit tape in such a way that when the contents of that tape are printed, the list will be printed as a column, one word per line, down the left side of the page.

If a *LEFTOVERS TAPE card is used, a tape to receive leftover-list output should be provided and machine-operator instruction 7 (Table 4.B) should be issued. The instruction should specify that the tape should be readied either on unit B6 (if there is no argument in field 5 of the *LEFTOVERS TAPE card) or on the unit explicitly specified in field 5.

The format of a *LEFTOVERS card should be as follows:

	Field	*Contents*
	1	*LEFTOVERS
	2	Blank.
Either	3	TAPE in order to cause a special *LEFTOVERS tape (§4.35) to be written.
	4	Blank.
	5	Either blank if the *LEFTOVERS tape is to be written on unit B6; or Bx (Table 4.A, column III) if that *LEFTOVERS tape is to be written on a B-channel unit other than B6.
Or	3	ACROSS in order to cause the leftover list recorded on the Program-Audit tape (§4.32.3) to be printed in rows across the page.
Or	3	DOWN in order to cause the leftover list recorded on the Program-Audit tape (§4.32.3) to be printed in a column, one word per line, down the left side of the page.

Any number of *LEFTOVERS cards of any type can be inserted in the general input deck in order, for example, to have the list printed (from the Program-Audit tape) alternatively in row and column formats from one text document, or group of documents, to the next. Similarly, *LEFTOVER cards can be staggered throughout the text portions of the general input deck in order to switch the leftover list back and forth between the Program-Audit tape and one or more *LEFTOVERS tapes.

§4.23. *FREQUENCIES Control Cards

Any *FREQUENCIES control card instructs the program to write on tape entries in the resident dictionary (§ 4.3) together with the number of times each entry had been matched by text words since the dictionary was *first* compiled. Thus, in a run in which the input dictionary is submitted in uncompiled form (§ 4.16), the match-frequencies generated by any *FREQUENCIES card will be cumulative for tagging performed upon all text that precedes that card. Moreover, if the input dictionary is precompiled (§ 4.15), the match-frequencies generated by a *FREQUENCIES card will be cumulative not only for all text that precedes the given *FREQUENCIES card in the input deck of the present run but also for all text that had ever been tagged in previous runs with the given dictionary. By loading a *NEW dictionary tape file (§ 4.34) at the beginning of a run and then creating another *NEW dictionary tape file at the end of the run, the frequencies can be accumulated over a number of runs before they are printed.

Similarly, the entries recorded in response to a *FREQUENCIES card will reflect all dictionary editing (§ § 4.4; 4.13) performed on the resident dictionary since the dictionary was first compiled. Thus, an entry that had been deleted will nevertheless be recorded, together with a match-frequency that refers to all text tagged with the dictionary before that entry was deleted. An entry whose instruction had been replaced will be recorded only once and with a cumulative match-frequency for both its original and all subsequent instructions.

There are four types of *FREQUENCIES cards:

*FREQUENCIES COMPLETE PRINT
*FREQUENCIES COMPLETE TAPE
*FREQUENCIES SINGLE PRINT
*FREQUENCIES SINGLE TAPE

Either COMPLETE or SINGLE, and either PRINT or TAPE, must be specified on every card. A TAPE argument may, but need not, be followed by an explicit tape-unit specification (Ax or Bx), as later explained. Comments may be keypunched starting at least one blank column to the right of the last specification on the card. *FREQUENCIES cards of any type(s) may appear any number of times in the general input deck.

If COMPLETE is specified, all entries in the resident dictionary will be transcribed, together with match-frequencies for each entry. (If the entries in the dictionary had been in alphabetic order when the dictionary was first compiled, the entries and match-frequencies will be transcribed in alphabetic order.) If SINGLE is specified, only those entries in the resident dictionary that are keypunched in columns 1-71 of cards following the given *FREQUENCIES SINGLE card will be transcribed (together with their match-frequencies). Any number of cards may be used to specify the SINGLE entries that are to be transcribed. Each entry should be keypunched without an equals sign or instruction (§ 2.5) but should be separated from the next entry by one or more blank card columns. The last card used to specify SINGLE entries must be immediately followed by a card with *END.

If PRINT is specified, requested entries and their match-frequencies will be transcribed onto the Program-Audit tape for subsequent printing (§ 4.32.2, d). If TAPE is specified but is not followed by an explicit tape-unit specification, requested entries and their match-frequencies will be transcribed as a single file onto a special *FREQUENCIES tape (§ 4.37) either on unit B7 (if the current *FREQUENCIES TAPE card is the first such card in the general input deck) or on the unit explicitly specified on the last previous *FREQUENCIES TAPE card in the deck. On the other hand, if TAPE is followed by a tape-unit specification of the form Ax or Bx (Table 4.A, column III), the file will be written on the specified unit.

Machine-operator instruction 5 (Table 4.B) must be issued if one or more *FREQUENCIES TAPE cards are present in the general input deck. A tape to receive frequencies output must be provided for each different unit specified (implicitly or explicitly) on a *FREQUENCIES TAPE card. If more than one *FREQUENCIES TAPE card specifies one and the same unit, the tape thereon need not be changed since each set of entries and match-frequencies will be written in a separate file after, not over, any previous set.

§4.24. *AUTODOC Control Cards

This card can instruct the program: (a) to ignore end-document cards (§ 3.5) that follow it in the general input deck; (b) to check at the end of every text sentence the number of words and/or sentences that have been processed in the current document, and/or any specified position in the sentence identification code (§ 3.8) of the current sentence; and (c) to end the current document and start a new one if the sentence or word count exceeds a specified limit, or if the character in the specified code position is different from the character in that same position for the preceding sentence. Thus, the *AUTODOC option results in documents of tagged text that are either equal in length, as measured in number of words or number of sentences, or that correspond in length to changes in sentence-identification codes. In all other respects, however, an end-of-document condition brought about by this "automatic documenting" procedure is the same as one brought about by an end-document card (§ 3.5).

Any number of *AUTODOC control cards may be placed in the general input deck. Each one will affect tagging of all text which follows it until another *AUTODOC card with a different specification is encountered.

The format of a *AUTODOC control card should be:

Field	*Content*
1	*AUTODOC
2	Blank.
3	Either the character W if the program is to determine the length of documents by number of words; or the character S if the program is to determine the length of documents by number of sentences; or the character I if the program is to determine the length of documents according to changes in sentence-identification codes; or blank in order to cancel all specifications on previous *AUTODOC cards and to signal that subsequent end-document cards should be recognized as valid end-of-document instructions. If W or S is punched, it should be followed by the number of words or sentences, respectively, to be included in each document of tagged

text. The first digit of this number, which must not be greater than 32768, should be keypunched in the columns immediately following the W or S. If zero (0) is punched, all subsequent text will be treated as a single document. If an I is punched, it should be immediately followed by a number indicating the column of the identification code that is to be tested.

4 Blank.

5. . . Other documenting limits in fields as just described for field 3. More than one test can be applied at the same time.

The specifications on one *AUTODOC card will only be canceled by those on the next *AUTODOC card if the same alphabetic characters (S, W, I) are specified, or if none of these characters is specified. But two end-document cards, one immediately after the other, temporarily supersede the last *AUTODOC specification by causing the current document to be terminated and to be immediately followed on the tape in Format One (§ 4.36) by a dummy (blank) document. (The two end-document cards do not cause counts of words or sentences to be reset to zero.)

§4.25. *UNEDITED Control Card

An *UNEDITED card instructs TAGGING not to delete slashes and subscripts (§ § 3.10; 3.12.1) from sentence records in the output tape in Format One (§ 18.3, positions n+2 to x). This card affects all text that follows it in the input deck. See further § 4.32.5, no. 19 and § 7.5.2.

§4.26. *FINISHED Control Card

A *FINISHED card instructs the program: (a) to write a RUN SUMMARY on the Program-Audit tape (§ 4.32.2, f) and a terminal file (§ 18.6) on the tape in Format One (§ 4.36), if any, (b) to terminate all other tapes, and (c) to accept no further input whatsoever. In *every* run, such a card should be the last program control card in the general input deck and should follow all data input. The *FINISHED card may, however, be followed or replaced by an end-of-file card (§ 4.10), if monitor system procedures so require.

SAMPLE RUNS: DECKS, TAPES, AND INSTRUCTIONS

§4.27. Introduction to Examples

The decks, tapes, and machine-operator instructions illustrated in Figures 4.C-4.F and briefly discussed in § §4.28-4.31 are representative rather than exhaustive of ways in which TAGGING can be used. If questions arise about a figure but are not answered in the respective discussion, the reader is referred to sections cited in the figure itself.

§4.28. Dictionary-Compilation Runs (Figure 4.C)

Schematic I in Figure 4.C illustrates a run performed only for the purpose of dictionary compilation (§ 4.3). The input dictionary is

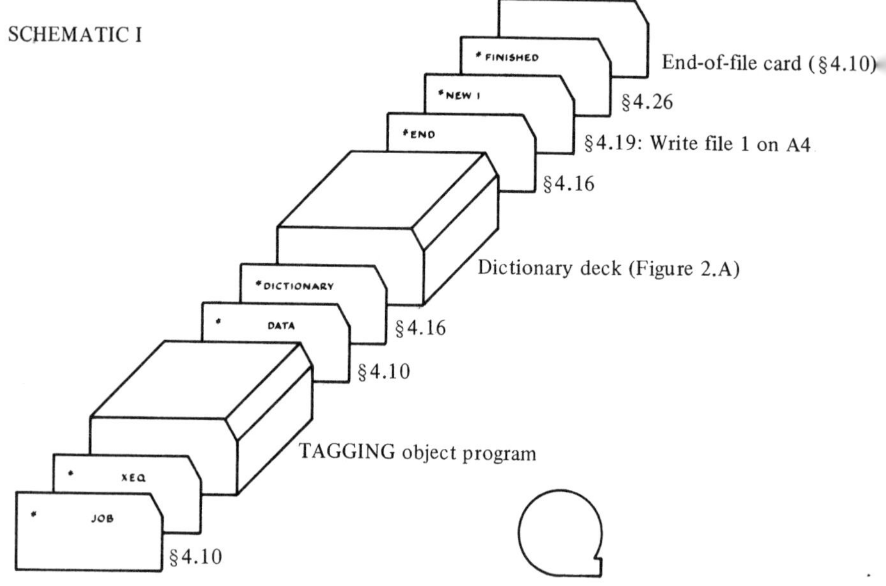

Machine-operator instructions (seeTable 4.B):
4. Ready tape for output on unit A4 (ring in).

FIGURE 4.C. *Decks, tapes, and instructions for typical dictionary-compilation runs. For general explanation see §4.28. The Program-Audit tape (§4.32), which in*

submitted on cards and is the only data input in the general input deck. The *NEW tape on which the resident dictionary is to be transcribed has not previously been written upon, and this tape is readied on unit A4, the unit on which the program initially expects a *NEW tape to be found (§ 4.8; Table 4.A, column II). Therefore, file 1 is specified on the *NEW card, but no tape-unit specification is necessary.

Schematic II illustrates a run for the same exclusive purpose, but here two uncompiled dictionaries—each on a separate optional input

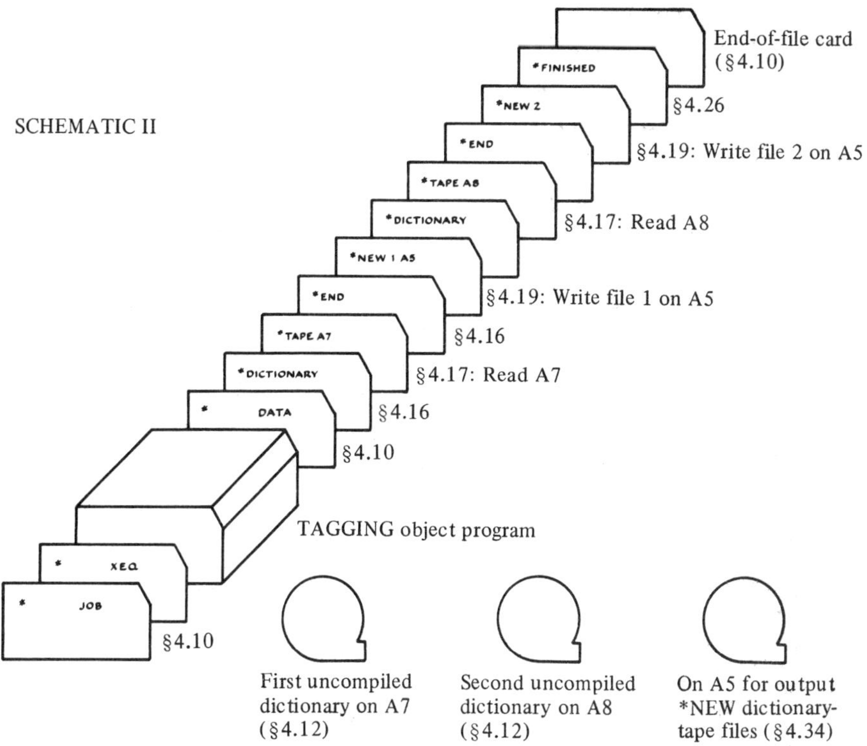

Machine-operator instructions (see Table 4.B):
2. Ready first optional input tape on unit A7 (ring out).
2. Ready second optional input tape on unit A8 (ring out).
4. Ready tape for output on unit A5 (ring in).

any monitored run is automatically written on unit A3 (monitor print tape), is not illustrated here (§4.9).

tape (§ 4.12)—are compiled and transcribed one after the other. Assignment of the dictionary input tapes to units A7 and A8 as opposed to other available units on channel A (Table 4.A, column III) is arbitrary. Each compiled—that is, output—dictionary will be recorded in a separate file of the same *NEW tape on unit A5. Unit A5 must be specified on the first *NEW card (since A5 is not the unit on which the program initially expects a *NEW tape will be found) but need not be specified on the second *NEW card (since a reassignment remains valid until explicitly changed). But file numbers must, as always, be specified on both *NEW cards and must in this case be consecutive.

§4.29. Permanent Dictionary-Editing Run (Figure 4.D)

For the sake of distinguishing a run performed solely to edit a dictionary (§ 4.4) from a compilation run (§ 4.28), the input dictionary in Figure 4.D is precompiled. But the same editing operation could be performed if the input dictionary in Figure 4.D were a deck or optional input tape as in schematic I or II of Figure 4.C.

The editing cards in Figure 4.D specify additions, replacements, and deletions. The *NEW card follows all editing cards so that the resident dictionary may be edited before being transcribed unto tape.

The input dictionary will be read from the thirty-fourth and *last* file of a *NEW dictionary tape on unit A6; the edited version of the dictionary will replace the unedited version in that same file. Therefore, the *LOAD and *NEW cards both specify file 34, though only the former need specify A6. Since the same tape is used for input and output, only one machine-operator instruction is necessary, but it must specify "ring in" so that the tape can be both read and written upon.

§4.30. Tagging Run Without Supplementary Output-Tape Options (Figure 4.E)

Since tagging is presumed to be the only operation performed in the run illustrated in Figure 4.E, a precompiled dictionary has been specified as input. Note that if tagging is to be performed, machine-operator instruction 6 must always be issued and a tape to receive the tagged text on unit B5 (or some other available unit) must be provided. The tagging operation begins as soon as the program encounters text.

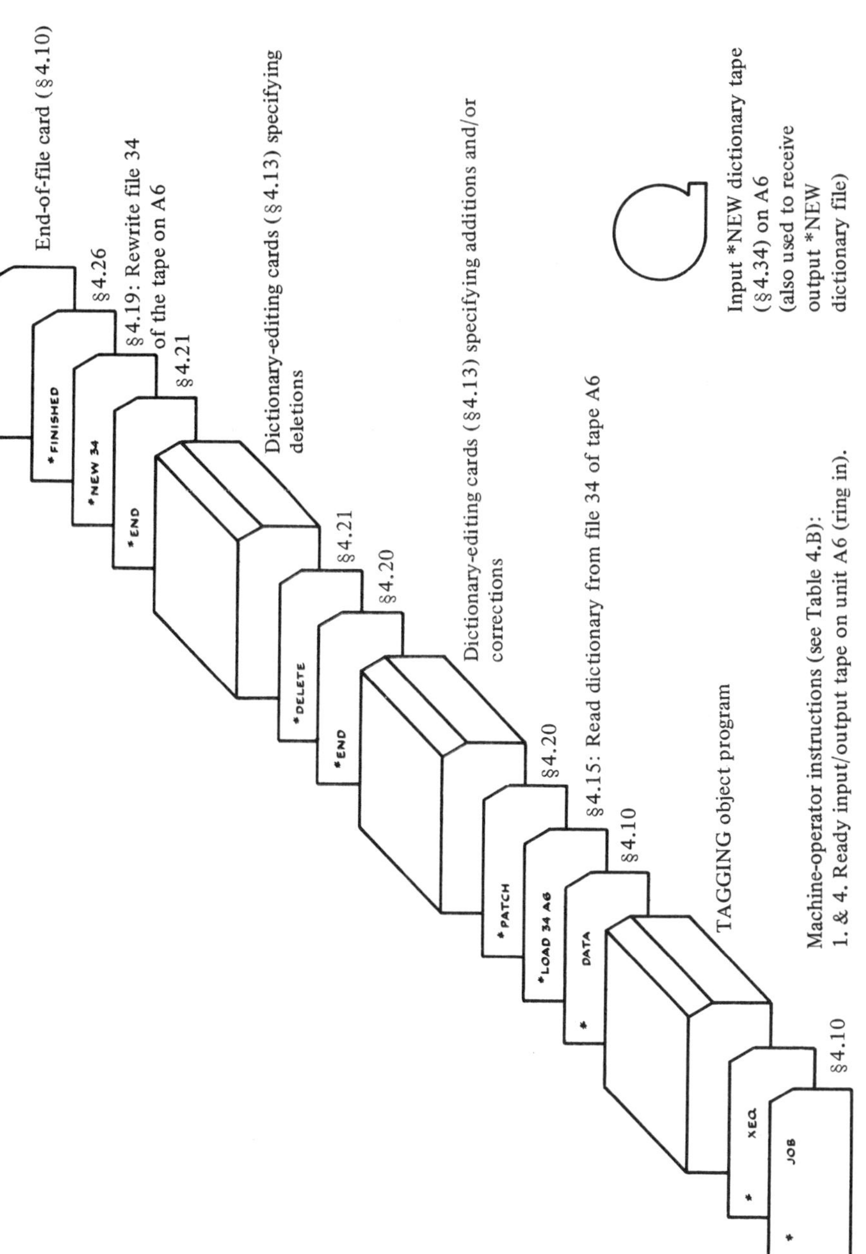

FIGURE 4.D. *Deck, tapes, and instructions for typical permanent dictionary-editing run. For general explanation see §4.29. The Program-Audit tape (§4.32), which in any monitored run is automatically written on unit A3 (monitor print tape), is not illustrated here (§4.9).*

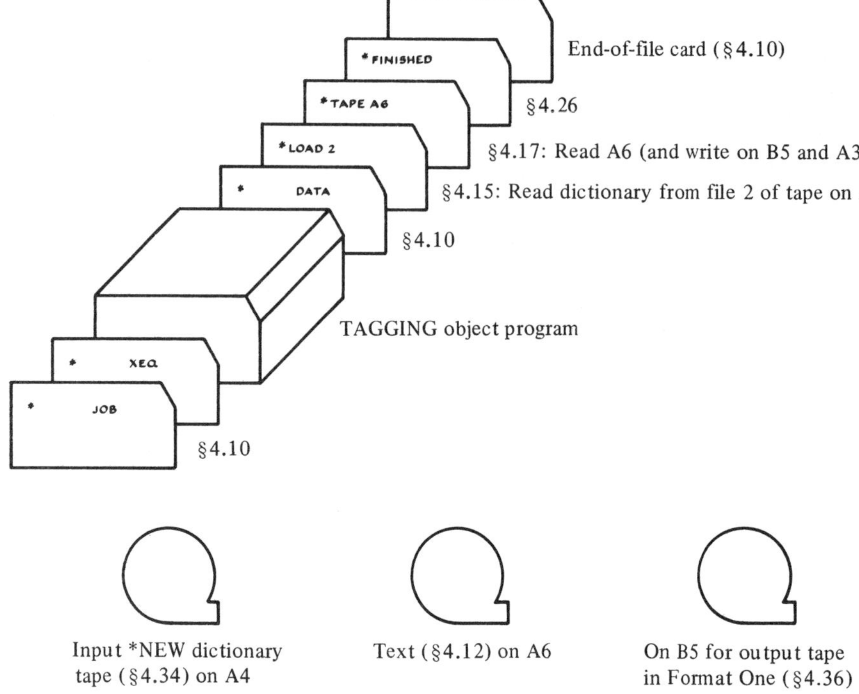

Machine-operator instructions (see Table 4.B):
1. Ready input tape on unit A4 (ring out).
3. Ready optional input tape on unit A6 (ring out).
6. Ready tape for output on unit B5 (ring in).

FIGURE 4.E. *Deck, tapes, and instructions for tagging run without supplementary output tape options. For general explanation see §4.30. The Program-Audit tape (§4.32), which in any monitored run is automatically written on unit A3 (monitor print tape), is not illustrated here (§4.9).*

§4.31. Tagging Run with Supplementary Output-Tape Options (Figure 4.F)

The tagging run illustrated in Figure 4.F differs from the one in Figure 4.E in that the supplementary output tape options (§ 4.2) are elected. Thus, instead of being written on the Program-Audit tape, the leftover list is written on a special *LEFTOVERS tape readied on unit B6. Also generated (on unit B7) is a *FREQUENCIES tape with frequencies for *all* entries in the resident dictionary. Note that tapes to receive these supplementary outputs must be provided and instructions 5 and 7 must be issued so that the operator will ready the tapes on the correct units.

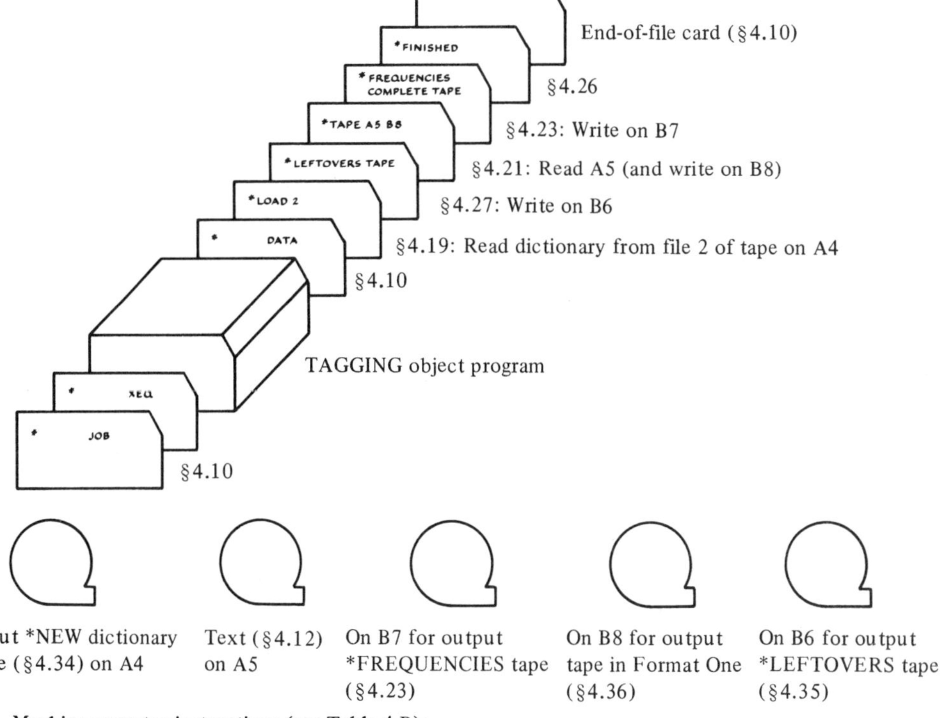

Machine-operator instructions (see Table 4.B):
1. Ready input tape on unit A4 (ring out).
3. Ready optional input tape on unit A5 (ring out).
5. Ready tape for output on unit B7 (ring in).
6. Ready tape for output on unit B8 (ring in).
7. Ready tape for output on unit B6 (ring in).

FIGURE 4.F. Deck, tapes, and instructions for tagging run with supplementary output tape options. For general explanation see §4.31. The Program-Audit tape (§4.32), which in any monitored run is automatically written on unit A3 (monitor print tape), is not illustrated here (§4.9).

Since each of these supplementary output tapes is to be written on the unit initially reserved for it (Table 4.A, column II), neither the *LEFTOVERS TAPE control card nor the *FREQUENCIES COMPLETE TAPE control card has to specify a tape unit. However, it is assumed that B5, the unit initially reserved for tagged-text output, is unavailable during the current run. Therefore, a *TAPE A5 B8 card is used to signal the program not only to read text input from an optional input tape on unit A5 but also to write tagged-text output (the tape in Format One) on unit B8.

§4.32. Program-Audit Tape (A3) and On-Line Print-Out

On the Program-Audit tape, which must be written on unit A3, a running description of the progress of a run will be recorded. This description may consist of five general types of information (§ §4.32.1-4.32.5), two of which are also printed out on-line for the benefit of the machine operator (§ §4.32.1; 4.32.4). The contents of a Program-Audit tape can be properly printed only by a program that accepts unblocked input records of variable length, which are headed by FMS-convention carriage-control characters (§4.9).

§*4.32.1. Program Control Cards (Program-Audit Tape and On-Line Print-Out).* Program control cards (§ §4.14-4.26) are recorded in the order in which they are encountered in the general input deck. So too are title cards (§3.3) when these are encountered in text.

Control cards are also printed out on-line in their entirety. This is of particular significance if a *STOP control card is used (§4.18).

§*4.32.2. Data Summaries.* Certain control cards, when encountered in the general input deck, cause the program to immediately write on the Program-Audit tape messages or lists that summarize the volume of data on which the operations initiated by the control cards have been performed. Each message or list can be produced as many times as the given type of data and control card appear in the input. When the contents of the Program-Audit tape are printed, each message or list will be immediately preceded by the image of the control card (§4.32.1) that caused the message to be written. Following is a description of these messages or lists:

a. Each *END card (§ §4.16; 4.20; 4.21) and *PATCH card (§4.20) will be followed by the message DICTIONARY HAS n WORDS IN IT. Here n will be the total number of all types of entries (§ §2.6-2.8) in the resident dictionary.
b. Each *PATCH card (§4.20) will be followed by a summary of the run up to that point (messages a and e) and by a list of any entries in the resident dictionary whose instructions were corrected by the dictionary-editing cards (§4.13) encountered between this last *PATCH card and the next *END card.
c. Each *DELETE card (§4.21) will be followed by a list of the entries deleted from the resident dictionary as a result of dictionary-

editing cards (§ 4.13) encountered between this last *DELETE card and the next *END card.

d. Each *FREQUENCIES PRINT card (§ 4.23) will be followed by a list of the requested entries in the resident dictionary, together with the cumulative match-frequency for each entry.

e. After each end-document card (§ 3.5) in text input, or when an automatic end-document condition (§ 4.24) is reached, the following message is written: END OF DOCUMENT. IN THE PRECEDING DOCUMENT THERE WERE ϕ WORDS, AND χ SENTENCES. LAST ID SEEN WAS ψ. This type of message interrupts the leftover list (§ 4.32.3) when all leftover words for a given document have been recorded. On the meaning of SENTENCES, see § 3.11; on that of LAST ID SEEN, see § 3.8. No more than six digits can be printed for the values ϕ and χ.

f. Each *PATCH card (§ 4.20) and the *FINISHED card (§ 4.26) will be followed by the message: RUN SUMMARY. α DOCUMENTS, β SENTENCES, γ WORDS. DICTIONARY FILLS δ COMPUTER WORDS. ϵ COMPUTER WORDS STILL AVAILABLE. THERE WERE ζ WORDS CHOPPED, η WORDS LEFTOVER, AND θ SCAN POINTS. Here α, β, γ, ζ, η, and θ are totals that refer to all text input processed thus far in the run. In ζ and η, WORDS mean English words. With β and γ, compare ϕ and χ in message e. On COMPUTER WORDS in δ and ϵ, see § 2.21 with note 15. Both δ and ϵ refer to (the last edited version of) the resident dictionary: Compare the value n recorded in message a. The symbol ζ refers to the total number of text words from which suffixes were "removed" (§ 2.8.1) in the tagging operation, regardless of whether suffix "removal" resulted in any one case in a successful match between the uninflected ("chopped") form of the text word and a regular dictionary entry or word-test specification (§ 2.10.3). The symbol η represents the total number of words in the leftover list (§ 4.32.3) for all text documents processed in the run. The symbol θ is the number of comparisons between text and dictionary that were made in the process of tagging. If the dictionary is organized by frequency, fewer comparisons will have to be made and processing will be somewhat faster. No more than six digits can be printed for any one of the values α-θ.

§ *4.32.3. Leftover List.* If tagging (§ 4.2) is performed in a run, each text word which does not match a regular entry (§ 2.8) in the resident dictionary is recorded as soon as the program determines that a match is impossible.[13] Thus, a leftover list of untagged words accumulates as the tagging operation progresses. This leftover list, which is not printed out on-line, is recorded on the Program-Audit tape unless a *LEFT-OVERS TAPE control card (§ 4.22) is used to request a special *LEFT-OVERS tape (§ 4.35).

Title cards (§ 3.4) interrupt the leftover list whenever they are encountered in the text. So too do end-document messages (§ 4.32.2, e). Thus, the leftover list—like other important listings generated by the system (§ 1.9; Figure 1.A)—is organized by text document.

All other types of Program-Audit information (§ § 4.32.1-4.32.2; 4.32.4-4.32.5) can also interrupt the leftover list, depending on the position of the text input in relation to control cards in the general input deck and on the sequence of the tagging operation in relation either to operations initiated by control cards or to error conditions.

*LEFTOVER ACROSS cards and *LEFTOVER DOWN cards (§ 4.22) can alter the format in which the leftover list will be printed.

§ 4.32.4. I/O Tape Messages (Program-Audit Tape and On-Line Print-Out). These messages refer to adverse conditions on tapes from which input is (or should be) read, or on which output is (or should be) written. None of these messages is written until 20 consecutive attempts have been made to read input from, or write output on, the specified tape. If these attempts fail, the run is usually halted until a substitute tape is provided; then processing continues normally. The messages are also printed out on-line so that the operator can take immediate action. Following is a list of the I/O tape messages:

a. INPUT PARITY ERROR ON *NEW TAPE. This means that an input *NEW tape of either type (§ 4.34) is physically damaged, or is defective as a result of some other condition. The run is terminated.
b. INPUT PARITY ERROR x. Here x will be the physical number (Tabl 4. A.) of a physically damaged input tape. The damaged portion of the tape will be skipped.
c. BAD x. DIAL NEW TAPE AND PRESS START. Here x will be the physical number (Table 4.A) of a damaged or defective output tape. The tape removed from unit x will be finalized with two end-of-file

[13]However, text words which match regular entries defined by the operator N (§ § 2.8.2; 2.10.4) are deliberately excluded from the leftover list. On the special treatment of alphabetically subscripted text words, see § 3.10 with note 13.

marks, and will contain some valid output. The run will be interrupted but can be resumed if the operator follows the instruction.

d. TAPE x AT END. DIAL NEW TAPE AND PRESS START. Here x will be the physical number (Table 4.A) of an output tape that is full. The tape will be finalized with two end-of-file marks. The run is interrupted but can be resumed if the operator follows the instruction.

§ *4.32.5. Data and Control-Card Error Messages.* The image of a dictionary, text, or control card on which some specification has been violated is written on the Program-Audit tape and is immediately followed by the message ERROR n ON ABOVE CARD. Here n will be the code number (1-20, 30-32) of the particular error discovered in the preceding card. If n is 1-14 or 30-32, a second message will immediately follow the first. The second message either will specify which word on the preceding card violates a specification (and also the serial number of the defective card) or will briefly describe the error. Following is a list of the code numbers that can appear in the first message together with descriptions of the corresponding error conditions, and of the ways in which TAGGING processes the defective card in each case.

1. An alphabetic subscript (§ 3.10) is not an optional special entry (§ 2.7) in the resident dictionary. The undefined subscript is ignored.
2. A slash (/) is not followed by an alphanumeric character or another slash; or a slash follows an alphabetic or numeric subscript (§ § 3.10; 3.12). The defective subscript(s) will be ignored.
3. More than one numeric subscript (§ 3.12) has been applied to a single text word. The extra subscript(s) will be ignored.
4. A tag of more than two digits has been specified in a dictionary instruction other than those instructions associated with required special entries (§ 2.6). The tag is ignored.
5. The operator N (§ 2.8.2) has been keypunched after at least one unparenthesized tag in a dictionary instruction. If the error occurred in an unconditional instruction (§ 2.9), only the tag(s) preceding N are assigned, but N and all tags after it are ignored. If the error occurred in a conditional instruction (§ 2.10.4), the entire entry is deleted.
6. A required special entry is not defined (§ 2.6). If the error is encountered by the program while processing an unconditional instruction, the incorrect special entry and all following card columns

are ignored. If the error is encountered during processing of a conditional instruction, the entire entry is deleted.

7. Either an equals sign (=) or a blank is not found before column 72 of a dictionary or dictionary-editing card (§ § 2.5; 4.13) or a blank is not found before column 72 of a card that follows a *FREQUENCIES SINGLE control card (§ 4.23). The entire card is ignored.
8. An entry specified on a card which follows a *DELETE control card (§ 4.21) or a *FREQUENCIES SINGLE control card (§ 4.23) is not found in the resident dictionary. The entry that cannot be found is ignored.
9. An alphabetic character other than S, V, Ø,U (§ 2.9), or N (§ § 2.8.2 2.10.4) is specified in a dictionary instruction; yet it is not located within that part of a word-test conditional expression (§ 2.11) which is reserved for words. If the error occurred in an unconditional instruction (§ 2.9), the improper alphabetic character and card columns that follow it are ignored. If the error occurred in a conditional instruction (§ 2.10), the entire entry is deleted.
10. An uncompiled input dictionary (§ 4.16) or additions to the resident dictionary that are specified on dictionary-editing cards (§ 4.13) have just overflowed the area in core allotted for storage of the resident dictionary (§ 2.19). The run is terminated immediately. Compare 31 of this list.
11. The equals sign (=), or a comma, on a dictionary or dictionary-editing card (§ § 2.5; 4.13) is immediately followed by a blank. All card columns after the blank are ignored.
12. On a dictionary or dictionary-editing card (§ § 2.5; 4.13), either the equals sign (=) is followed by a nonalphanumeric character other than a left parenthesis or blank (cf. 11 of this list) or a tag is followed by any character other than a comma or blank (§ § 2.9; 2.10.2). If the error occurred in an unconditional instruction (§ 2.9), the improper character and card columns that follow it are ignored. If the error occurred in a conditional instruction (§ 2.10), the entire entry is deleted.
13. The control word on a program control card (§ 4.6) is misspelled. The entire card is ignored. Compare 30 and 31 of this list.
14. A dictionary card (§ § 2.5; 4.16) specifies an entry that was specified on a previous dictionary card. The card with the redundant entry is ignored.
15. The character after the left parenthesis in a conditional expression

(§ § 2.11-2.12) is not W or T. The expression is skipped and processing continues.

16. An expected comma is not found in a conditional expression (§ § 2.11; 2.12). Processing continues.
17. Not used as an error code.
18. A nonalphanumeric character other than a comma, blank or plus (+) is specified within the enclosing parenthesis of a conditional expression (§ § 2.11; 2.12). The entire entry is deleted.
19. The current text sentence, together with all tags that have been assigned to it (§ 4.2), is too long to be written in a single sentence record (§ 18.3). This can result from either of two conditions: (1) the text of the sentence is longer than 810 characters, after any regular deletions (§ § 3.3-3.3.2) and requested optional deletions (§ 4.25) have been made; or (2) more than 270 tags have been assigned to the sentence, thus making the tag string longer than 810 characters (since each tag is assigned as a two-digit number followed by one of the four alphabetic syntax markers [§ 2.9]). If either of these conditions occurs, the input sentence is divided into as many output sentence records as necessary, and no information is lost. If the user wishes to increase the 810-character maximum of either the text field or the tag string field, he should consider the possible effects of this change upon subsequent programs in the system (§ 5.10).
20. In a word-test expression (§ 2.11), the first nonblank character after a word is neither a comma, an alphanumeric character, nor a right parenthesis. The improper character is ignored.

21-29. Not used as error codes.

30. An argument following the control word on a control card is wrong. There are five possibilities, any one of which results in the given card being ignored: (1) a *TAPE card (§ 4.17) does not specify at least one physical tape number; (2) a file number is not specified in field 3 of a *LOAD card (§ 4.15) or a *NEW card (§ 4.19); (3) the file number specified on a *LOAD card is zero (0); (4) *AUTODOC (§ 4.24) is not followed by either S, W, I, or an unbroken series of blanks; or (5) an argument on a *LEFTOVERS (§ 4.22) or *FREQUENCIES (§ 4.23) card is misspelled.
31. A compiled dictionary cannot be written on, or read from, a *NEW dictionary tape file (§ 4.34). There are four possibilities, *any one of which results in immediate termination of the run:* (1) the file

number on a *NEW card (§ 4.19) is greater by more than one than the number of files already on the *NEW dictionary tape that is supposed to be written on; (2) the file number on a *LOAD card (§ 4.15) is greater than the number of the last file on the *NEW dictionary tape that is supposed to be read; (3) the precompiled dictionary specified on a *LOAD card exceeds current storage capacity (§ 2.21); or (4) the tape on the unit specified (implicitly or explicitly) by a *LOAD card is not a *NEW dictionary tape.

32. Tagging of a sentence has exceeded the program's capacity. The sentence is ended but some tags of the last word are lost.

§4.33. Special Sentence-Summary Messages on Program-Audit Tape

If the investigator chooses to incorporate a sentence-summary subroutine (§ 27.1) into TAGGING, he has the option of recording special messages on the Program-Audit tape by means of the OCWRIT command function (§ 27.11). The information that is regularly recorded on the Program-Audit tape (§ 4.32) would be interrupted by such special OCWRIT messages whenever the text satisfied a test on which the OCWRIT command was contingent.

§4.34. *NEW Tape

There are two types of *NEW tapes—a *NEW dictionary tape, to which a dictionary file can be added by a *NEW control card (§ 4.19) with a file designation from 1 to 99, and a *NEW self-loading program tape, which is created in response to a *NEW card with a file designation of zero (0).

A *NEW self-loading program tape consists of a one-record file containing 32,768 machine words, followed by two end-of-file marks. The file will include the object program and whatever other information was in core when the *NEW 0 card was encountered. This type of *NEW tape may only be used as a self-loading program tape in nonmonitored runs (§ 4.11).

The other, and more common, type of *NEW tape consists of from one to 99 precompiled-dictionary files. Each dictionary file consists of two records, with the storage parameters of the dictionary in the first record and the precompiled dictionary itself in the second record. The first dictionary file on the tape is preceded by a header file consisting of one binary word (*NEWTP), and the last file on the tape is followed by two end-of-file marks.

§4.35. *LEFTOVERS Tape

A *LEFTOVERS tape is generated only if the general input deck contains a *LEFTOVERS TAPE control card (§ 4.22). On this tape will be written the leftover list of untagged words derived from all text input that follows the given *LEFTOVERS TAPE card in the general input deck until the program encounters a *LEFTOVERS ACROSS or *LEFTOVERS DOWN card. Leftover words written on a *LEFTOVERS tape cannot be simultaneously recorded on the Program-Audit tape (§ 4.32.3).

A *LEFTOVERS tape will consist of one file of leftover words for each file of tagged text that is written (simultaneously) on the tape in Format One (§ 4.36). In other words, the leftover list will be organized by document according to end-document-card (§ 3.5) or *AUTODOC-card (§ 4.24) specifications. The last file on a *LEFTOVERS tape will be followed by two end-of-file marks.

The file for each document will consist of a series of 42-position records in the following format:

Position	*Contents*
1-6	Blank.
7	Blank or asterisk. (On leftover words to which TAGGING prefixes an asterisk, see § 3.10.)
8-42	One leftover word, left-adjusted and followed by blanks.

§4.36. Tape in Format One (Tagged Text)

The program starts writing this tape during a tagging operation (§ 4.2) as soon as it encounters text input that had been preceded in the general input deck by any form of input dictionary. Writing of this tape continues until all text input has been processed, but it can be temporarily interrupted at any time if the text input is itself interrupted by other kinds of data input or by control cards. In such cases, when text input is next encountered in the general input deck, writing of tagged text in Format One resumes at the point on the tape at which writing had last been interrupted.

A tape must be provided—and a machine-operator instruction (Table 4.B, no. 6) to ready that tape on unit B5 or some unit specified on a *TAPE control card (§ 4.17) must be issued—in advance of a run in which a tape in Format One is to be written. Format One is described in § § 18.1-18.6.

§4.37. *FREQUENCIES Tape

A *FREQUENCIES tape is one that is written when the program encounters a *FREQUENCIES TAPE control card (§ 4.23) in the general input deck. On the specified tape will be written requested entries that are in the resident dictionary (§ 4.32.5, no.8) when the given *FREQUENCIES TAPE card was encountered in the general input deck. Next to each entry will be written the number of times it had been matched by any words in all text during any tagging operation since the current resident dictionary was first compiled.

A tape must be provided—and a machine-operator instruction to ready that tape (on unit B7 or some other unit specified on the *FREQUENCIES TAPE card) must be issued—in advance of a run in which the *FREQUENCIES tape is to be written.

One file will be created on a *FREQUENCIES tape for each *FREQUENCIES TAPE card which specifies that tape. The last file will be followed by two end-of-file marks.

Each file will consist of a series of 42-position records in the following format:

Position	*Contents*
1-6	Match-frequency (right-adjusted and preceded, if necessary, by leading blanks) of the entry in positions 8-42 of this record.
7	Blank.
8-42	Entry, left-adjusted and followed by blanks.

TECHNICAL CONSIDERATIONS

§4.38. Run Termination

A run can be terminated by the error conditions described in § 4.32.4 a and § 4.32.5, nos. 10 and 31.

A program halt can be caused by the conditions described in § 4.32.4 c and d, and by a *STOP control card (§ 4.18).

§4.39. Running Time

A tagging operation (§ 4.2) is performed at approximately 20,000 words—about one box of text cards (§ 3.3)—per minute. Many conditional instructions in the dictionary (§ 2.10) and/or many sentence-summary tests (§ 4.5) can reduce this estimated rate—but not accordin to linear parameters. This rate can be increased slightly if regular entries had been arranged in the dictionary deck (§ 2.4) in order of decreasing frequency on the basis of *FREQUENCIES data (§ § 2.17; 4.23).

Compilation (§ 4.3) of an uncompiled input dictionary (§ 4.16) does not require more than one minute of running time. Assembling the source program (§ 4.43) requires about two minutes.

§ 4.40. Language

TAGGING is written in IBM 7094 FAP or MAP. It is completely compatible with both languages and with FMS and IBSYS monitors.

§ 4.41. Machine Requirements

The object program should be executed on an IBM 7094 with two data channels (A and B), seven index registers, and a 716 Printer on channel A. The program can also be run on certain models of the IBM System/360 (§ 4.7 with note 10).

§ 4.42. Installing TAGGING for Execution under Monitor System Control

The only major restriction on the type of monitor system under which the object program can be executed is that the monitor must be able to load either a BSS-type relocatable binary deck or an IBSYS-type relocatable binary deck. The Fortran Monitor System (FMS) in any version will leave more room in core available for storage of the program and dictionary (§ 2.21) than IBSYS or other standard monitor systems. FMS is therefore generally recommended.

Once the object program has been loaded, it operates independently of the monitor. When processing is successfully completed or is terminated by an error condition (§ 4.38), the program expects to return control to the monitor by calling "EXIT". This call is issued by the FIN routine of the main subprogram (§ 4.45). That routine must be modified if "EXIT" is not the name of the subroutine whereby the monitor resumes control after a job.

The program has its own initial physical tape assignments (Table 4.A), which agree with FMS assignments. These initial assignments should be modified if they are inconsistent with assignments expected by a monitor under which TAGGING is to be run. The program's assignments are located at the very beginning of the main subprogram (§ 4.45).

§4.43. Assembling the Source Program

To assemble the source program, use normal FMS or IBSYS procedures. On compilation of sentence-summary source tests, see §27.12.

§4.44. Program Organization

TAGGING is organized as one FAP/MAP assembly (§4.40). A replaceable dummy subroutine for sentence-summary tests is also provided (§27.13). (The name STSUM must be given to any summary test subroutine implemented by the investigator.) TAGGING itself subsumes three subprograms—a main subprogram (§4.45) and two I/O subprograms (§4.46).

Except for minor revisions which may be necessary to install the program for execution under a particular monitor system (§4.42), it would be well to restrict modifications to the options at the beginning of the program. The source deck of the program is well annotated.

§4.45. Major Sections of Main Subprogram

The major operations performed by the main subprogram are: initializing a run, "compiling" a dictionary (§4.3), encoding input text words, preparing a limited number of buffers, and taking action on a variety of special conditions.

The important sections and their functions are as follows:

GENINQ	Initializes various core constants when processing begins.
LO	Reads in the first input record and switches to the proper routine. At various times—usually after end-document (§3.5) and control-card records (§4.14)—again reads the next input record (see STAR in this list).
BILDCT	Reads BCD dictionary input (§4.16). Encodes entries and picks out all tags.
BL101	Determines that redundant or otherwise incorrect dictionary entries are not loaded (§4.32.5, no. 14) and edits dictionary (§4.13).
BIDOM	Performs special processing of idiom expressions (§§2.11-2.12).

TEXT — Controls all important operations concerned with encoding input text words (§ 3.3). Notes any special conditions (Table 3.A)—particularly, subscripts (§ § 3.10; 3.12). Orders a dictionary lookup for each text word (see SUFFIX in this list). Maintains execution parameters. Reinitializes constants upon the end of each word (§ 3.3) and each sentence (§ 3.11).

LFTVRS — Accumulates and outputs leftover words as necessary (§ § 3.10 with note 13; 4.2; 4.32.3).

TITLE — Processes title cards (§ 3.4) and writes them on Program-Audit tape (§ 4.32.1) and tape in Format One (§ § 4.36; 18.4).

STAR — Reads any record whose first nonblank position is an asterisk. If the given record is the image of an end-document card (§ 3.5), bookkeeping is performed and control is then transferred to LO to read the next record. If the given record is the image of a control card (§ 4.14), it is processed.

ERROR — Processes errors, prints out error messages (§ 4.32.4), and writes them on Program-Audit tape (§ § 4.32.4-4.32.5).

SUFFIX — If LOOKUP fails to match a text word to a dictionary entry or idiom word, SUFFIX attempts to "remove" suffixes from the text word in the possibility that the uninflected form can then be matched (§ § 2.8.1; 2.10.3). See § 4.47.

INTRPT — Interprets control tags, which have a value between 101 and 127. Among the various internal operations affected by these control tags are: appending syntax markers to assigned tags in accordance with the priorities enumerated in § 2.9 (IL4); excluding untagged words from the leftover list (§ 2.8.2) (IL10); indicating the end of a dictionary instruction (§ § 2.9-2.10) (IL9); and differentiating between word-test and tag-test conditional expressions (§ § 2.11-2.12). The syntax-marker and leftover-list functions just mentioned are specified by the five required special dictionary

	entries (§ 2.6). Depending on the nature of the control tag, normal program logic flow may be altered.
IL5	Writes a *NEW tape (§ 4.34).
IL12	Evaluates a tag-test conditional expression (§ 2.12) by examining tag buffers for the presence of the tag θ specified in the expression.
IL13	Evaluates a word-test conditional expression (§ 2.11) by examining text buffers for the presence of the text word(s) specified in the expression.
IL17	Loads (§ 4.15) precompiled dictionary from *NEW dictionary tape file (§ 4.34) into core.
CVINT	Performs binary-decimal conversion.
FETCH	Gets the next character from the input buffer by incrementing the character count or reading the next card.
GET	Gets the next seven-bit tag field from a dictionary instruction (§ § 2.9-2.10).
IDT	Reads initial positions of each input text card record (§ 3.3). If position 1 has a legitimate ID character, the entire ID field of the card record replaces the previous one in storage (§ 3.8).
RCARD	Inputs and unpacks another data record. Each character is encoded in a special buffer (TBUF) for rapid determination of its class.
LOOKUP	Attempts to match a given text word to a dictionary entry. Keeps on looking for a match until one is found or it is determined that none can be found. In either case, transfers control to the appropriate processing routine—for instance, SUFFIX in this list. In NEWTAG adds another seven-bit tag to the instruction being built for an entry. See BLDICT in this list.
NUM	Composes a binary number from one or more BCD characters.
PTWER PTPER	Packs a backward-stored packed string. (Cf. WRITE in this list.)

WRITOT	Writes a sentence-record on tape in Format One (§ 4.36).
WRITE	Packs and then outputs words of characters onto the Program-Audit tape (§ 4.32). (Cf. PTWER, PTPER in this list.)
ZERO	Zeros out all available storage at the beginning of execution (cf. § 4.16).
FIN	Rewinds and unloads tapes and returns control to the monitor by calling "EXIT" (§ 4.42).

§ 4.46. I/O Subprograms

All channel-trap handling and tape selection is done by the I/O subprogram TRIGR, a select-stacker and error-diagnosis routine developed at the University of Chicago. PRNLN, the other I/O subprogram, converts to row-binary and prints on-line messages (§ § 4.32.1; 4.32.4) using TRIGR.

§ 4.47. Modifying Suffix "Removal"; Implementing Prefix "Removal"

The suffix-"removal" procedures (§ § 2.8.1; 2.10.3) used in the current version of the program can be modified by adding or changing tests in the routine SUFFIX of the main subprogram (§ 4.45). The code in that routine should make evident how the removal procedures are executed.

A routine for "removing" prefixes from text words in order to match them to dictionary entries could be inserted immediately before the instruction L314 of the routine TEXT. The prefix-"removal" routine would have to perform the operations that are annotated following instruction L314 of the source deck.

TEXT-TAG LIST Operational Summary

Machine:

IBM 1401 with 8K, Advanced Programming, High-Low-Equal compare, two tape units, and 1403 Model 2 or 3.

Input Schematic:

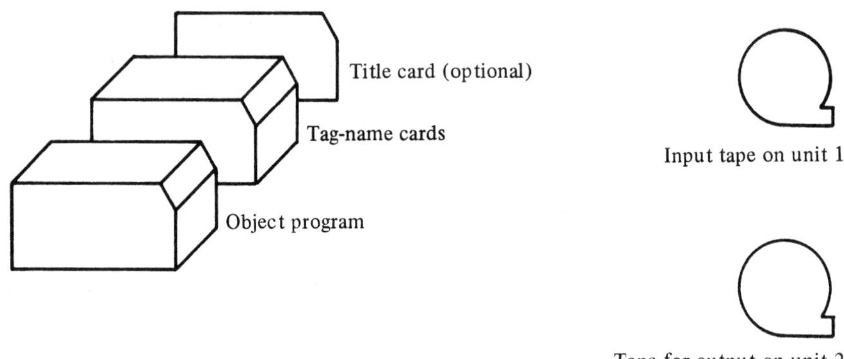

Machine-Operator Instructions:

1. Place card input in 1402 read hopper.
2. Set sense switches on 1401.
   A: Always up.
   B, C, D, E: Ignored.
   F: Suppression of syntax markers in listing (§5.7.2). Ignored if sense switch G is up.
   G: Suppression of listing. This switch may be repeatedly reset during program execution (§5.8).
3. Ready input tape on unit 1 (ring out). Position tape correctly (§5.10). When read, tape will automatically rewind and unload.
4. Ready tape for output on unit 2 (ring in). Tape does not automatically rewind or unload at end of run (§5.10).
5. On 1403 ready continuous forms for desired number of copies of the output listing (usual maximum four copies) and for diagnostic messages.
6. Press START RESET on 1401.
7. Press CHECK RESET and LOAD on 1402.
8. Press START to process last two cards of input deck.
9. For procedures in case of defective input, see §5.11 and §26.3.

CHAPTER 5

Text-Tag List[1]

INTRODUCTION

§5.1. Function

The contents of a tape written by TAGGING in Format One (§ § 4.36;18.1) are printed by this program in a "bilingual" listing (Figure 5.A) with separate sentences on the left side of the page and the names of the tags assigned to each sentence on the right side. The tags for each sentence are printed in one or more rows immediately to the right of the sentence in the order the tags were assigned. The program obtains the tag names associated with tag numbers from a set of cards that is part of the input deck (§ 5.4). Thus, the name associated with any given number may vary, depending on the investigator's dictionary.

The program also transcribes the contents of the input tape onto an output tape in Format Two (§ 5.2).

§5.2. System Considerations

The "bilingual" text-tag listing provides the investigator with feedback on the validity of the various strategies he has adopted in preparing the dictionary, editing the text, and specifying sentence-summary instructions for TAGGING (§ 4.5). Inspection of the listing may tend to confirm preliminary hypotheses about the data and may suggest both changes that should be made in the dictionary when it is next revised and possible patterns of within-sentence tag co-occurence that can be systematically examined in retrieval questions (§ 7.1). Tag-tally

[1]Stone, Philip J., Dexter C. Dunphy, Marshall S. Smith, Daniel M. Ogilvie, with associates, *The General Inquirer: A Computer Approach to Content Analysis* (Cambridge, Mass.: The M. I. T. Press, 1966), pp. 96,262-265.

```
        SENTENCE   1     TOTAL WORDS=  2     IDENTIFICATION 192

DEAR MARY.                                          AFFECTION    U  SIGN-ACCEPT  U  FAMILY       U

        SENTENCE   2     TOTAL WORDS=  4     IDENTIFICATION 192

(YOU ARE CONVINCED THAT )                           OTHER        S  COMMUNICATE  V  SIGN-AUTH    V

        SENTENCE   2     TOTAL WORDS=  6     IDENTIFICATION 192

SINCE YOU ARE CONVINCED THAT YOU ARE AN INVALID     TIME-REF     U  OTHER        S  BAD          S  DISTRESS     S  SIGN-WEAK    S
(SICK) +

        SENTENCE   3     TOTAL WORDS=  6     IDENTIFICATION 192

AND NO ONE CAN HELP YOU.                            NOT          U  QUAN-REF     S  GUIDE        V  SIGN-STRONG  V  SIGN-ACCEPT  V
                                                    OTHER        O

        SENTENCE   4     TOTAL WORDS=  2     IDENTIFICATION 192

(I HOPE )                                           SELF         S  SIGN-ASCEND  V  URGE         V

        SENTENCE   4     TOTAL WORDS=  9     IDENTIFICATION 192

I HOPE MY THREE THOUSAND DOLLARS OF INSURANCE WILL  SELF         S  QUAN-REF     S  OVERSTATE    S  MESSAGE-FORM S  ECONOMIC     S
HELP YOU +                                          MESSAGE-FORM S  SIGN-STRONG  S  ECONOMIC     S  GUIDE        V  SIGN-STRONG  V
                                                    SIGN-ACCEPT  V  OTHER        O

        SENTENCE   5     TOTAL WORDS=  7     IDENTIFICATION 192

TO (YOU) SEE THE TRUTH ABOUT YOURSELF +             OTHER        S  SENSE        V  IDEAL-VALUE  O  ACADEMIC     O  OTHER        U

        SENTENCE   6     TOTAL WORDS=  8     IDENTIFICATION 192

AND (YOU) GET RID OF YOUR MENTAL SICKNESS.          OTHER        S  GET          V  SIGN-REJECT  V  EXPEL        V  OTHER        O
                                                    THINK        O  ACADEMIC     O  DEVIATION    O  MEDICAL      O
```

FIGURE 5.A. *Sample text-tag listing of syntax-edited text. For detailed explanation see §§5.7-5.7.1.*

tables (§ 6.2; Figure 6.A) and graphs of tag tallies (§ 10.1; Figure 10.A) can facilitate analysis of the text-tag listing.

In transcribing tagged text from Format One (§ 18.2) to Format Two (§ 19.2), TEXT-TAG LIST serves as a required intermediary step between TAGGING and programs that can only process tapes in Format Two–that is TAG TALLY (§ 6.1) and RETRIEVAL (§ 7.1) as well as certain time-sharing procedures.[2] Printing may be suppressed under sense switch control (§ 5.8) if only the tape-format conversion is desired.[3]

INPUT AND OUTPUT SPECIFICATIONS

§5.3. Input

Input normally consists of a tape written by TAGGING in Format One (§ § 4.36; 18.1), the object-program deck, tag-name cards, and a title card. Care should be taken that the input tape unit is set for the same tape-storage density (556 or 800 bits per inch) as was used by the IBM 7094 in writing the tape.

§5.4. Tag-Name Cards

One tag-name card should be prepared for each tag appearing in the dictionary. Each card specifies a tag number and the name of the tag. These same cards are used by other programs; their format is given in Appendix Two (§ 24.2). The cards may be arranged in any order for this program.

These cards may be omitted if printing is suppressed throughout the run (§ 5.8). On processing of defective tag-name cards, see § 5.11.

§5.5. Title Card (Optional)

Information on a title card, if one is included at the end of the input deck, is used by the program until a title record (§ 18.4) appears on the input tape. That is, title card information is printed at the top of each page of the listing until the first title record on the input tape is encountered. This new title is then printed instead. Each subsequent

[2] *Ibid.*, pp. 119-133.

[3] The print-suppress option is generally used only when a tape in Format One has to be processed for a second time in order to generate a replacement for a damaged tape in Format Two. Print suppression greatly increases processing speed.

title encountered on the tape similarly replaces the previous title for the pages that follow. Title card format is:

Card Columns	*Contents*
1	$ [dollar sign]
2	Blank.
3-80	Title (any alphanumeric and/or special characters).

§5.6. Output

Output consists of the "bilingual" text-tag listing and a tape of tagged text in Format Two.

§5.7. Text-Tag Listing[4]

See samples (Figures 5.A, 5.B). Each sentence is preceded by a line giving its serial number within the document in which it occurs (§ § 1.8.2; 18.3, positions 4-6), the number of words it contains (§ 18.3, positions 1-3), and its sentence-identification code, if any (§ 18.3, positions 7 to n). In one or more rows to the right of each sentence appear the names of the tags assigned to that sentence (§ 18.3, positions x+2ff.). The tag names are printed in the order the tags were assigned to the sentence. Names of sentence-summary tags, if any, are thus printed last (§ 27.1). There will be gaps in the rows of tag names if a tag-name card (§ 5.4) for any tag had been omitted from the input deck. A new page is started at the beginning of each document (§ § 1.9; 18.5).

Each document (that is, each file on the input tape) is numbered serially by the program. The serial number of the document being printed appears at the top of each page. If processing is interrupted and the program has to be reloaded, the serial counter is reset to one, whether or not the input tape is changed.

§ *5.7.1. Syntax Markers.* Each tag name may be followed by a syntax marker (S,V,Ø, or U) indicating the syntactic position of the text word assigned that tag (Figure 5.A). If the text had not been edited with numeric subscripts (§ 3.12) or if syntax markers had not been specified in dictionary instructions (§ 2.9), all tag names will be followed by the syntax marker U.

[4] See Table 3.A, columns V and VI, for a summary of the treatment of special characters by the IBM 1403 Printer.

```
        SENTENCE  25      TOTAL WORDS= 22      IDENTIFICATION 364

THE NEEDS WE SEEK TO FILL, THE HOPES WE SEEK TO     URGE          SELVES         ATTEMPT        SIGN-ACCEPT    SIGN-ASCEND
REALIZE, ARE NCT OURS ALCNE, THEY ARE THOSE OF OUR  URGE          SELVES         ATTEMPT        SIGN-ACCEPT    SENSE
PEOPLE.                                             NOT           SELVES         QUAN-REF       OTHER          QUAN-REF
                                                     SELVES       LARGE-GROUP    COMMUNITY

        SENTENCE  26      TOTAL WORDS=  8      IDENTIFICATION 364

MOST AMERICANS WANT MEDICAL CARE FOR OLDER          QUAN-REF      OVERSTATE      NEUTER-ROLE    POLITICAL      URGE
CITIZENS.                                           MEDICAL       GUIDE          TIME-REF       HIGHER-STAT    NEUTER-ROLE
                                                    POLITICAL     PEER-STATUS

        SENTENCE  27      TOTAL WORDS=  4      IDENTIFICATION 364

AND SO DO I.                                        SELF

        SENTENCE  28      TOTAL WORDS=  9      IDENTIFICATION 364

MOST AMERICANS WANT FAIR AND STABLE PRICES FOR      QUAN-REF      OVERSTATE      NEUTER-ROLE    POLITICAL      URGE
FARMERS.                                            GOOD          UNDERSTATE     IDEAL-VALUE    SIGN-STRONG    QUAN-REF
                                                    ECONOMIC      JOB-ROLE       TECHNOLOGICL

        SENTENCE  29      TOTAL WORDS=  4      IDENTIFICATION 364

AND SO DO I.                                        SELF

        SENTENCE  30      TOTAL WORDS= 12      IDENTIFICATION 364

MOST AMERICANS WANT A DECENT HOME IN A DECENT       QUAN-REF      OVERSTATE      NEUTER-ROLE    POLITICAL      URGE
NEIGHBORHOOD FOR ALL.                               SOCIAL-PLACE  FEMALE-THEME   FAMILY         SOCIAL-PLACE   COMMUNITY
                                                    QUAN-REF      OVERSTATE

        SENTENCE  31      TOTAL WORDS=  4      IDENTIFICATION 364

AND SO DO I.                                        SELF
```


FIGURE 5.B. *Sample text-tag listing of text not edited for syntax. For detailed explanation see* §§ 5.7-5.7.2.

§ *5.7.2. Suppression of Syntax Markers (Sense Switch F).* If sense switch F is set up before the program run begins, the places on the listing where syntax markers normally appear will be blank, as in Figure 5.B. If sense switch F is set down, a syntax marker will be printed after every tag name. This option obviates printing all the U markers when syntax identification had not been used.

§5.8. Suppression of Text-Tag Listing (Sense Switch G)

If sense switch G is set up at any time during the program run, printing of the text-tag listing (§ 5.7) immediately ceases. If sense switch G is set down, printing of the listing resumes. This switch may be repeatedly reset during the program run in order to display the "bilingual" listing on a sample basis. It may also be used to suppress the listing completely. See § 5.2, note 3. The setting of this switch does not affect the print-out of error messages or of defective input records (§ § 5.11; 26.3).

§5.9. TEXT-TAG LIST Output Tape (Format Two)

See Appendix One (§ § 19.2; 19.4-19.8) for the format of this tape, and see § 1.8.5 with Figure 1.C for an explanation of the difference between Formats One and Two.

The setting of sense switches F and G (§ § 5.7.2; 5.8) do not affect the generation of this tape.

TECHNICAL CONSIDERATIONS

§5.10. Language and Processing

The source program is written in 1401 Tape Autocoder. The program reads in the tag-name cards and the optional title card before beginning to process the tape. The files on the input tape are processed consecutively without interruption. The program halts upon encountering the terminal file on the input tape (§ 18.6).

The operator should make sure the tapes are rewound (or positioned as desired) at the beginning of the run. At the end of the run, the input tape automatically rewinds and unloads. The output tape halts, but does not rewind, after the terminal file (§ 19.8) is written, in case the investigator wishes to add further information to the same tape.

In processing defective records on the input tape, the program follows procedure two (§ 26.3).

TEXT-TAG LIST cannot process an input sentence record (§ 18.3) longer than 1701 characters. If the program encounters an input record longer than this, the run will be terminated immediately. However, this situation obviously cannot occur if TAGGING's current maximum of 1698 positions per output record is not increased (§ 4.32.5, no. 19).

The maximum length of a sentence record written by TEXT-TAG LIST is 1800 characters. This maximum is well within the input restrictions of both programs that read tapes in Format Two—that is, TAG TALLY, which could theoretically accept a sentence record of as many as 3000 characters, and RETRIEVAL, which could accept a record of up to 1942 characters (§ 7.15 with note 7).

§5.11. Processing of Defective Tag-Name Cards

If the characters in columns 1-2 of a tag-name card (§ § 5.4; 24.2) are not both numeric, TEXT-TAG LIST halts and prints the message BAD CARD PRESS START TO IGNORE. The bad tag-name card is the last card in the stacker.

TAG TALLY Operational Summary

Machine:

IBM 1401 with 8K, Advanced Programming, High-Low-Equal compare, Multiply-Divide, at least one tape unit (but two if tape-output option is exercised), and 1403 Model 2 or 3.

Input Schematic:

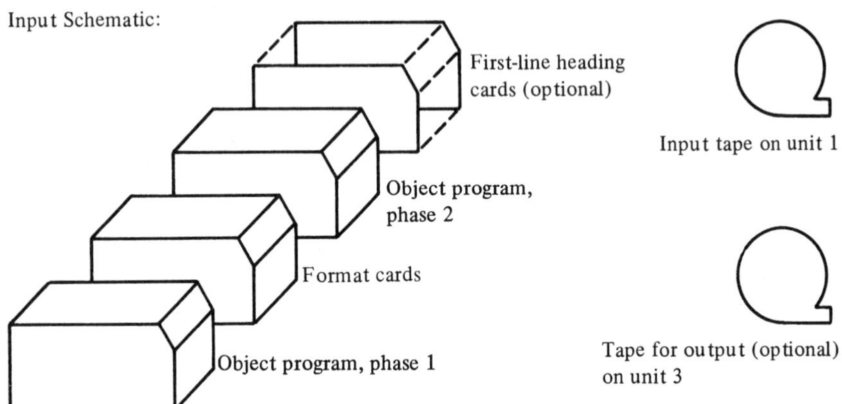

Machine-Operator Instructions:

1. Place card input in 1402 read hopper; ready 1402 punch if sense switch E is to be set up.
2. Set sense switches on 1401. All switches may be repeatedly reset at fixed points in the program execution cycle (§6.7).
   A: Ignored.
   B: Suppression of tag tally table (§6.9).
   C: Table-heading card option (§6.6).
   D: Tape-output option (§6.10).
   E: Punched-output option (§6.11).
   F: Ignored.
   G: Word-count scores versus sentence-count scores (§6.8).
3. Ready input tape on unit 1 (ring out); position tape correctly (§6.12).
4. Ready tape for output on unit 3 (ring in) if sense switch D is to be set up.
5. On 1403 ready continuous forms for desired number of copies of the printed output (usual maximum four copies), and for run summary (§6.7) and possible diagnostic messages.
6. Press START RESET on 1401.
7. Press CHECK RESET and LOAD on 1402. Press START to process last two cards in input deck.
8. For procedures in case of defective input, see §§6.13-6.14 and §26.3.
9. After last file is processed, program will halt and tapes will rewind and unload.

CHAPTER 6

Tag Tally[1]

INTRODUCTION

§6.1. Function

This program counts how often each tag had been assigned to the sentences in each file of tagged text. The primary input is a tape in Format Two (§ 19.1)—that is, either a TEXT-TAG LIST output tape (§ 5.9) or a RETRIEVAL output tape (§ 7.13). The investigator can choose to calculate tag scores with reference to either the number of sentences (§ 1.8) or the number of words in each file. Input files are processed separately but consecutively until a terminal file is encountered.

The tag scores for each file may be recorded in printed tables (Figure 6.A), on punched cards, or on magnetic tape. Further analysis of these counts may be performed by other statistical programs.

§6.2. Types of Total and Subtotal Tag Scores

If the investigator chooses the number of sentences in the input file to be the basis of computation, the two types of tag scores computed for each tag will be:

1. *Total sentence-count raw score:* the number of sentences in the file to which the tag had been assigned.
2. *Total sentence-count index score:* the total sentence-count raw score as a percentage[2] of the number of sentences in the file.

[1] Stone, Philip J., Dexter C. Dunphy, Marshall S. Smith, Daniel M. Ogilvie, with associates, *The General Inquirer: A Computer Approach to Content Analysis* (Cambridge, Mass.: The M.I.T. Press, 1966), pp. 96-104, 226-232.

[2] This percentage is rounded to the nearest tenth of a percent, so that, for example, 7.85 percent becomes 7.9 percent but 7.84 percent becomes 7.8 percent.

GENERAL INQUIRER SENTENCE TAG TALLY LETTERS FROM JENNY. SECTION ONE.

DOCUMENT 1 FIRST ID 00130 4541 WORDS 502 SENTENCES

	RAW SCORES					INDEX SCORES AS PERCENT				
	SUB	VRB	OBJ	UCL	TOTAL	SUB	VRB	OBJ	UCL	TOTAL
SELF	216	1	39	105	309	43.0	.2	7.8	20.9	61.6
SELVES	13			3	16	2.6	.0	.0	.6	3.2
OTHER	35	1	17	29	76	7.0	.2	3.4	5.8	15.1
MALE-ROLE	77		14	23	106	15.3	.0	2.8	4.6	21.1
FEMALE-ROLE	43		20	22	75	8.6	.0	4.0	4.4	14.9
NEUTER-ROLE	15		6	14	34	3.0	.0	1.2	2.8	6.8
JOB-ROLE	2		2	3	7	.4	.0	.4	.6	1.4
GROUPS										
SMALL-GROUP	2		2		4	.4	.0	.4	.0	.8
LARGE-GROUP	6	1		8	14	1.2	.2	.0	1.6	2.8
PHYSICAL OBJECTS										
BODY-PART	11		5	4	20	2.2	.0	1.0	.8	4.0
FOOD	1		1	1	3	.2	.0	.2	.2	.6
CLOTHING	1		7	6	13	.2	.0	1.4	1.2	2.6
TOOL	9	2	5	8	22	1.8	.4	1.0	1.6	4.4
NATURAL-OBJ	24		8	8	38	4.8	.0	1.6	1.6	7.6
NON-SPC-OBJ	6	3	8	71	86	1.2	.6	1.6	14.1	17.1
PHYSICAL QUALIFIERS										
SENSORY-REF	7		1	4	12	1.4	.0	.2	.8	2.4
TIME-REF	14	5	7	138	154	2.8	1.0	1.4	27.5	30.7

	RAW SCORES					INDEX SCORES AS PERCENT				
	SUB	VRB	OBJ	UCL	TOTAL	SUB	VRB	OBJ	UCL	TOTAL
AROUSAL	3	2		5	10	.6	.4	.0	1.0	2.0
URGE	2	16	3	10	30	.4	3.2	.6	2.0	6.0
AFFECTION	4	5	3	10	22	.8	1.0	.6	2.0	4.4
PLEASURE	8	2	2	3	15	1.6	.4	.4	.6	3.0
DISTRESS	17	17	1	4	37	3.4	3.4	.2	.8	7.4
ANGER	2	3			5	.4	.6	.0	.0	1.0
THOUGHT										
SENSE		15		10	25	.0	3.0	.0	2.0	5.0
THINK	5	19	4	33	59	1.0	3.8	.8	6.6	11.8
IF	3	1	1	43	48	.6	.2	.2	8.6	9.6
EQUAL	2	7	1	7	16	.4	1.4	.2	1.4	3.2
NOT	4	4	3	73	84	.8	.8	.6	14.5	16.7
CAUSE				7	7	.0	.0	.0	1.4	1.4
DEF-MECH						.0	.0	.0	.0	.0
EVALUATION										
GOOD	20	1	7	14	41	4.0	.2	1.4	2.8	8.2
BAD	10			3	13	2.0	.0	.0	.6	2.6
OUGHT		5	1	48	54	.0	1.0	.2	9.6	10.8
SOCIAL-EMOTIONAL ACTIONS										

FIGURE 6.A. Sample sentence-count tag tally table for syntax-edited text. See § 6.2 on types of scores and § § 6.5-6.6 on format and headings.

If the number of words in the input file is chosen as the basis of computation, the two types of tag scores computed for each tag will be:

3. *Total word-count raw score:* the number of words (or multiword units [§ 2.10.1]) in the file to which the tag had been assigned.
4. *Total word-count index score:* the total word-count raw score as a percentage[3] of the number of words in the file.

Note that both types of index scores are based on the size of the file currently being processed, and not necessarily on the size of the original document (§ 1.9). In cases where an input file is a set of retrieved sentences written on a RETRIEVAL output tape, the file will usually be either a small portion of the original document, or a small portion of several documents (§ 7.13).

The sentence-count/word-count option also applies to the computation of subtotals for each of the four syntax categories, S, V, Ø, and U (§ § 2.9; 3.12.1). In all, ten sentence-count scores *or* ten word-count scores are computed for each tag. As illustrated in Figure 6.A, these ten types of scores are: four raw score subtotals, the total raw score, four index score subtotals, and the total index score.

If neither numeric subscripts were used in editing the text nor syntax specifications were included in dictionary instructions (§ § 2.9; 3.12.1), the subtotals for syntax categories S, V, and Ø will be zero. As indicated in Figure 6.B, these null subtotals will not be printed and the subtotals for category U will equal the totals for each tag.

If sentence-count scores are requested, the sum of raw or index subtotals for a tag can exceed the corresponding total score. This is because a tag that has been assigned to a given sentence more than once—yet not with the same syntax marker each time—will be counted once in the computation of each relevant subtotal, but only once in the computation of the total score. For example, if tag 48 had been assigned to a given sentence twice with the marker V and five times with the marker U, then that sentence would be counted once in the raw score verb subtotal, once in the unclassified subtotal, but again only once in the raw score total. The same would be true for the sentence-count index scores for tag 48.

[3] See footnote 2.

GENERAL INQUIRER SENTENCE TAG TALLY

DOCUMENT 1 FIRST IC 11811 — 5572 WORDS — 263 SENTENCES

	RAW SCORES SUB	VRB	OBJ	UCL	TOTAL	INDEX SCORES AS PERCENT SUB	VRB	OBJ	UCL	TOTAL
PRODUCT PROPERTIES										
STRENGTH				35	35				13.3	13.3
VERSATILI				65	65				24.7	24.7
ECONOMY				25	25				9.5	9.5
RELIABILI				7	7				2.7	2.7
BEAUTY				79	79				30.0	30.0
GOOD				78	78				29.7	29.7
TOTAL ASSET				172	172				65.4	65.4
WEAKNESS				16	16				6.1	6.1
EXPENSE				20	20				7.6	7.6
BAD				22	22				8.4	8.4
T. LIABILIT				52	52				19.8	19.8
QUANTITY										
MANY-LARG				61	61				23.2	23.2
FEW-SMALL				24	24				9.1	9.1
METRICS				103	103				39.2	39.2
RELATIONA				52	52				19.8	19.8
TOTAL-QUANT				152	152				57.8	57.8
HIGH-RATE				31	31				11.8	11.8
LOW-RATE				11	11				4.2	4.2

	RAW SCORES SUB	VRB	OBJ	UCL	TOTAL	INDEX SCORES AS PERCENT SUB	VRB	OBJ	UCL	TOTAL
INSTITUTIONAL REFERENCE										
ROLES				34	34				12.9	12.9
ORGANIZAT				31	31				11.8	11.8
MANAGEMEN				26	26				9.9	9.9
FINANCE				14	14				5.3	5.3
MARKETING				11	11				4.2	4.2
CONSUMPTI				8	8				3.0	3.0
SCIENTIFI				81	81				30.8	30.8
TECHNOLOGI				65	65				24.7	24.7
STYLE										
EMPHASIS				88	88				33.5	33.5
UNDEREMPHA				37	37				14.1	14.1
EMOTIONAL				6	6				2.3	2.3
CHANGE										
INCREASE				51	51				19.4	19.4
DECREASE				14	14				5.3	5.3
STASIS				8	8				3.0	3.0
TRANSFORM				73	73				27.8	27.8
TOTAL-CHANG				122	122				46.4	46.4
SUM-DECLINE				6	6				2.3	2.3
SUM-IMPROVE				30	30				11.4	11.4

FIGURE 6.B. *Sample sentence-count tag tally table for text not edited for syntax (null subtotals suppressed). See* § 6.2 *on types of scores and* § § 6.5-6.6 *on format and headings.*

§ 6.3. System Considerations

This section relates TAG TALLY to RETRIEVAL procedures, and to the secondary programs for processing TAG TALLY output.

§ *6.3.1. TAG TALLY and RETRIEVAL.* After TAG TALLY information has been obtained, the investigator may want to make retrievals. If RETRIEVAL (§ 7.1) is instructed to find all sentences containing *one* specific tag, the number of sentences with that tag that are retrieved from a given file should be the same as TAG TALLY's original total sentence-count raw score for that same tag in that same file. The investigator should check the tag tally scores beforehand to make sure there were enough assignments of the given tag to make a retrieval procedure worthwhile.

At the end of each file, RETRIEVAL can print out raw and index scores for each retrieval question (§ 7.11; Table 7.C). If a retrieval question (§ 7.5) refers to the co-occurrence of two or more tags, the index score for that question can be compared with TAG TALLY's sentence-count index scores for each of the tags specified in the question. If, for example, a sentence-count tag tally table indicates that tag a occurred in 18.5 percent of the sentences in a given file and tag b occurred in 12.2 percent of these sentences, we would expect tags a and b to co-occur in 2.3 percent (18.5 percent x 12.2 percent) of the sentences. The retrieval index score will show whether in fact co-occurrence is more or less than expected.

§ *6.3.2. Processing TAG TALLY Output.* Under sense switch options (§ 6.7), TAG TALLY can record scores on tape (§ 6.10) and/or on cards (§ 6.11). The output tape contains all the types of scores that are printed on the tag tally table (Figure 6.A), whereas only total index scores can be punched onto cards.

The tag tally information recorded on either cards or tape can be used as input in subsequent statistical analyses—for example, analysis of variance, factor analysis, or stepwise multiple regression.[4] These analyses can be performed by standard statistical programs that are available at most computation centers. When such programs are used, it is generally necessary to prepare special control cards that describe how the data are arranged on cards or tape. These control cards should

[4]See Stone *et al., op. cit.*, p. 643, for an index of discussions in that book of many statistical procedures for analyzing tag scores.

follow the TAG TALLY output format specifications given in Appendices One and Two (§ § 20.1; 25.1).

In addition, several secondary programs have been prepared to generate graphs, means, ranges, and standard deviations of tag scores that have been transposed from tag-within-document to document-within-tag order (§ 1.5; Figure 1.B). These programs and their capabilities are described in Part Three of this manual (§ § 10.1; 12.1).

§ *6.3.3. Suggestions for File Maintenance.* The tape or punched cards generated by TAG TALLY do not indicate whether sentence-count or word-count scores have been recorded on them. Similarly, there is no indication of whether the scores are based on a complete document or a subset of sentences resulting from a retrieval. Therefore, it is recommended that both output cards and output tapes be fully labeled when they are first produced.

Printed tag tally tables are automatically labeled as to whether they contain sentence-count or word-count scores. The identification field of the first sentence in each input file—the document-identification code (§ § 1.8.3; 3.6)—is also printed at the top of each table. An option (§ 6.6) permits additional header information to be printed at the top of the table.

Should the investigator find that he has mixed together unlabeled tapes or card decks, he can usually determine what data they contain by printing a few cards or a few tape records and comparing the identification fields with those appearing on the tag tally tables. Sentence-count scores can usually be distinguished from word-count scores because the latter tend to be of a higher order of magnitude.

INPUT AND OUTPUT SPECIFICATIONS

§ 6.4. Input

The input tape of tagged sentences is in Format Two (§ 19.1). Card input is as follows: the first part of the program, the tag tally table format cards,[5] the second part of the program, and finally any optional first line table heading cards.

[5] These cards may be omitted if sense switch B (§ 6.9), which suppresses the printing of tables, remains *up* throughout the program execution.

§6.5. Format Cards[6]

The format of all tag tally tables produced during a single run is defined by a set of format cards. This control of table layout begins after the fourth printed line (Figures 6.A, 6.B), where the table divides in half vertically. One format card is made for each line of the table beginning at this point. The card indicates to the program which tags should be printed on that line or whether titles or spacing should appear instead. If the approximately 50 lines on a single page[7] are not enough to complete the table, the table may be continued onto a second page.

§ *6.5.1. Columns 78-80 of Format Cards.* Each format card should have a page number (1 or 2) in column 78 and a line number (01 to a maximum of approximately 50) in columns 79-80. The cards must be arranged so that columns 78-80 are in ascending numerical order. It is not necessary, however, that the numbers in columns 79-80 be consecutive. If cards are not in ascending order, the program run will be terminated after an error message has been printed out (§ 6.13).

§ *6.5.2. Columns 1-77 of Half-Line Format Cards.* Most format cards will provide separate information for the left and the right sides of that line in the table which is identified in columns 78-80 of the card (§ 6.5.1). The information for the left side of the line is specified in columns 1-40 of the card; information for the right side is in columns 41-77. Either field of a format card may specify any one of three types of half-line instructions: a tag to be printed, a title, or a space (blank half line). Thus, any one of nine different combinations of half-line instructions may be punched on one format card. The formats for the left and right fields, and the actions taken by the program in response to each type of format, are shown in the table on page 124.

Not all tags used in the dictionary need be specified in the format cards. Thus, the investigator has the option of deliberately excluding the scores for certain tags from the table. The tags may be printed in the table in any order. The printed order of tags (as well as whether or not a tag appears at all in the table) does not affect the appearance and ordering of tags on tape or card output (§ § 6.10;6.11).

§ *6.5.3. Columns 1-77 of Centered-Heading Format Cards.* If a format card has a period in column 1, any information keypunched

[6] See footnote 5.

[7] The exact number of lines available depends on the carriage-control tape used by the printer. If the exact number is needed, the operator should be consulted. A special carriage-control tape can easily be prepared.

Left-Field Card Columns		Right-Field Card Columns		Contents	Action
Either	1-12 34-35	*Either*	41-52 74-75	Tag name[8] Tag number (01-99)	Tag name, and a row of ten scores for that tag, are printed.
Or	1-37	*Or*	41-77	Title[9]	The title is printed.
Or	1-40	*Or*	41-77	Blank	The half line is left blank for spacing.

in columns 2-77 will be printed in the middle of that line in the table that is specified in columns 78-80 of the card (§ 6.5.1).

§6.6. Optional Table Heading Card (Sense Switch C)

Seventy print positions on the right of the first line of the table (see Figure 6.A) can be filled by a table heading obtained from a heading card placed at the end of the input deck. If sense switch C is up when the program begins to process a file on the input tape (§ 6.7), the contents of the heading card will be printed at the top of the table. This same heading will be used to title the following tables unless sense switch C is kept up and a new heading card is read in for the next input file. If sense switch C is down throughout a run, the right side of the first line of all tables will remain blank.

The title is taken from columns 1-70 of the heading card; columns 71-80 are ignored.

§6.7. Output: Setting and Resetting Sense Switches

The setting of sense switch G determines whether word-count or sentence-count scores are generated (§ 6.8). Sense switches B, D, and E control whether the scores are recorded in tables, on tape and/or on punched cards (§ § 6.9-6.11).

[8] If there is a tag number in columns 34-35 (or 74-75) but no tag name in columns 1-12 (or 41-52), the program halts and prints out an error message (§6.14).

[9] Columns 34-35 (or 74-75) of titles may be blank or contain alphabetic characters but should *not* contain numbers. If numbers appear in these columns, the program will not interpret them correctly.

A final run summary is printed giving the total number of input files processed,[10] the total number of sentences processed, the total number of words processed, and the average number of words per sentence.

All sense switches are consulted immediately before a file is read from the input tape—that is, just before the first record in the file moves under the read head of the tape unit. Thus, the settings that are to govern the output for a given file may be made at any time during the processing of the *preceding* file.

§6.8. Sentence-Count Versus Word-Count Scores (Sense Switch G)

If sense switch G is up when an input tape file begins to be processed, then only sentence counts are made and the words GENERAL INQUIRER SENTENCE TAG TALLY are printed at the head of the table for that file. If sense switch G is down when an input tape file begins to be processed, then word counts are made and the message GENERAL INQUIRER WORD TAG TALLY is printed at the top of the table.

§6.9. Tag Tally Table (Sense Switch B)

If sense switch B is up when an input tape file begins to be processed, a tag tally table (Figures 6.A, 6.B) will *not* be printed for that file. This does not affect the production of an output tape (§ 6.10), the punching of output cards (§ 6.11), or print-out of the run summary (§ 6.7) and error messages (§ § 6.13; 6.14; 26.3). Therefore, the printer should not be turned off.

If sense switch B is down when an input tape file begins to be processed, a tag tally table for that file will be printed in accordance with format card instructions (§ § 6.5-6.5.3) and table heading cards, if any (§ 6.6).

§6.10. Tag Tally Output Tape (Sense Switch D)

If sense switch D is up when an input tape file begins to be processed, all the scores for each tag will be written on tape unit 3. Six output

[10]When a TAG TALLY output tape is used as input to TRANSPOSE, it is necessary to specify on the TRANSPOSE control card how many documents are on the input tape (§ 9.4, columns 4-6). This number will be equal to the number of files processed by TAG TALLY, if sense switch D (§ 6.10) was up throughout the entire run in which the tape was generated.

records are produced for each input file; this output is in Format Three, as described in Appendix One (§ § 20.3-20.4). If sense switch D is down when an input tape file begins to be processed, no scores for that file are written on the output tape. If sense switch D is to be down throughout a run, an output tape need not be mounted on unit 3.

§ 6.11. Summary Cards (Sense Switch E)

If sense switch E is up when an input tape file begins to be processed, the total index scores for that file will be punched onto a set of seven cards. The format of these cards is given in Appendix Two (§ § 25.2-25.4). Note that if raw scores (total or subtotal) are wanted on cards, they can be generated later from the tag tally output tape (§ 6.10) by SUMMARY PUNCH (§ 8.1). If sense switch E is down throughout the run, the punch motor may be turned off.

TECHNICAL CONSIDERATIONS

§ 6.12. Language and Processing

The program is written in 1401 Tape Autocoder. All files on the input tape are processed separately but consecutively until the terminal file (§ 19.8) is reached. The program does not rewind either the input tape (unit 1) or the output tape (unit 3) at the beginning of the run. At the end of the run, the program will clear the 1402 punch (if punched output was produced), rewind and unload the input tape, and rewind and unload the output tape (if tape output was produced). On acceptable input record length, see § 5.10. On defective input records, see § 26.3.

§ 6.13. Processing of Unsorted Format Cards

If the program encounters a format card that is not in correct order (§ 6.5.1), the message LAST CARD OUT OF SEQUENCE...SORT ON 78-80 is printed and the program halts. The format cards should be put in order and the input deck reloaded.

§ 6.14. Processing Defective Half-Line Format Cards

If a half-line format card (§ 6.5.2) contains numbers in columns 34-35 (or 74-75) but no category name in columns 1-12 (or 41-52), the program halts and prints the message NO LABEL IN TAG CARD. If START is pressed, a line of scores will be printed without a tag name.

RETRIEVAL Operational Summary

Machine:

IBM 1401 with 8K, Advanced Programming, High-Low-Equal compare, and at least one tape unit (but two or more if tape-output options are exercised).

Input Schematic:

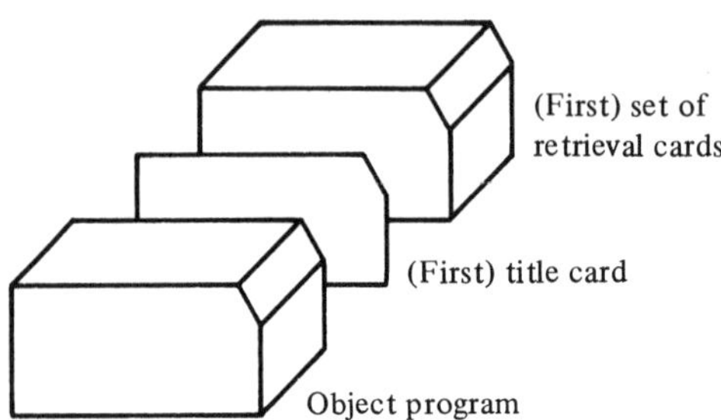

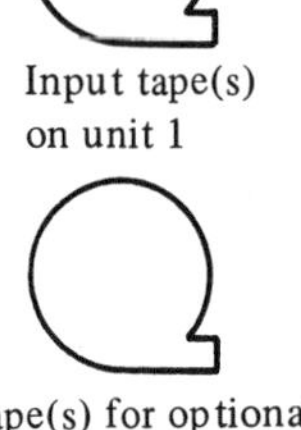

Machine-Operator Instructions:

1. Place card input in 1402 read hopper; ready 1402 punch if optional punched output is requested (§ 7.14). Place only one set of retrieval cards in hopper at a time; each set must be preceded by a title card.
2. Set sense switches on 1401. Note that if either F or G is up, additional operator instructions must be supplied.
   A: Always up (§ 7.15).
   B; C, D, E: Suppression of title records and end-of-file marks on output tapes (if any) on units 2-5 (§ 7.13).
   F: Multiple-tape input option (§ 7.6).
   G: Single-file processing option (§ 7.7).
3. Ready first and each subsequent input tape on unit 1 (ring out); position each tape correctly.
4. Ready tape(s) on units 2, 3, 4, and/or 5 (ring in) if optional tape output is wanted (§ 7.13).
5. On 1403, ready continuous forms for desired number of copies of printed output (usual maximum four copies) and for diagnostic messages.
6. Press START RESET on 1401.
7. Press CHECK RESET and LOAD on 1402. Press START to process last two retrieval cards in each set.
8. For procedures in case of defective input tape records, see § 26.2.
9. Input tapes are not automatically rewound before being read, but output tapes are rewound before being written upon. No tape is rewound after a program halt or at the end of the run.

CHAPTER 7

Retrieval[1]

INTRODUCTION

§7.1. Function

This program consecutively examines all files on a Format Two (§ 19.1) input tape—either a TEXT-TAG LIST output tape (§ 5.9) or the output of a previous RETRIEVAL run (§ 7.13)—in order to locate and count sentences that satisfy specifications made by the investigator about one or more of the following: (a) tags assigned or not assigned to the sentence; (b) parts of words, words or phrases occurring or not occurring in the text of the sentence; and (c) information in the sentence identification code. The investigator prepares these specifications as a set of one or more "questions."

Each retrieval question is keypunched on a single "retrieval card" (§ 7.5) and must immediately be followed on that card by an output instruction (§ 7.5.4). All sentences satisfying every specification within a question are counted, and may also be recorded on any or all of six output media, as specified by the investigator's output instruction for the given question. The six output media are: a printed listing (§ 7.10; Figure 7.B), as many as four tapes (§ 7.13), and punched cards (§ 7.14). The counts for each question can be printed at the end of each file (§ 7.11; Figure 7.C). Final totals of the counts for each question as applied to all files are also printed at the end of the run (§ 7.12).

The program automatically counts how many sentences have been recorded in each output medium, and prints these counts both for each file processed and in aggregate total at the end of the run.

[1] Stone, Philip J., Dexter C. Dunphy, Marshall S. Smith, Daniel M. Ogilvie, with associates, *The General Inquirer: A Computer Approach to Content Analysis* (Cambridge, Mass.: The M. I. T. Press, 1966), pp. 107-119, 162-265.

During a single run, the program can successively process more than one input tape and/or more than one set of retrieval cards (§ 7.6-7.7).

§7.2. System Considerations

Sentences sent to any of the output tapes will be recorded in Format Two (§ 19.1) and can be subjected to further analyses by both TAG TALLY (§ 6.1) and RETRIEVAL itself. Since an output file of sentences retrieved from a single input document (§ 1.9) may be very short, the investigator may wish to exercise the option of suppressing (on the output tape) the end-of-file marks that normally separate sentences of different documents (§ 7.13). This results in the grouping of all retrieved sentences as one file from which over-all tag tally scores (§ 6.2) and further retrieval scores can be obtained.

The percentage scores prepared by RETRIEVAL for each input file (§ 7.11; Figure 7.C) are directly comparable with the sentence-count index scores computed by TAG TALLY (§ 6.3.1). Retrieval questions may be suggested by examination of the text-tag listings (Figure 5.A), tag tally tables (Figure 6.A), and graphs derived from the tag tally tables (Figure 10.A).

Note that when sentences retrieved from several documents are merged into a single output file, comparison with tag tally scores for the original documents becomes more complicated. Output tapes should be carefully labeled so that necessary identification is available when they are used as input to TAG TALLY.

INPUT AND OUTPUT SPECIFICATIONS

§7.3. Input

Input consists of one or more tapes in Format Two (§ 19.1), the object program, and one or more sets of retrieval cards, with each set preceded by a title card. See further § 7.15 and Figure 7.A.

§7.4. Title Card

One title card must appear in front of each set of retrieval cards.

§ *7.4.1. Title Card: Columns 1-79.* The contents of columns 1-79 of the title card will be printed at the top of every page of the listings printed during that pass through the data (Figures 7.A-7.C). Any alphanumeric or special characters may be keypunched in columns 1-79.

§ *7.4.2. Title Card: Column 80.* Tables of input-file retrieval scores (§ 7.11; Figure 7.C) will be printed if column 80 of the title card is blank but will not be printed if column 80 contains any character other than blank. This option permits the investigator to reduce the volume of printed output when many short files are to be processed and the investigator is interested in retrieved sentences to the exclusion of retrieval counts. Suppression of the tables for each input file does not suppress printing of the final table for all files on the input tape (§ 7.12).

§7.5. Retrieval Cards

Each retrieval card must contain a retrieval question beginning in column 1 followed by an output instruction ending in or before column 80. Card columns that remain to the right of the output instruction may, at the investigator's option, contain a comment.

The retrieval question may consist of any combination of specifications as to tags (§ 7.5.1), letters or words in the text (§ 7.5.2), or sentence-identification codes (§ 7.5.3). Any of these three types of specifications may appear more than once in, or be wholly absent from, a retrieval question. Each specification must be preceded by a plus (+) or a minus (-) to indicate whether its presence or absence in an input sentence is the criterion for retrieval. An input sentence must satisfy every specification in a retrieval question in order to be considered as "matching" the question—that is, in order to be counted and retrieved.

The last specification in a question should be followed by an equals sign (=), which, in turn, should be followed by an output instruction (§ 7.5.4). The output instruction is a list of output devices on which matching sentences are to be recorded. The end of this list of output devices must be followed by a blank column.

We will now consider the different instruction features for retrieval questions and output. General format rules and other points to check in preparing retrieval cards are listed in § 7.5.6. It is suggested that the user always check his proposed retrievals against this list until he is thoroughly familar with retrieval procedures.

In considering retrieval procedures, the following sample retrieval cards will be discussed in detail:

Example One: +04=P

Example Two:

+03/EJ4-33+11S+(PARENT(=PC24   AFFECTION/HOSTILITY

§ *7.5.1. Retrieval Questions: Tag Specifications.* The presence or absence in each sentence on the input tape of any word tagged by a particular category is tested by specifying the two-digit tag (01-99) for that category. This two-digit tag specification is punched with a preceding plus or minus sign. In example one, all input sentences to which tag 04 had been assigned by TAGGING (§ 4.2) will satisfy the specification +04. Since this is the only specification in the question, all sentences assigned tag 04 will be considered to have "matched" the question.

In example two, the specification -33 can only be satisfied by sentences to which tag 33 had *not* been assigned. However, no sentence will match this question unless the sentence satisfies all the other specifications in the question.

The two-digit tag specification may be further restricted by the addition of a syntax marker (S, V, Ø, U). In example two, only sentences to which tag 11 has been assigned in the syntax position of subject can satisfy the specification +11S. A sentence to which tag 11V, 11Ø, or 11U–but not 11S–has been assigned will not satisfy the specification +11S. (See § 2.9 and § 3.12.1.)

§ *7.5.2. Retrieval Questions: Text Specifications.* This feature permits examining the text of sentences on the input tape for a specified string of letters, a word, or a string of words. The letters or words to be searched for should be enclosed within a pair of parentheses, and a plus (+) or a minus (-) should precede the first parenthesis in order to indicate whether the presence or absence of the specified alphabetics should be the criterion for retrieval. The two parentheses function independently of each other as boundary markers and can be paired in any of the four combinations illustrated here:

+(CONSIDER) +(CONSIDER(+)CONSIDER) +)CONSIDER(

In these examples, each left (or right) parenthesis that faces the text specification is a closed boundary, and indicates that the immediately adjacent character of the specification must be the first (or last) character[2] of a word in any sentence that is to satisfy the specification. Each left (or right) parenthesis that does not face the text specification is an open boundary and indicates that the immediately adjacent character of the specification need not be the first (or last) character[3] of

[2] The first (or last) character of a word is the one preceded (or followed) by a blank.

[3] See footnote 2.

a word in any sentence that is to satisfy the specification. For example, text words whose presence would satisfy each of the four examples just given are:

+(CONSIDER):	only consider
+(CONSIDER(:	consider, considers, considered, considering, considerable, considerate, consideration, etc.
+)CONSIDER):	consider, disconsider, reconsider, etc.
+)CONSIDER(:	all of the preceding, and reconsiders, reconsidered, reconsideration, unconsidered, etc.

Thus, in example two (§7.5), the text specification +(PARENT(could be satisfied by any input sentence that contained PARENT, PARENTS, PARENTAL, or PARENTHOOD; but it could not be satisfied by GRANDPARENT or GRANDPARENTS.

A multiword text specification is written with blanks as it would appear in the sentence. For example,

+(EQUAL OPPORTUNITY EMPLOYER(

would be matched by either EQUAL OPPORTUNITY EMPLOYER or the plural EQUAL OPPORTUNITY EMPLOYERS. Note that if two text words had been separated by more than one blank when they were keypunched, this would have been reduced to a single blank by TAGGING (§3.3). Similarly, all subscripts and slashes (§§3.10; 3.12) are normally removed by TAGGING and need not be considered in preparing text specifications for RETRIEVAL. However, if TAGGING's *UNEDITED control-card option was exercised (§4.25), slashes and subscripts will be included in the text processed by RETRIEVAL, and the investigator may, but need not, specify subscripts in retrieval card text specifications. For example, the specification +(FATHER/1) would be satisfied by sentences containing FATHER/1 but not by those containing FATHER/1A, FATHER/5 or FATHER. On the other hand, the "open-bounded" specification +(FATHER(would be satisfied by sentences containing any subscripted or unsubscripted form of FATHER, FATHERS, FATHER-IN-LAW, FATHERLAND, etc.

§ *7.5.3. Retrieval Questions: Sentence-Identification-Code Specifications.* The presence or absence in the identification code assigned to a sentence (§3.8) of one or more consecutive code characters is tested by a specification in the following format: (a) a plus or minus sign, (b) a two-digit number (01-70) indicating the column of the first code character to be searched for, (c) a slash (/), and (d) the code character or the string of consecutive code characters to be searched for. Thus, in example 2 of § 7.5, the code specification +03/EJ4 could be satisfied only by a sentence that had EJ4 as the third through fifth characters of its identification code.

§ *7.5.4. Retrieval Cards: Output Instructions.* The output instruction that must follow each retrieval question indicates whether sentences on an input tape satisfying all specifications in the given question are merely to be counted (§ § 7.11-7.12) or are also to be recorded on one or more specified output units. The number of times sentences have been recorded on each output unit are printed (Figure 7.C) for each input file (§ 7.11) and for the data as a whole (§ 7.12).

Each output instruction should consist of at least one of the characters listed in Table 7.A. An equals sign (=) must intervene between the last character of the retrieval question and the first character of the output instruction. No character should appear more than once in a single output instruction. The output instruction must end on the same card on which the retrieval question began. The formats of retrievals to each kind of output unit are described in § 7.10 and § § 7.13-7.14.

TABLE 7.A. Characters Used in Output Instructions on Retrieval Cards

Character	*Meaning*	
P	Print all sentences that match the retrieval question on this card (§ 7.10; Figure 7.B).	
2	Transcribe all sentences which match the retrieval question on this card onto the output tape (§ 7.13) on:	tape unit 2
3		tape unit 3
4		tape unit 4
5		tape unit 5
C	Punch onto an output card (§ 7.14) numerical information about each sentence that matches the retrieval question on this card.	
X	Sentences matching the retrieval question on this card are not to be recorded on any output medium but are to be counted in pertinent scores (§ § 7.11-7.12; Figure 7.C).	

In example one of § 7.5, the output instruction P specifies that all sentences matching the question are to be printed. In example two, the instruction PC24 specifies that matching sentences are to be printed and transcribed onto tapes readied for this purpose on units 2 and 4 and that numerical information about each matching sentence is to be punched onto a card.

§ *7.5.5. Comments.* A comment keypunched at least one blank column after the end of the output instruction can facilitate inspection of all listings and tables produced by the program (Figures 7.A-7.C), since each comment will always be printed together with the retrieval question to which it pertains. For example, when tags are specified in retrieval questions (§ 7.5.1), it is often useful to keypunch a comment that includes the names of the tag categories. Or if the retrieval question is fairly complicated, it can be helpful to have a comment identifying the purpose of the question, especially when many questions are processed together as a set.

Comments may consist of one or more words (any alphanumeric and/or special characters). Inasmuch as comments are stored in the computer's memory during processing, the amount of space they occupy lessens the space available for retrieval questions. Numerous comments thus can seriously reduce the maximum number of retrieval questions that can be processed together as a set. See further § 7.16.

§ *7.5.6. General Format Rules: Points to Check in Preparing Retrieval Cards.* Except for blanks occurring within a multiword text specification (§ 7.5.2) like +(EQUAL OPPORTUNITY EMPLOYER(, there should be no blank columns between column 1 of the retrieval question and the last column of the output instruction. The program considers a blank (if not within parentheses) as indicating the end of the retrieval directions. If one equals sign (§ 7.5.4) does not occur before the first blank, the program will reject the question and stop with an error message. The computer will also stop with an error message if there is no output instructions (§ 7.5.4) or if an illegal character—that is, one not specified in Table 7.A—is found in the instruction.

The retrieval specifications on any one card are tested from left to right on each input sentence. If any specification is not satisfied, the attempt at matching is considered to have failed and testing of further specifications is omitted. Therefore, it makes sense to put first on the retrieval card those specifications that can be quickly tested and have a fairly high probability of failing. Tag specifications (§ 7.5.1) and sentence-identification-code specifications (§ 7.5.3) are tested many times faster than text specifications (§ 7.5.2). See § 1.8.5. Whenever a text specification occurs, the computer has the lengthy task of running through the entire text of each sentence. Text specifications should therefore appear last in the retrieval questions, in order to minimize running time. If there are words in the text specification that have been assigned tag(s), it saves considerable time to test for the presence of the tag(s) *before* searching the text.[4]

Before submitting his retrieval cards for processing, the investigator should check that:

a. A title card (§ 7.4) precedes each set of questions.
b. No other title cards and no blank cards are mixed in with the retrieval cards.
c. A plus or minus sign precedes each specification on each card.
d. Parentheses appear on both sides of each text specification.
e. An equals sign separates the last specification in each question from the beginning of the output instruction.
f. Each output instruction contains only valid characters (Table 7.A).
g. Each output instruction is followed by at least one blank.

The program does not completely analyze a question to confirm that it "makes sense" and may therefore attempt to process what are obvious mistakes in keypunching. If the retrievals are radically different from, or fewer than, what was expected, the investigator should check to make sure the retrieval cards were keypunched correctly.

Whenever a set of retrieval cards is read in, the program will halt before processing the last two cards. Pressing START on the 1402 will cause the last two cards in the set to be processed and will complete the listing of the cards (§ 7.9). The user should check the numbered listing to make sure the questions are as intended. If some questions lack an equal sign (§ 7.5.4) or have inappropriate output instructions, an error message will be printed and a halt will occur at this time. The defective question should be corrected and reentered in the card reader.

§7.6. Multiple-Tape Input Option (Sense Switch F)

If sense switch F is set down when the terminal file (§ 19.8) on an input tape is reached, the table of retrieval scores for the last input

[4] For example, if we specified +(FRANCE) and the word FRANCE had been assigned tags 35 and 54 by TAGGING (§4.2), then processing would be much quicker if the retrieval question were expanded to +35+54+(FRANCE). In this case, the search for the text word FRANCE will not begin unless both tags 35 and 54 have been assigned to a sentence. Even then the word FRANCE may not be found because those tags might also have been assigned to other words. Since the tag specifications have been put first, the number of sentences in which the text word FRANCE is then searched for would usually be a small subset of the number of sentences in the file.

data file (§ 7.11) will be followed by a table of aggregate scores for all data files on the tape (§ 7.12). The program will then halt, ready to read in a new set of questions when START is pressed. If sense switch F is up, only the table for the last file is printed, and the computer halts. If a new input tape is readied and START is pressed, the computer will process the new input tape with the same questions, aggregating the across-file counts with those from the previous tape.

If sense switch F is set up and START RESET and START are pressed in that order, the aggregate totals will be printed and the counters cleared before the new tape is processed with the same questions as used for the previous tape.

§7.7. Single-File Processing (Sense Switch G)

If sense switch G is set down, the program continues to process each consecutive document on the input tape with the same set of questions. If, however, sense switch G is set up at any time, the program will halt upon reaching the next end-of-file mark (§ 19.7) on the input tape. When START RESET and START are pressed, a table of aggregate scores will be printed for the files so far processed, the counters will be cleared, and a new set of retrieval questions can be read in. If only START is pressed, the aggregate totals are not printed and the counters are not cleared; instead, the counts for each question number (§ 7.9) will be aggregated with the counts for the next set of questions.

In this way, if it is necessary to halt the operation after a particular file is processed (for example, to skip a file or change the input tape), the last question set can be reloaded upon pressing START and the aggregate counting across files continued. In some cases, the investigator may want to change certain questions before processing of a new file begins. For example, the names of people occupying key roles in different countries or time periods may change, so that the names in the text specifications (§ 7.5.2) of retrieval questions should also be changed.

§7.8. Output

Output is for the most part determined by the output instructions (§ 7.5.4) on retrieval cards. We here consider printed output first and then describe tape and card output. If tape or card output is not called for by any output instructions, tape units 2-5 or the card punch should be switched off throughout the run.

§7.9. Numbered Listing of Retrieval Cards

When the first and any subsequent set of retrieval cards is read in (§7.7), the entire image of each card (§§7.5-7.5.5) is immediately listed under the title (§7.4.1) for the given set, as well as the heading QUESTIONS BEING PROCESSED (Figure 7.A). The cards in the set are numbered serially, with the numbering starting at one for the first card in each set.[5]

```
LETTERS FROM JENNY.  MODES OF PERCEIVING ATTACK ANC ANGER.


QUESTIONS BEING PROCESSED

   1. +01S+32V=P       (SELF AS SUBJECT, ANGER AS VERB)
   2. +C1S+48V=P       (SELF AS SUBJECT, ATTACK AS VERB)
   3. -01S+32V=P       (SELF NOT AS SUBJECT, ANGER AS VERB)
   4. -01S+48V=P       (SELF NOT AS SUBJECT, ATTACK AS VERB)
   5. +32S=P           (ANGER AS SUBJECT)
   6. +48S=P           (ATTACK AS SUBJECT)
   7. +32O=P           (ANGER AS OBJECT)
   8. +48O=P           (ATTACK AS OBJECT)
```

FIGURE 7.A. Sample numbered listing of retrieval cards. See §7.9 with note 5.

§7.10. Listing of Retrieved Sentences

After a set of questions has been read in from the card reader and printed in a numbered listing (§7.9; Figure 7.A), the search of the input tape begins. Each sentence that matches a retrieval question followed by an output instruction that includes the character P (§7.5.4 is printed (Figure 7.B) in the order in which the sentence occurs on the input tape.

Next to the question set title (§7.4.1) at the top of each page of the listing are printed a document serial number and a page number. The former refers to the ordinal position (in the entire sequence of files on the input tape) of the file from which the matching sentences printed on the page have been retrieved (§1.9). Each time there is a match from a new input file, a new page is begun and the document serial number is incremented by one. The page number refers to the page of the listing for that file, and thus begins again with "1" for each new file. On the second printed line of each page, the title record (§19.6), if any, last encountered by the program on the input tape is listed.

[5] If different sets of retrieval questions are run successively without clearing the aggregate counters (§7.7), the final aggregate total will represent the counts for the different questions associated with a particular question number, even though the listing of questions (Table 7.A) will display only the last question associated with each number.

```
                                                                              DOCUMENT   8   PAGE   1

          SENTENCE   8      TOTAL WORDS=  8     IDENTIFICATION 04510

NC, WE (CODE J 9) (CODE R Z) CIC NOT COME (FIGHT) TO BLOWS.

          QUESTICN      -01S+48V=P     (SELF NOT AS SUBJECT, ATTACK AS VERB)

          SENTENCE   9      TOTAL WORDS= 19     IDENTIFICATION 04510

RCSS (CODE R Z) WAS SURPRISED AND INDIGNANT TO (ANGRY) THINK THAT THERE WAS ANYTHING UNKIND OR UNUSUAL ABOUT WHAT HE SAID.

          QUESTICN      +32S=P         (ANGER AS SUBJECT)

          SENTENCE  14      TOTAL WORDS= 16     IDENTIFICATION 04510

BUT EVEN SUPPCSE IT (ROSS (CODE R Z) LETTER) WAS ALL RIGHT, YET KNCWING THAT IT HURT ME, AND +

          QUESTICN      -01S+48V=P     (SELF NOT AS SUBJECT, ATTACK AS VERB)

          SENTENCE  19      TOTAL WORDS= 24     IDENTIFICATION 04510

(HE) (CODE R Z) SAIC IT WOULC NOT BE ME IF I WERE NOT ,,KICKING UP A FUSS, ABOUT SCMETHING, AND WALKED OUT OF (ANGRY) THE ROOM.

          QUESTICN      +32S=P         (ANGER AS SUBJECT)

          SENTENCE   5      TOTAL WORDS= 16     IDENTIFICATION 04830

I DC NCT KNCW ABOUT THE CRIVER, OR IF ANYONE WAS INJURED IN THE CTHER CAR.

          QUESTICN      +48S=P         (ATTACK AS SUBJECT)

          SENTENCE  10      TOTAL WORDS=  7     IDENTIFICATION 05010

(I)  NEVER ASK AN EMBARRASSING QUESTION.

          QUESTICN      +48O=P         (ATTACK AS OBJECT)

          SENTENCE  21      TOTAL WORDS= 1C     IDENTIFICATION 05110

HE (CODE R Z) HAS NEVER (CISLIKE) CARED ANYTHING AT ALL FOR ME +

          QUESTICN      -01S+32V=P     (SELF NOT AS SUBJECT, ANGER AS VERB)

          SENTENCE  45      TOTAL WORDS= 1C     IDENTIFICATION 05110

BUT RCSS (CCDE R Z) WOULC BE VERY ANGRY, AND RESENT IT DREADFULLY.

          QUESTICN      -01S+32V=P     (SELF NOT AS SUBJECT, ANGER AS VERB)
                        +32S=P         (ANGER AS SUBJECT)
```

FIGURE 7.B. Sample listing of retrieved sentences. For detailed explanation see § 7.10.

Above every retrieved sentence are printed, from left to right: the within-document serial number originally assigned to the sentence by TAGGING (§ § 1.8.2; 18.3, positions 4-6; 19.4); the number of words in the sentence (§ § 18.3, positions 1-3; 19.4); and the sentence-identification code, if any (§ § 18.3, positions 7 to n; 19.4). Beneath each retrieved sentence is printed the retrieval question or questions (§ 7.5) which that sentence has matched. These questions are printed with comments (§ 7.5.5) that may have appeared on the retrieval card.

The listing of retrieved sentences may be interrupted by an error message and print-out of the defective input tape record which has caused that message (§ 26.2).

§7.11. Table of Input-File Retrieval Scores

If column 80 of the title card for the question set being processed is blank (§ 7.4.2), retrieval scores for each question and summaries of the number of sentences sent to each output unit are printed (Figure 7.C) each time an end-of-file mark is encountered on the input tape.

The top of the table is labeled SUBTOTAL SUMMARY to distinguish

```
     LABOR LEADERS SPEECHES                                    DOCUMENT 86


SUBTOTAL SUMMARY

  210 SENTENCES PROCESSED
 1260 ATTEMPTED MATCHES

QUESTION                                 TALLY                PERCENT

+(STRIKE(+(NEA)=P                          12                    5.7
+(UNION(+(NEA)=P                            5                    2.4
+76+(NEA)=P                                17                    8.1
+40=P                                      25                   11.9
+76=P                                      94                   44.8
+56=P4                                    130                   61.9


FINAL OUTPUT DEVICE USAGE

DEVICE                                   TALLY                PERCENT

PRINTER
  QUESTIONS                               283                   22.2
  SENTENCES                               194                   92.4
PUNCH                                                             .0
TAPE UNIT 2                                                       .0
TAPE UNIT 3                                                       .0
TAPE UNIT 4                               130                   61.9
TAPE UNIT 5                                                       .0
```

FIGURE 7.C. Sample table of input-file retrieval scores. For detailed explanation see §7.11.

it from the FINAL SUMMARY of aggregate counts across files (§ 7.12), and the document serial number is given. The number of sentences in the file is printed next to the words SENTENCES PROCESSED. The number identified as ATTEMPTED MATCHES represents the number of sentences in the file multiplied by the number of questions in the question set. Note that this multiplication is by the total number of questions, not just the number of questions having a P in their respective output instructions (§ 7.5.4).

Under the heading QUESTION, the set of retrieval cards, including their comments, is listed together with a TALLY for each retrieval question (that is, the number of times the question was matched) and a PERCENT for each question (that is, the respective TALLY divided by the number of SENTENCES PROCESSED).[6]

Under the heading DEVICE are listed the six output devices: printer, card punch, and tape units 2, 3, 4, and 5. The TALLY for the card punch and for each tape unit is the number of sentences recorded on the given device; the PERCENT for the card punch and each tape is the respective TALLY divided by the number of SENTENCES PROCESSED. The output to the printer is summarized by two lines of scores. In the first line, which is labeled QUESTIONS, the TALLY gives the number of matches between a sentence and any retrieval question whose output instruction (§ 7.5.4) specified the printer. (Note that if a listed sentence matched more than one question, each such match will be counted separately in this score.) The PERCENT score opposite QUESTIONS is the respective TALLY divided by the product of the number of SENTENCES PROCESSED times the number of questions that do include a P in their output instructions. The second line of scores associated with the printer, labeled SENTENCES, simply gives the number of sentences sent to the printer both as a raw score and as a percent of the number of SENTENCES PROCESSED.

Percentage scores are computed with reference to the total number of sentences in the input-tape file. As previously discussed (§ 6.3.1), these percentages correspond to TAG TALLY's sentence-count index scores.

§7.12. Table of Aggregated Input-Tape Retrieval Scores

The across-file aggregate scores are printed in the same format (Figure 7.C) as the tables produced for each file (§ 7.11). However, the across-

[6] All scores in the PERCENT column are rounded to the nearest tenth of a percent so that, for example, 7.85 percent becomes 7.9 percent but 7.84 percent becomes 7.8 percent.

file table is titled FINAL SUMMARY rather than SUBTOTAL SUMMARY. These aggregate scores are normally printed at the end of a run, but can also be printed at other times under control of sense switches F and G (§ § 7.6-7.7).

§7.13. Retrieval Output Tape(s) in Format Two and Suppression of Title Records and End-of-File Marks on Output Tapes

Each sentence that has matched a retrieval question whose output instruction includes one of the digits 2, 3, 4, or 5 (§ 7.5.4; Table 7.A) is transcribed onto the output tape on the tape unit specified by that digit. If an output instruction includes two, three, or all of these four digits, a sentence matching the retrieval question associated with that instruction is simultaneously transcribed onto each of the output tapes specified by those digits. However, no sentence, even if matching more than one retrieval question, can be written more than once on any one output tape (cf. § 7.15). Each output tape is written in Format Two (§ § 19.1; 19.3) and can in turn be used as input to RETRIEVAL and TAG TALLY.

For purposes of preventing transcription of certain information from an input tape to one or more output tapes, sense switch B corresponds to the output tape on tape unit 2, sense switch C to the tape on unit 3, sense switch D to the tape on unit 4, and sense switch E to the tape on unit 5. Title records and end-of-file marks (§ § 19.6; 19.7), when encountered on the input tape, will not be transcribed onto any output tape for which the corresponding switch had been set up, but will be transcribed onto any tape for which the corresponding switch had been set down.

Note carefully that the matching sentences transcribed by RETRIEVAL from two or more input tapes onto an output tape without intermediate end-of-file marks will constitute a single output file. Secondary tag tally tables for that file will not be readily comparable with the tables originally generated for each separate document. See further § 7.2.

The settings of sense switches B-E are mutually independent and are also unaffected by the settings of sense switches G and F (§ § 7.6-7.7).

§7.14. Punched Output

Numerical information concerning each sentence that matches a retrieval question whose output instruction includes the character C

(§7.5.4; Table 7.A) will be punched onto a single card in the format given in this section. One card is punched for each match. Thus, if one sentence matched three questions (whose output instructions included the character C), three separate cards would be punched for that one sentence. The format of each card is as follows:

Card Columns	*Contents*
1-3	Serial number of the input document (§1.9) from which the matching sentence specified in columns 5-7 has been retrieved.
4	Blank.
5-7	Serial number of the matching sentence (§§1.8.2; 18.3, positions 4-6; 19.4) within the input document specified in columns 1-3.
8-13	Blank.
14-16	Serial number of the retrieval question (§7.9) which the sentence specified in columns 5-7 has matched.
17	Blank.
18-80	As many as 63 initial characters of the document- or sentence-identification code (§§3.6; 3.8; 18.3, positions 7 to n) of the sentence specified in columns 5-7.

The punched output option is intended particularly for those cases in which retrieval information is to be tabulated against information in sentence-identification codes. For example, sentence completion test responses may be retrieved and then compared with information identifying the stimulus and various characteristics of the responses that were encoded in the identification field.

TECHNICAL CONSIDERATIONS

§7.15. Language and Processing

The source program is written in 1401 Tape Autocoder. Sense switch A must always be set up in order to enable the program to confirm that the last card in a set of retrieval cards (§§7.5; 7.7; 7.16) has been read into core. When the last retrieval card has been read in, the first sentence record is compared with *all* the retrieval questions in core. Then the second and each successive sentence record is similarly compared with all retrieval questions. A tape record longer than 1942 positions cannot be properly processed.[7]

Note that only one set of retrieval questions, consisting of a title card followed by retrieval cards, should be placed in the card reader at one time. It is the reading of the last retrieval card (with no more cards in the hopper) that signals the end of the question set and causes the computer to begin processing the input tape. While the input tape is being processed, the next question set (title card plus retrieval cards) can be placed in the reader.

At no time when the program halts are any of the input tapes rewound. If several question sets are to be processed on the same input tape, rewinding of that tape must be initiated by the operator before each pass.

§7.16. Maximum Size of Question Sets

On an IBM 1401 with 8K memory, a maximum of 833 characters is available for storing each set of retrieval cards. Each retrieval card in a set is stored in 9+n core characters, where n is the total number of characters in the retrieval question proper (§§7.5.1-7.5.3), the output instruction (§7.5.4), and comments, if any (§7.5.5), as well as any blanks between the end of the output instruction and the beginning of the comments. For example, if a set of 35 retrieval cards were keypunched in an average of 12 columns each, the total core requirement would be 35(9+12), or 735 core positions. This would fit with 98 core positions to spare.

If the question set requires more than the available 833 core positions, the message INPUT STORAGE AREA FILLED is printed out and the computer halts. The program must then be reloaded with a smaller question set.

[7] TEXT-TAG LIST will not write a Format Two tape record of more than 1800 characters (§5.10). Sentence records written by RETRIEVAL on tape are exact copies of the records read and selected by the program, and will thus in no case exceed 1800 characters in length, although the theoretic maximum is 1942 characters.

PART THREE

SECONDARY PROGRAMS FOR PROCESSING TAG TALLY OUTPUT

SUMMARY PUNCH Operational Summary

Machine:

IBM 1401 with 4K, Advanced Programming, High-Low-Equal compare, and one tape unit.

Input Schematic:

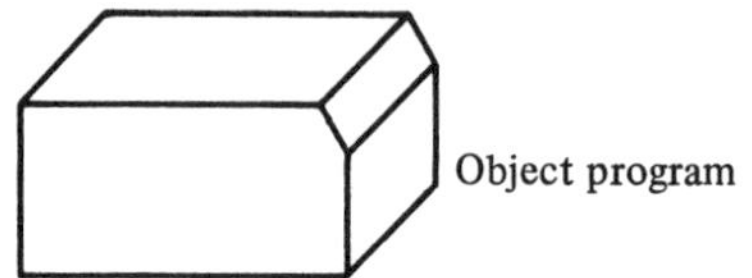
Object program

Input tape on unit 3

Machine-Operator Instructions:

1. Place card input in 1402 read hopper.
2. Ready 1402 punch.
3. Set sense switches on 1401.
   A: Ignored
   B, C, D, E, F: Specification of type of raw score to be punched (§ 8.5).
   G: Suppression of output listing (§ 8.6).
4. Ready input tape on unit 3 (ring out).
5. On 1403 ready continuous forms for desired number of copies of the optional output listing and for diagnostic messages.
6. Press START RESET on 1401.
7. Press CHECK RESET and LOAD on 1402.
8. For procedures in case of defective input tape records, see § 26.2.

CHAPTER 8

Summary Punch

INTRODUCTION

§8.1. Function

This program can punch onto summary cards one or more of the five types of sentence-count or word-count raw tag scores that are recorded on an input tape in Format Three (§ 20.1). The five types of raw scores are the total score and the subtotals for the four syntax markers (§ 6.2; Figure 6.A). For each document on the input tape, each type of raw score for tags 01 through 99 can be punched onto a separate set of seven summary cards. Thus, as many as five seven-card sets can be generated for each input document, depending on how many of the five types of scores the investigator requests by means of sense-switch settings (§ 8.5). The program also prints, at the investigator's option, a listing of the document-identification codes (§ 3.6) of all documents on the input tape.

§8.2. System Considerations

This program cannot distinguish whether the scores on the input tape in Format Three had been computed by TAG TALLY on the basis of a sentence count or a word count (§ § 6.3.3; 6.8).

SUMMARY PUNCH complements the punched-output capability of TAG TALLY since the latter can only generate summary cards containing total sentence-count or word-count index scores (§ 6.11). The summary cards produced by both programs are largely identical in format and are designed to serve as input to standard statistical analysis programs (§ 6.3.2, note 4).

INPUT AND OUTPUT SPECIFICATIONS

§8.3. Input

Input consists of a tape in Format Three (§ 20.1) and the object program.

§8.4. Output

For each document on the input tape, output consists of one set of seven summary cards for each type of raw score that is requested by the appropriate sense switch setting (§ 8.5). The format for a set of summary cards is given in Appendix Two (§ § 25.2-25.4). Another sense switch option controls the printing of a listing of document-identification codes of all documents on the input tape (§ 8.6).

§8.5. Specification of Type (s) of Raw Score to Be Punched (Sense Switches B-F)

Sense switches B-F correspond to the five types of raw scores (and to OUTPUT REQUESTED messages) as follows:

Sense Switch Up	*Type of Raw Score*	*OUTPUT REQUESTED Message*
B	Raw score subtotal for tags assigned with syntax marker S.	SUBJECT CARDS
C	Raw score subtotal for tags assigned with syntax marker V.	VERB CARDS
D	Raw score subtotal for tags assigned with syntax marker Ø.	OBJECT CARDS
E	Raw score subtotal for tags assigned with syntax marker U.	UNCLASSIFIED CARDS
F	Total raw score.	TOTAL CARDS

If one of these switches is up at the beginning of the run, the corresponding type of raw score will be punched onto one set of seven summary cards for each document on the input tape. For example, if only switches B and F were up at the beginning of a run for which an input tape consisting of scores for 100 documents had been submitted, then output would consist of 200 seven-card sets: one set per document for the subtotals for tags assigned with the marker S and one set per document for total scores.

Sense switches B-F are consulted at the beginning of the run, and an OUTPUT REQUESTED message is printed for each switch found to be up. If all are found to be down at that time, the message OUT-

PUT REQUESTED–NONE, SET SENSE SWITCHES THEN PRESS START is printed.

§8.6. Listing of Document-Identification Codes (Sense Switch G)

If Sense switch G is set up, a listing of the document-identification codes of all documents on the input tape will be printed (§ § 3.6; 20.3, positions 8-77). If sense switch G is set down, no listings will be printed.

TECHNICAL CONSIDERATIONS

§8.7. Language and Processing

The program is written in 1401 Tape Autocoder. When the program reaches the end-of-file mark on the input tape (§ 20.2), the program clears the 1402 punch by producing one blank card, which will fall in the normal stacker. The program then halts.

If the program encounters defective records on the input tape, they are processed according to procedure one (§ 26.2).

TRANSPOSE Operational Summary

Machine:

IBM 1401 with 8K, Advanced Programming, High-Low-Equal compare, and three tape units.

Input Schematic:

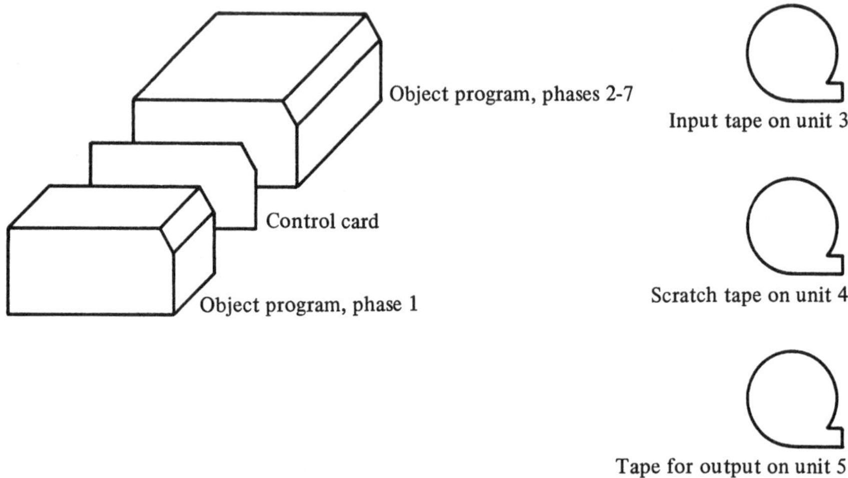

Machine-Operator Instructions:
1. Place card input in 1402 read hopper.
2. Ready input tape on unit 3 (ring out).
3. Ready scratch tape on unit 4 (ring in).
4. Ready tape for output on unit 5 (ring in).
5. Ready 1403 printer for diagnostic messages only.
6. Press START RESET on 1401.
7. Press CHECK RESET and LOAD on 1402.
8. For procedures in case of error conditions, see § §9.7-9.7.2 and §26.2.

All sense switches are ignored.

CHAPTER 9

Transpose[1]

INTRODUCTION

§9.1. Function and Storage Considerations

All tag scores of any one of the ten types (§ 6.2) that are recorded in tag-within-document order on an input tape in Format Three (§ 20.1) are sorted by this program into document-within-tag order and then written on an output tape in Format Four (§ 21.1). (See § 1.5 with Figure 1.B for a general discussion of this operation.) The output format will consist of one logical record[2] for each tag, beginning with tag 01 and continuing in ascending order through the highest numbered tag used in dictionary definitions. Each logical record will contain the specified type of score from each document on the input tape, as well as all or part of the document-identification code (§ 3.6) and the number of sentences or words[3] in each document. The type of tag scores as well as the columns of the identification code to be transferred are specified on a control card (§ 9.4).

[1]Stone, Philip J., Dexter C. Dunphy, Marshall S. Smith, Daniel M. Ogilvie, with associates, *The General Inquirer: A Computer Approach to Content Analysis* (Cambridge, Mass.: The M. I. T. Press, 1966), pp. 104,106.

[2]The terms "logical record" and "physical record" refer to two different ways of considering information recorded on magnetic tape. Consecutive physical records are separated from each other on magnetic tape by gaps of about 3/4 of an inch, in which no data are recorded. Consecutive logical records are recurring lists of information on tape. A logical record may be broken into several physical records, as in the case of TRANSPOSE tape output, (§ 21.5). Conversely, several logical records may be grouped ("blocked") into the same physical record, as in the case of KWIC BLOCKS tape output (§ 24.1) and CROSS-SORT RECORDS tape output (§ 16.17). The size of the physical record is determined by the programmer on the basis of the amount of input-output area of computer memory available after other program storage requirements have been ascertained.

[3]This depends, of course, on whether a sentence-count or a word-count tag tally was used to produce the Format Three tape (§ 6.8). Cf. § 4.32.2, e, ϕ and χ.

Two other variables that must be specified on the control card (§9.4) are the number of documents on the input tape (columns 4-6) and the columns of identification code that are to be written for each document on the output tape (columns 11-80). These variables affect storage requirements that must be met during processing. Before beginning the final phase of processing, the program solves several equations in order to determine the number of passes (§9.6) needed to make the sort. If many identification columns are to be transcribed onto the output tape and if there are a large number of documents, it is recommended that one equation (§9.7.2) be solved manually before a program run is attempted. The number of identification-code columns to be transcribed onto the output tape may have to be reduced.

The program processes only that number of documents on the input tape specified in columns 4-6 of the control card. This number may be lower than the actual number of documents on the input tape.

§9.2. System Considerations

This program cannot distinguish whether the scores on the input tape had been computed by TAG TALLY on the basis of a sentence count or a word count (§§6.3.3; 6.8), or whether the count is of an entire document or merely a subset of sentences produced by RETRIEVAL (§§1.9; 7.13). This information, as well as the type of score that was transposed—that is, raw or index, total or subtotal for one syntax position (§6.2)—should be written on the output tape to avoid later confusion.

The scores on an output tape generated by this program may be displayed in different ways by GRAPH (§10.1) and MEANS-DEVIATIONS (§12.1) and may be further rearranged by SORTED TRANSPOSE (§11.1).

INPUT AND OUTPUT SPECIFICATIONS

§9.3. Input

Input consists of the object program, one control card, and a tape in Format Three (§20.1).[4]

[4] In addition to the input tape and a tape on which output will be recorded in Format Four, a scratch tape must be supplied on which the program records intermediate data during processing (§9.6).

§9.4. Control Card

The items of information on this card are used by the program to determine values for variables in the two equations on the basis of which storage requirements and number of passes over the scratch tape (§ 9.6) are determined. The format of the control card is:

Card Columns	*Contents*
1-3	Number of tags to be processed (001-099). If only consecutive tags had been used in dictionary definitions and the first of these tags had been 01, the number in columns 1-3 will equal the last tag.
4-6	Number of documents to be processed (001-999). The number of documents on the input tape (§ 6.7 with note 10) may be greater, but may not be smaller, than the number specified in columns 4-6 (§ 9.7.1).
7	Either the character R if a total or subtotal raw score is to be transcribed onto the output tape, or the character I if a total or subtotal index score is to be transcribed onto the output tape (cf. § 6.2 and column 8).
8	The type of raw scores (if column 7 = R) or of index scores (if column 7 = I) to be transcribed onto the output tape, according to the following key: S = Raw or index score subtotals for tags assigned with syntax marker S. V = Raw or index score subtotals for tags assigned with syntax marker V. Ø = Raw or index score subtotals for tags assigned with syntax marker Ø. U = Raw or index score subtotals for tags assigned with syntax marker U. T = Total raw or index scores.
9-10	Ignored.
11-80	These columns correspond to the 70 positions of every document-identification field on the

Card Columns	Contents
11-80 (cont.)	input tape (§ 20.3, positions 8-77), and control which document-identification-code characters are to be transferred to entry d of every logical record on the output tape (§ 21.4). If the character X is punched in any one of these columns, the document identification-code character in the corresponding position on the input tape will be transferred to the output tape as part of entry d in each logical record. Whether or not the character X is punched in consecutive columns on the control card, the code characters thus specified will be written in entry d in the same order, but without intervening blank positions. See further § § 9.2; 10.5, columns 11-80; 11.5, columns 10-39.

§9.5. Output

Output consists of a tape in Format Four (§ 21.1), which will contain a maximum of 99 logical records arranged in ascending tag order (01-99). Each logical record contains for a single tag all scores of the type specified in columns 7 and 8 of the control card (§ 9.4). The scores for each tag—that is, in each logical record—are written in the order in which the documents to which those scores apply were encountered on the input tape. On the length of physical records on a tape in Format Four, see § 21.5.

TECHNICAL CONSIDERATIONS

§9.6. Language and Processing

The program is written in 1401 Autocoder. If the program encounters defective records on the input tape, they are processed according to procedure one (§ 26.2).

Due to the limited capacity of core storage, the program processes in six core overlays (that is, a total of seven phases) and generates intermediate data on the scratch tape on unit 4. The scratch tape may be processed in several passes. The seven phases of the program are:

1. Calculating the buffer, the input-output and processing area sizes that will be needed (§ 9.7.2) and the number of passes necessary to process the intermediate data to be written on the scratch tape. At the end of this phase messages are printed out specifying: the number of documents to be processed; the number of different tags for which scores are recorded on the input tape; the number of tags to be processed in each pass over the scratch tape; and the total number of passes.
2. Reading the input tape on unit 3, building strings of document-identification-code characters in core, and writing intermediate data on the scratch tape. The input tape unloads at this point.
3. Checking for error conditions encountered during the first and second phases. If error conditions were encountered, the program halts and prints out appropriate error messages (§ § 9.7.1-9.7.2); if not, phase four is begun.

4. & 6. Perform housekeeping–that is, address modification–in preparation for phases 5 and 7.

5. & 7. Reading intermediate data from the scratch tape into core (as many passes are made as are necessary to process all tags) and writing the output tape.

When the fourth phase is completed the output tape on unit 5 rewinds. The program then halts.

§9.7. Processing of Error Conditions

Error conditions encountered during the first and second phases of processing (§ 9.6, 1-2) result in print-out of various error messages and in programmed halts, as appropriate.

§ *9.7.1. Defective Control Card.* If the number of documents on the input tape (§ 20.2) is less than the number specified in columns 4-6 of the control card (§ 9.4), the message NUMBER DOCS FOUND (   ) NOT EQUAL NUMBER SPECIFIED ON PARAMETER CARD is printed out and the program then halts. If the number of documents on the input tape is greater than the number of documents specified in columns 4-6 of the control card, only that specified number will be processed.

§ *9.7.2. Excessive Storage Requirements or Number of Passes.* The following calculation is made by the program during the first phase of processing (§ 9.6, 1) in order to determine whether storage requirements for the volumes of input and output specified on the control card (§ 9.4) exceed actual storage capacity:

$$c = 6600\ [2z + d(6 + i + k)]$$

The variables in this equation are:

- c Remaining core.
- z Number of tags to be processed (§ 9.4, columns 1-3).
- d Number of documents to be processed (§ 9.4, columns 4-6).
- i Number of control-card columns in which the character X has been keypunched (§ 9.4, columns 11-80).
- k $3z$ if column 8 of the control card (§ 9.4) contains S, V, Ø, or U; or $4z$ if column 8 contains T; but if $3z$ (or $4z$, as the case may be) is less than 80, let k equal 80.

If the program determines that c is less than zero, the message BUFFER LEN + 2(NUM TAGS) +(NUM DOCS) (DOC ID LEN) GREATER THAN 6600. REPAIR AND RESTART is printed out with the current value for each expression in the third phase of processing (§ 9.6, 3), and the program halts.

In this case, the program run should be begun again with a new control card. In this new card, the number of documents (columns 4-6) and/or the number of columns in which the character X is keypunched (columns 11-80) should be less than the corresponding number(s) of the previous control card. The equation just given should then be solved manually with the value(s) for d and/or i derived from the new control card. If with these new values c is greater than or equal to zero, the next program run will probably prove successful.

GRAPH Operational Summary

Machine:

IBM 1401 with 4K, Advanced Programming, Modify Address, High-Low-Equal compare, Multiply-Divide, one tape unit, and 1403 Model 2 or 3.

Input Schematic:

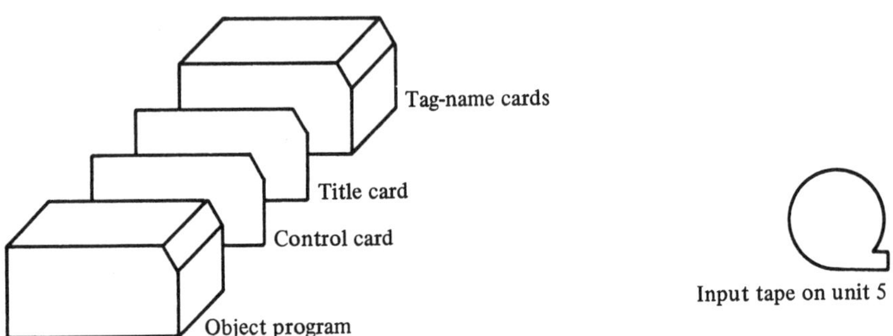

Machine Operator-Instructions:

1. Place card input in 1402 read hopper.
2. Ready tape input on unit 5 (ring out).
3. On 1403 ready continuous forms for desired number of copies of graphs (usual maximum four copies) and for diagnostic messages.
4. Press START RESET on 1401.
5. Press CHECK RESET and LOAD on 1402. Press START to process last two cards of input deck.
6. On procedures in case of defective input tape records, see § 26.4.

All sense switches are ignored.

CHAPTER 10

Graph[1]

INTRODUCTION

§10.1. Function

This program consecutively plots one horizontal bar graph (Figure 10.A) for each tag score recorded on an input tape in Format Four (§ 21.1) or Five (§ 22.1). The length of each bar will be proportional to the magnitude of the given score.

The page (or consecutive pages) on which the bar graphs for a single tag are printed will be titled with the name of that tag. For this purpose, tag-name cards must be supplied as part of the input deck. Other title information, including the name of the study, and the type of scores (§ 6.2) being graphed, may be specified on a title card (§ 10.6). Each bar will be labeled with the scaled tag score that has been plotted, with specified columns of the identification code of the document to which that score refers, and with the number of words or sentences in that document (depending on whether the scores on the input tape are of the word-count or sentence-count type).

§10.2. Scale Factor

Each bar is printed as a series of consecutive hyphens and may have a maximum length of 100 hyphens. Asterisks at the top and bottom of the graph identify every tenth hyphen position. The value of each hyphen is determined by a scale factor specified on the control card (§ 10.5). If word-count index scores are to be plotted, the scale factor is usually one, and each hyphen in a bar will accordingly represent a

[1]Stone, Philip J., Dexter C. Dunphy, Marshall S. Smith, Daniel M. Ogilvie, with associates, *The General Inquirer: A Computer Approach to Content Analysis* (Cambridge, Mass.: The M. I. T. Press, 1966), pp. 106-107, 262-264.

GENERAL INQUIRER TAG TALLY GRAPH.   TAG 22   IDEAL-VALUE

COLLEGE STUDY   APRIL 15, 1967   SCALE FACTOR 1   PAGE 2

DOCUMENT IDENTIFICATION	Value	-N-
608	70	100
609	31	508
610	40	302
621	1*-----5	105
625	58	395
701	39	228
702	64	94
703	39	432
704	27	335
706	35	228
708	35	574
709	29	311
710	27	110
801	31	388
802	26	117
803	26	196
804	42	192
805	46	219
806	19	257
807	63	557
808	48	525
809	31	321
811	49	245
901	15	982
902	27	331
903	74	256
904	59	695
905	59	238
906	57	211
907	46	196
908	63	380
909	52	210
911	85	307
912	54	314
916	44	315
920	30	234
922	65	138
923	38	130

FIGURE 10.A. *Sample GRAPH output. For detailed explanation see §10.2 and §10.8.*

tenth of a percentage point. Although 10.0 percent would thus be the highest score that could be graphed on a line, word-count index scores rarely exceed that maximum.

If sentence-count index scores are graphed, a higher maximum can usually be anticipated. If these scores range as high as 30.0 or 40.0 percent, the scale factor should then be 3 or 4, in order that almost all of the scores may be plotted within the 100 positions provided. For example, if a sentence-count index score is 27.6 and the scale factor is 3, the bar will be plotted as 276/3 or 92 hyphens. In general, when raw scores are to be plotted, the maximum score will depend on the length of the document, and the scale factor should be set to make an appropriate allowance.

If the program encounters a raw score exceeding 100 times the specified scale factor, the second and third digits of the score will be graphed as though they constituted a two-digit score, and the first digit of the score (the hundreds position) will be divided by the scale factor. The quotient of this division will be printed immediately before the first hyphen in the bar. For example, if a raw score of 540 is encountered during a program run for which a scale factor of five has been specified, the graph for that score will be printed as the digit one followed by eight hyphens and the number 08.

§10.3. System Considerations

If a tape in Format Four (§21.1) is used as input, the order in which the tag scores of various documents are graphed will be the order in which those documents had been processed by TRANSPOSE (§9.1), TAG TALLY (§6.1), TEXT-TAG LIST (§5.1), and, originally, TAGGING (§4.1).

However, if a tape in Format Five (§22.1) is used as input, the order in which tag scores of various documents are graphed will be the order in which those documents had been sorted by SORTED TRANSPOSE (§11.1).

GRAPH labels each bar with the total number of sentences or words in the document to which the score represented by the bar applies. These totals, which are printed in a column headed N (Figure 10.A), can be used to check whether a particular bar is based on a significant amount of data.

INPUT AND OUTPUT SPECIFICATIONS

§10.4. Input

Input consists of the object program, a control card, a title card, a set of tag-name cards, and a tape in either Format Four (§21.1) or Five (§22.1).

§10.5. Control Card

On this card are specified: the scale factor in accordance with which all tag scores on the input tape will be plotted (§10.2); a maximum of 20 document-identification-code characters with which each bar will be labeled; and spacing between bars.

Card Columns	*Contents*
1-2	Scale factor (01-99). See §10.2.
3-10	Ignored.
11-80	These columns, which correspond to the maximum of 70 positions of which every document-identification code on the input tape may consist, control the code columns that are to be printed to the left of every bar graph and certain vertical spacing capabilities. Note that the actual positions in every identification code on a given input tape are only the columns transferred by TRANSPOSE (§9.4, columns 11-80) in the run that generated either the tape in Format Four now to be processed by GRAPH or the tape in Format Four from which the tape in Format Five now to be processed by GRAPH had been transcribed by SORTED TRANSPOSE (§11.1). Columns 11-80 of this GRAPH control card thus correspond to consecutive identification-field positions 1-70 as they are on the input tape, not to their original positions (among other columns that may have been dropped) on the antecedent tape in Format Three (§20.3, positions 8-77). Columns 11-80 should be punched accord-

Card Columns	*Contents*
11-80 (cont.)	ing to the key given in the following four paragraphs. The characters 1 and/or 3 may be punched in a maximum of 20 columns, but there are no restrictions on the number of columns in which the character 2 may be punched. The document-identification-code columns specified with a 1 or a 3 will be printed by GRAPH from left to right without intervening blanks. 1-The character in the input-tape document-identification-code position that corresponds to this card column should be printed as part of the label for every bar graph. 2-Every time a character in the input-tape document-identification-code position that corresponds to this card column changes from one code to the next, one blank line should be skipped between the sets of bar graphs for the two documents thus differentiated. However, characters in the differentiating positions should not be printed. 3-Both 1 and 2, as just specified—that is, both print a character in the input-tape document-identification-code position that corresponds to this card column and skip a line whenever the character in that position changes from one document to the next. Any other character (including blank)-The character in the input-tape document-identification-code position corresponding to this card column will be ignored.

§10.6. Title Card

The image of columns 1-80 of this card, in which any alphanumeric and/or special characters may be keypunched, will be printed in the second printed line of every page of output.

§10.7. Tag-Name Cards

Tag-name cards in the format prescribed in Appendix Two (§24.2) should be submitted for processing. The cards should be ordered in ascending tag-number sequence. One card should be included for each tag used in the dictionary. A tag name will be printed at the top of every output page in order to specify the particular tag to which the scores plotted on that page refer.

§10.8. Output

Output consists of one bar graph for every tag score on the input tape and various diagnostic messages (§§10.9-10.10).

All scores for one and the same tag will be plotted (Figure 10.A) in successive bar graphs on one or more consecutive and numbered pages. The graphs for different tags are plotted in ascending (though not necessarily consecutive) numerical order—that is, the order in which the tags are organized on the input tape. The page(s) in which the graphs of the scores for a given tag are displayed will be titled with the name of that tag (§10.7), the scale factor specified on the control card (§10.5, columns 1-2; cf. §10.2), and an image of the title card (§10.6).

Within each set of graphs of the scores for a given tag in various documents, the graphs will be sequenced in the order in which those scores are recorded on the input tape. This order will correspond either to the order in which documents had been originally processed by TAGGING if the input tape is in Format Four (§21.1), or, if the input tape is in Format Five (§22.1), to the order in which the document-identification codes of the various documents to which the scores for each tag apply had been sorted by SORTED TRANSPOSE (§10.3). In either case, the bar graph for each score will be labeled with three items of information. To the left of the bar will be printed a maximum of 20 characters of the document-identification code. Immediately to the right of the bar will be printed the score itself, and far to the right, in the column headed N, the total number of sentences or words in the document specified by the code printed to the left of the bar (§10.3). This total may be replaced by an error message (§26.4).

Normally, bars are printed in successive lines. However, one line will be skipped between the bars printed for any two documents whose identification codes contain different characters in the position corresponding to a column on the control card in which the character 2 or 3 has been keypunched (§10.5, columns 11-80).

§10.9. Language and Processing

The language of the source program is 1401 Tape Autocoder. The program consecutively processes all records on the input tape. Upon encountering the end-of-file mark on the input tape (§ 21.2 or § 22.2), the program prints the terminal message C'EST FINI and halts. If defective records are encountered on the input tape, they are processed according to procedure three (§ 26.4).

§10.10. Error Conditions

If the program encounters on the input tape a tag score (§ 21.4 or § 22.4, entry b) that is not accompanied by a document-identification-code (§ 21.4 or § 22.4, entry d), the message INPUT ERROR is printed out and processing is terminated and cannot be resumed with the given input tape. The program that generated the defective input tape should be rerun in order to generate a new tape with the same data.

If the program encounters an unsorted tag-name card (§ 10.7), processing halts after the following messages have been printed out:

NAME CARD OUT OF SEQUENCE
ON CARD.
ON TAPE.

The message ON CARD will be immediately preceded by the tag in columns 1-2 of the unsorted tag-name card, and the message ON TAPE by the tag of the input-tape logical record (§ 21.2 or § 22.2) that the tag in columns 1-2 of the unsorted card should have matched. The tag-name cards should be correctly resorted and the program run attempted again from the beginning.

SORTED TRANSPOSE Operational Summary

Machine:

IBM 1401 with 8K, Advanced Programming, High-Low-Equal compare, Multiply-Divide, and two tape units.

Input Schematic:

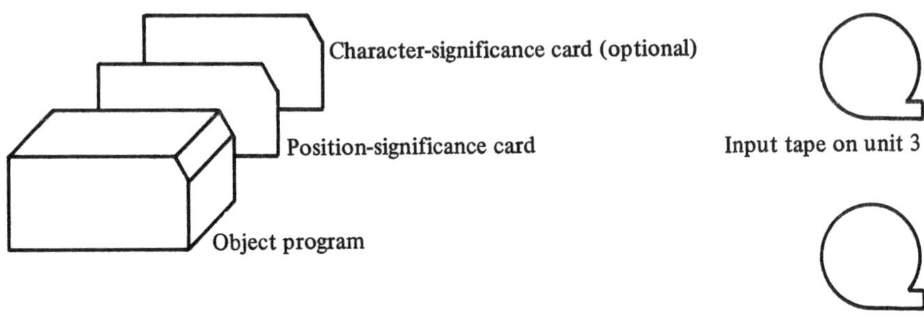

Machine-Operator Instructions:

1. Place card input in 1402 read hopper.
2. Set sense switches on 1401.
   A: Always up (§ 11.8).
   B, C, D, E, F, G: Ignored.
3. Ready input tape on unit 3 (ring out).
4. Ready tape for output (ring in) on unit 4.
5. Ready 1403 printer for diagnostic messages only.
6. Press START RESET on 1401.
7. Press CHECK RESET and LOAD on 1402. Press START to process last two cards of input deck.
8. For procedures in case of error conditions, see § § 11.9-11.10 and § 26.2.

CHAPTER 11

Sorted Transpose[1]

INTRODUCTION

§11.1. Function

This program sorts the document-identification codes (§3.6) within each logical record of an input tape in Format Four (§21.1) and transcribes in sorted order the tag scores associated with those codes onto a logical record on a tape in Format Five (§22.2). The tape in Format Five will thus contain precisely the same information as the antecedent tape in Format Four—one logical record containing all scores for each tag, with the logical records being sequenced in ascending tag order (01-99).

The sort-transpose operation allows the same tag scores to be ordered for inspection in two or more different ways. For example, in an analysis of political party platforms, if document-identification codes had been designed to include both year and party information, the tag scores could be ordered and graphed (§10.1) by year or by party.

§11.2. Sorting

§*11.2.1. Character Significance.* Sorting denotes resequencing information according to arbitrary rules. In sorting the characters of document-identification codes, SORTED TRANSPOSE observes two rules—one of character significance and another of position significance. The first rule specifies the relative significance of the characters that can occur in a code. Unless the investigator chooses to specify a special

[1] Stone, Philip J., Dexter C. Dunphy, Marshall S. Smith, Daniel M. Ogilvie, with associates, *The General Inquirer: A Computer Approach to Content Analysis* (Cambridge, Mass.: The M. I. T. Press, 1966), p. 107.

sequence on an optional character-significance card (§ 11.6), this program automatically observes the following sorting sequence[2] of decreasingly significant characters:

blank .) + $ * – / , (= ' ? A *through* Z 0 *through* 9

If only *one* position (§ 11.2.2) of the document-identification codes were specified as significant, the codes would be resequenced by SORTED TRANSPOSE according to the relative significance of the characters occurring in that one position. The ordering in that column, for example, of the characters * A X N 9 C 4 1 + M would be resorted into + * A C M N X 1 4 9.

§ *11.2.2. Position Significance.* However, since various positions in which code characters occur may be significant bases for rearranging the codes, a rule of position significance must specify the relative significance of those positions. The maximum length of document-identification codes on the input tape in Format Four is seventy positions (§ 9.4, columns 11-80). A maximum of ten positions may be assigned relative significance on a position-significance card (§ 11.5). For example, if that card specifies the fifth position in all codes to be the most significant, and the fourth and second positions to be next in *decreasing* significance (and if the program is allowed to observe the sequence of character significance given in § 11.2.1), then codes occurring in each logical record on the input tape in the order

6+M.=
22)B/
31NB/
3ZMB/
7?G4*

would be resequenced in each logical record on the output tape in the order

7?G4*
3ZMB/
31NB/
22)B/
6+M.=

§ *11.2.3. System Considerations.* Careful application of SORTED TRANSPOSE will enable the investigator not only to control the order in which GRAPH is to print bar graphs of tag scores for various docu-

[2] This is the IBM 1401 collating sequence. In this sequence, the first character after *blank* is a period, and the sixth character after *blank* is a minus sign, not a dash.

ments (§ § 10.1; 10.3) but also to determine those documents whose scores are to be grouped together by MEANS-DEVIATIONS in the computations performed by that program (§ § 12.1-12.2).

§11.3. Calculating Storage Requirements

Storage requirements dictated by the volume of data on the input tape will exceed actual storage capacity if an equation solved by the program (§ 11.9) yields a value for c that is greater than 6800. In that event, the program run terminates prematurely, and it will be impossible for SORTED TRANSPOSE to process the given input tape successfully.

Therefore, if it is anticipated that a tape to be generated by TRANSPOSE will at some time be processed by SORTED TRANSPOSE, the TRANSPOSE control card values found to yield satisfactory solutions to the equations in § 9.7.2 should be tested for the equation in § 11.9 in order to confirm that the tape to be generated by TRANSPOSE can later be successfully processed by SORTED TRANSPOSE.

INPUT AND OUTPUT SPECIFICATIONS

§11.4. Input

Input consists of the object program, one position-significance card, a tape in Format Four (§ 21.1) and, at the investigator's option, a character-significance card.

§ 11.5. Position-Significance Card

Columns 10-39 of this card should specify at least one and no more than ten significant positions (§ 11.2.2) on which all document-identification codes (§ § 9.4, columns 11-80; 21.4, entry d) within every logical record on the input tape are to be sorted. The positions should be specified in order of decreasing significance. The score associated with each code will be transcribed onto the output tape in the sorted order of that code.

If this card is omitted from or misplaced in the program deck, the program run will terminate prematurely (§ 11.10).

The format of a position-significance card is:

Card Columns	*Contents*
1	F
2-9	Ignored.
10-12	Of all positions to be sorted, the number (001-070) of the most significant position in document-identification codes.
13-39	Nine three-column fields, in which the numbers (001-070) of as many as nine other significant positions may be specified in order of decreasing significance.
40-80	Ignored.

§11.6. Character-Significance Card (Optional)

If the program is *not* to observe the sequence of decreasingly significant characters listed in § 11.2.1, the investigator may specify in columns 10-34 of this card a special sequence of as many as 25 characters. Characters not specified in columns 10-34 will all be considered equally less significant than the last—and thus the least significant—of the specified characters.

Card Columns	*Contents*
1	S
2-9	Ignored.
10-34	As many as 25 significant characters in order of decreasing significance. Blank may be any of the specified characters except the last.

§11.7. Output

Output consists of a tape in Format Five (§ 22.1) containing exactly the same information as the antecedent tape in Format Four (§ § 21.1; 9.5). However, scores are written within each logical record in the sorted order of the document-identification codes with which those scores are associated.

As soon as it has been generated, the output tape should be correctly labeled as containing the type of tag score recorded on the input tape in Format Four (§ 9.2). This information should be available in order that output printed by GRAPH and MEANS-DEVIATIONS may be correctly titled (§ § 10.6; 12.5).

TECHNICAL CONSIDERATIONS

§11.8. Language and Processing

The source program is written in 1401 Tape Autocoder. If a defective record is written on the output tape, the latter is backspaced, the defective record erased, and another attempt to write the record is made. If defective records are encountered on the input tape, they are processed according to procedure one (§ 26.2).

§11.9. Excessive Storage Requirements

Storage requirements for the volume of data on the input tape exceed actual storage capacity and the program run terminates if c in the following equation does not yield a value less than or equal to 6800:

$$c = (d + 1)(k + i + 6)$$

The variables c, d, k, and i are as defined in § 9.7.2.

If the equation cannot be satisfactorily solved, the message DATA TOO BIG FOR CORE. USE SORT II. is printed out before the run terminates. It will be impossible for SORTED TRANSPOSE to process the given input tape successfully. ("Sort II" is an earlier version of Sort 7 for the IBM 1401.)

§11.10. Omitted or Misplaced Position-Significance Card

If the position-significance card (§ 11.5) is omitted from or misplaced in the input deck, the program halts with the message PARAMETER CARD MISSING. The card should be supplied or correctly placed in the input deck and the program run begun again.

MEANS-DEVIATIONS Operational Summary

Machine:

IBM 1401 with 8K, Advanced Programming, High-Low-Equal compare, Multiply-Divide, unit, and 1403 Model 2 or 3.

Input Schematic:

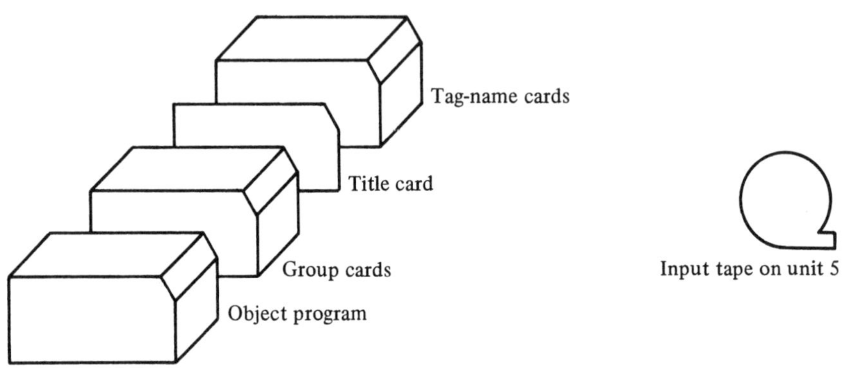

Machine-Operator Instructions:

1. Place card input in 1402 read hopper.
2. Ready the input tape on unit 5 (ring out).
3. On 1403 ready continuous forms for desired numbers of copies of printed output (usual maximum four copies) and for diagnostic messages.
4. Press START RESET on 1401.
5. Press CHECK RESET and LOAD on 1402. Press START to process last two cards of input deck.
6. For procedures in case of defective input tape records, see §26.4.

All sense switches are ignored.

CHAPTER 12

Means-Deviation[1]

INTRODUCTION

§12.1. Function

Processing an input tape in Format Four (§ 21.1) or Five (§ 22.1), this program reads groups of as many as 999 *consecutive* scores for the assignment of each tag to various documents, and computes the arithmetic mean, standard deviation, and range for each such group. The investigator must specify on a separate group card (§ 12.4) each group for which statistics are to be computed for every tag, and how many consecutive scores for every tag are to constitute each specified group. As many as 50 groups may be specified. (However, there need be only one group; that is, all scores for each tag may be processed as a single group.)

For each tag for which scores are recorded on the input tape—that is, for each logical record on the input tape—the program prints a table consisting of as many rows as the number of specified groups (Figure 12.A). The row for each group will contain the following seven entries: the name of the group as specified on the group card; the number of documents in that group; the arithmetic mean $\frac{\Sigma x}{n}$ where Σx is the sum of the scores in the group and n the number of those scores; the biased standard deviation $\sqrt{\frac{\Sigma (x-m)^2}{n}}$ where m is the arithmetic mean; the lowest score in the group; the highest score in the group; and the number of nonzero scores in the group.

[1] Stone, Philip J., Dexter C. Dunphy, Marshall S. Smith, Daniel M. Ogilvie, with associates, *The General Inquirer: A Computer Approach to Content Analysis* (Cambridge, Mass.: The M. I. T. Press, 1966), p. 107.

PALLEY COLLEGE STUDY TAG 09 LARGE-GROUP PAGE 1

GROUP NAME	NUMBER	MEAN	STANDARD DEV.	MINIMUM	MAXIMUM	1 OR MORE OCCJRANCES
HIGH LARGE QUAL	3	3.23	.69	2.6	4.2	3
MEDIJM HIGH QUALITY	11	1.95	1.33	.7	5.5	11
SMALL HIGH QUALITY	6	1.65	.57	.6	2.4	6
LARGE MEDIUM QUALITY	16	2.39	1.42	.0	4.5	15
MEDIUM MEDIUM QUALITY	10	2.77	.71	1.8	4.1	10
SMALL MEDIUM QUALITY	10	2.72	1.30	1.0	5.7	10
LARGE, LARGE QUAL	8	2.43	.91	1.1	3.6	8
MEDIJM LOW QUAL	10	2.19	.79	.9	3.2	10
LOW, LOW QUALITY	15	2.13	.84	.8	3.8	15

FIGURE 12.A. Sample of means and deviations. For detailed explanation see §12.7.

§12.2. System Considerations

Only tag scores that are *consecutively* recorded on the input tape can be specified for processing as a group (§ 12.4, columns 1-3). Thus, the original document order or the order in which SORTED TRANSPOSE (§ 11.1) had sorted scores according to their respective document-identification codes determines which particular document will be represented by the consecutive scores in any specified group. To obtain statistics for various groupings of a single set of scores, SORTED TRANSPOSE must be applied iteratively with different control-card specifications (§ 11.5) in order to produce appropriately sorted tapes in Format Five.

INPUT AND OUTPUT SPECIFICATIONS

§12.3. Input

Input consists of the object program, as many as 50 group cards, a title card, tag-name cards, and a tape in Format Four (§ 21.1) or Five (§ 22.1).

§12.4. Group Cards

As many as 50 group cards may be submitted, each card specifying the name of one group and how many scores consecutively recorded on the input tape are to constitute that one group for every tag. The order in which group cards are arranged should correspond to the order in which the scores for the documents in the successive groups are written in every logical record on the input tape.

If no group cards are submitted, all scores for each tag will be processed as a single group. See further § 12.7, no. 2.

The format of a group card should be:

Card Columns	*Contents*
1-3	Number (001-999) of consecutive scores which, in the case of every tag, are to be processed as a group.
4-25	Title (any alphanumeric and/or special characters) for the group of scores specified in columns 1-3 of this card. This title will label the row of entries printed in the table for the specified group (§ 12.7, no. 1).
26-80	Ignored.

§12.5. Title Card

The image of columns 2-80 of this card will appear in the first printed line of every page of output (Figure 12.A). For ease of future reference, it is advisable to specify on the title card the name of the study, as well as the type of tag scores recorded on the input tape, for which all statistics are thus to be computed (§§9.2; 11.7).

The format of a title card should be:

Card Columns	*Contents*
1	* [asterisk]
2-80	Any alphanumeric and/or special characters to be printed at the top of every page of output.

§12.6. Tag-Name Cards

Each tag-name card should contain a two-digit tag and the name of that tag, as described in Appendix Two (§24.2). There should be one card for each tag for which scores are recorded on the input tape (§22.2). These cards may be arranged in any order.

The tag and the name on each of these cards will appear in the first printed line of the one or two pages of output on which statistics for the given tag are tabulated (§12.7; Figure 12.A).

§12.7. Output

Output consists of one table of statistics for each tag–that is, for each logical record–on the input tape (§21.2 or §22.2). See Figure 12.A. The table for each tag is printed on one or two numbered pages. In the first printed line of all pages of all tables are printed the image of columns 2-80 of the title card (§12.5) the tag itself and its name (§12.6).

The table for each tag will consist of one row for each group specified on a group card (§12.4) and of seven columns. The seven entries in the row for a given group are printed from left to right under appropriate column headings as follows:

1. GROUP NAME–The name assigned on a group card (§12.4, columns 4-25) to the group of scores for which values are printed in this row. This entry will be blank if no group cards have been submitted.
2. NUMBER–The number of scores in this group, as specified on the group card (§12.4, columns 1-3). This entry will be blank if no group cards have been submitted.

3. MEAN–The arithmetic mean $\frac{\Sigma x}{n}$ (§ 12.1) of the scores in this group.
4. STANDARD DEV.–The biased standard deviation $\sqrt{\frac{\Sigma(x\text{-}m)^2}{n}}$ of the scores in this group.
5. MINIMUM–The lowest nonzero score in this group. This entry will be blank if a score of zero has been encountered in this group. Cf. 7.
6. MAXIMUM–The highest score in this group.
7. 1 OR MORE OCCURRENCES–The number of nonzero scores in this group.

The error message BAD RECORD will be printed to the right of the row for any group containing one or more scores derived from a defective record on the input tape (§ 26.4).

TECHNICAL CONSIDERATIONS

§12.8. Language and Processing

The source program is written in 1401 Tape Autocoder. All records on the input tape are processed consecutively. If defective records are encountered on the input tape, they are processed according to procedure three (§ 26.4).

PART FOUR

SECONDARY PROGRAMS FOR DICTIONARY CONSTRUCTION AND DISPLAY

KWIC RECORDS Operational Summary

Machine:

IBM 1401 with 4K, Advanced Programming, High-Low-Equal compare, and one tape unit.

Input Schematic:

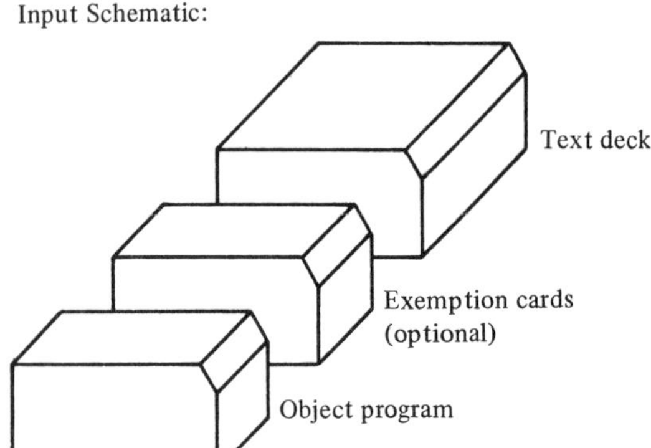

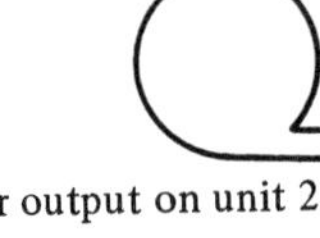

Tape(s) for output on unit 2

Machine-Operator Instructions:

1. Place card input in 1402 read hopper.
2. Set sense switches.
   A: Always up.
   B, C: Ignored.
   D,E: Exemption-card and programmed-exemption options (§ 13.5).
   G: Ignored.
3. Ready tape(s) for output (ring in) on unit 2. On procedures for reading successive output tape reels, see § 13.7.
4. Ready 1403 for diagnostic messages only.
5. Press START RESET on 1401.
6. Press CHECK RESET and LOAD on 1402. Press START to process last two cards of input deck.
7. For procedures in case of defective input, see § 13.10.

CHAPTER 13

Kwic Records[1]

INTRODUCTION

§13.1. Function

This program transcribes the entire contents of a text deck (§3.1) onto tape in Format Six (§23.2). In so doing, the program creates a separate 132-position record for every word in every sentence of the text, unless the investigator explicitly exempts the occurrences of specified words. The word for which any given tape record is created is the "key word" of that record. In each record, the key word always begins in record position 42, and positions before and after the key word contain the words which immediately preceded and followed it in the text. Thus each record contains a *k*ey *w*ord *i*n its original *c*ontext (whence the acronym "KWIC"). Each tape record also contains the sentence-identification code, if any, on the card in which the given key word occurred and also title information for the document in which the key word occurred.

These 132-character tape records can be alphabetically sorted on the key words (beginning in record position 42) by any standard computer sort program, and then printed as an alphabetized key-word-in-context index (Figure 15.A). A KWIC index makes possible studies of the variation in meaning and phraseology of conceptually significant words in the body of text to be subjected to content analysis.

[1] Stone, Philip J., Dexter C. Dunphy, Marshall S. Smith, Daniel M. Ogilvie, with associates, *The General Inquirer: A Computer Approach to Content Analysis* (Cambridge, Mass.: The M. I. T. Press, 1966), pp. 142, 155-160.

Words which frequently recur in the text, but which the investigator does not need to examine as key-words-in-context, can be exempted from processing by either or both of two procedures (§§13.5-13.5.3). The result of either procedure is to cause the program *not* to create a separate output tape record for each occurrence of the specified exemption words when they are found in the text input. Among words which are often exempted from key-word listing are articles prepositions, conjunctions, and parts of the verb "to be." By exempting as few as 80 such common words, the size of the final printed listing can be reduced by more than half.

§13.2. System Considerations

§*13.2.1. KWIC Processing.* Inasmuch as a separate line is printed for each occurrence of each word in the text (except exemption words), a small sample of text can generate a large amount of output. For example, if no exemption words are specified, 1000 cards (with about ten words of text per card) will generate 10,000 key-word records or about 200 pages of listing. KWIC RECORDS will process some 60 to 90 cards of text per minute depending on how many exemption words are specified and the speed of the tape units used with the computer (§1.10). Thus, creating the 10,000 records on tape will take at least ten minutes of computer time, with additional time needed for sorting (sorting time will vary with the sort program and computer used) and another ten to 15 minutes (depending on the speed of the printer) to make the listing. Given the large volume of material that is produced and the amount of computer time needed, the investigator should exercise some care in selecting his sample and choosing exemption words. We generally find that a sample of about 1000 cards, well chosen from throughout the text we are studying, is enough to give adequate context information about words of high and moderate frequency.

After the tape records have been created for each key word, we recommend that they be sorted by either the Sort 7 program for the IBM 1401 or by the standard IBSYS sorting program for the IBM 7090/94. It is suggested that about 35 positions of information be alphabetically sorted, beginning with record position 42. In this way, ordering is by the key word *and* following words within 35 positions (see Figure 15.A).

If larger amounts of data are to be sorted, it is more economical to use the faster computer, the 7090/94. If many reels of tape are to be sorted, it is recommended that tapes in Format Six (§ 23.2) generated by KWIC RECORDS be condensed ("blocked") by KWIC BLOCKS (§ 14.1) before sorting is performed. This procedure minimizes the number of times input-tape reels must be changed during the sorting operation and will thus reduce the 7090/94 processing time. The investigator should also consider taking advantage of the blocked-output options of the sort programs. If blocking is done by a factor of 45 (tape Format Seven [§ 23.3]), the alphabetized output tape can be printed by KWIC PRINT-STATISTICS (§ 15.1), which is specially designed for that purpose.

§ *13.2.2. Compatibility of TAGGING and KWIC RECORDS Input.* A text deck (§ 3.1) ready for processing by TAGGING (§ 4.2) can be processed by KWIC RECORDS without the necessary removal, insertion, or rearrangement of any cards. KWIC RECORDS, however, uses only the title information in columns 2-30 of title cards (§ 3.4) and allows for only the first 19 characters of sentence-identification information (§ 13.9).

Many lines of a key-word-in-context listing will include carry-over from one sentence to the next, if the key word for the given line is near the beginning or end of a sentence. But whenever an end-document card (§ § 3.5;13.4) is encountered, the two sentences on either side of that card are not joined in the KWIC listing.

§ *13.2.3. Anticipating Features of KWIC PRINT-STATISTICS in Preparing Title Cards.* If the investigator intends to process a number of different documents, he may wish to know whether the occurrences of key words in his sample come from only one document or from a number of different documents represented. This information can be obtained by inspecting the document titles printed to the right of each line in the KWIC index (Figure 15.A). In addition, KWIC PRINT-STATISTICS (§ 15.1) counts the number of different documents in which each key word occurred (§ 15.6). In order to do this, the program examines the character obtained from column 3 of the title card (§ 13.6) and counts the number of different characters in that position for each occurrence of the given key word. If two title cards have the same character in column 3, the documents represented by those title cards will be considered the same document. A maximum of 40 different characters in column 3 of title cards can be monitored by KWIC PRINT-STATISTICS. See further § 15.2.3.

Title cards also cause KWIC RECORDS to print certain program-audit messages (§ 13.8).

§13.3

INPUT AND OUTPUT SPECIFICATIONS

§13.3. Input

Input consists of the object program, optional exemption cards, and a text deck containing text cards, title cards, and end-document cards in the formats prescribed for TAGGING (§ 13.2.2).

§13.4. Asterisk Cards

Normal end-document cards (§ 3.5) as well as any other cards with an asterisk in column 1—that is, any TAGGING control card (§ 4.18)—may appear in the text deck. The messages on these cards are ignored by the program.

§13.5. Exemption Word Options

Words in the text input that the investigator does not wish to be treated as key-words-in-context (§ 13.1) can be specified either within the program source deck (§ 13.5.1) or on exemption cards placed between the program deck and the text deck (§ 13.5.2). Sense switches D and E permit individual or combined use of the two exemption procedures (§ 13.5.3).

Although it is important to specify exemption words in order to minimize the size of the eventual KWIC listing, it should be noted that a very long list of exemption words can considerably reduce the speed of the program. Regardless of the procedure used to specify exemption words, the total number of such words should normally not exceed about 100, although the program can accommodate as many as 300.

§ *13.5.1. Programmed Exemptions.* The distributed version of the program contains the following list of exemption words: A, AN, AND, ANY, AS, AT, BE, BUT, BY, ETC, FOR, FROM, HE, I, IN, IS, IT, OF, ON, ONE, OR, OTHER, SHE, SO, SOME, THE, THEM, THEY, THIS, TO, WAS, WERE, WITH, YOU. This internal list can be altered or removed by the programming procedures described in § 13.11. But if the investigator wants only to supplement or replace the list of programmed exemptions with his own exemption cards (§ 13.5.2), the simplest procedure is to choose the appropriate settings of sense switches D and E (§ 13.5.3).

§ *13.5.2. Exemption Cards.* Exemption words other than those already in the program (§ 13.5.1) can be specified on exemption cards placed between the program object deck and the text deck. Exemption cards should be keypunched in the following format:

Card Columns	*Contents*
1-10	Exemption word, which will not be processed as a key-word-in-context.
11-80	Ignored.

The last exemption card must be followed by an end-exemption card containing only a period in column 1.

See § 13.5.3 on using exemption words specified on exemption cards instead of, or in addition to, those already specified in the program's internal list.

§ *13.5.3. Separate and Combined Use of Exemption Options (Sense Switches D and E).* If the investigator wishes only the programmed exemptions (§ 13.5.1) to be used, sense switch D should be set down. When sense switch D is down, sense switch E will be ignored by the program, and no exemption cards (§ 13.5.2) should be present in the input deck.

If the investigator wishes his own exemption cards to be used in addition to the programmed exemptions (§ 13.5.1), sense switches D and E should both be set up. If he wishes his exemption cards to be used instead of the programmed exemptions, sense switch D should be set up and sense switch E should be set down.

§ 13.6. Output

Output consists of one or more successive tapes in Format Six (§ 23.2) and print-out of program-audit messages (§ 13.8). When an output tape reel has been completely filled, another reel of tape for output may be readied on unit 2 (§ 13.7).

In each record the key word begins in position 42. In positions 3-41 are written the text words that immediately preceded the key word; between the end of the key word and position 81 of the record are written the text words that immediately followed the key word. The context within which the key word is thus transcribed onto a record will begin and end with whole words.

Positions 83-102 of any record may contain as many as 19 characters of a sentence- or document-identification code (§ § 3.6; 3.8). Positions 83-102 of the record will be blank, if no code was keypunched on the card from which the last word in positions 3-81 was obtained.

In positions 104-132 of any given record are written the contents of columns 2-30 of the title card (§ 3.4) of the document in which the key word in that record occurred.

An end-of-file mark will follow the last record on every output tape.

TECHNICAL CONSIDERATIONS

§ 13.7. Language and Processing

The source program is written in 1401 Tape Autocoder. Sense switch A must always be set up in order to enable the program to confirm that the last input card has been read. When the end of a tape on which output has been written is reached, it is unloaded and the program halts. A new reel for output may then be readied on unit 2, and pressing START will cause the program to resume processing.

§ 13.8. Program-Audit Messages

Upon encountering a title card (§ 13.3), the program prints out the message END OF DOC. x CARDS READ. y RECORDS WRITTEN. In this message x will be the number of text cards (§ 13.3) processed, and y the number of output key-word-in-context records (§ 13.6) generated, since the last title card was encountered. The number of end-of-document messages produced in a run should be noted for future reference (§ 15.4, columns 15-16).

When all input is exhausted, the total numbers of input text cards, input text words and output key-word-in-context records are printed in the message END OF JOB. x TOTAL CARDS READ. y TEXT WORDS EXAMINED. z TOTAL RECORDS WRITTEN. The number of text words (y) should be noted for future reference (§ 15.4, columns 4-10).

§ 13.9. Sentence-Identification Code Longer than 19 Characters

If the program encounters a text card that contains a sentence-identification code (§ 3.8) longer than 19 characters, the twentieth and any subsequent code characters are ignored.

§ 13.10. Omission of End-Exemption Card

If an end-exemption card containing only a period in column 1 does not immediately follow the last exemption card (§ 13.5), the program halts and prints out the message IS THERE NO END TO THE DICTIONARY. Processing cannot be resumed. A new program run should not be attempted until the missing card has been properly inserted into the input deck.

§13.11. Implementing and Removing Programmed Exemption Words

If the program is to be run on a 4K 1401, a maximum of approximately 300 words to be exempted from processing as key words may be inserted just before the next-to-last card of the source program. No such word may be longer than ten characters. Each should be left adjusted within a ten-position field, with a word mark in the high-order position. Fields should usually be defined by use of DCN instructions. The last ten-position field should contain a period in position 1.

Any word or words in the current list of programmed exemption words (§ 13.5.1) can be deleted by simply removing from the source program the card(s) on which the given word(s) is (are) keypunched. The entire list of programmed exemption words can be deleted by simply removing from the source program all cards after the last major instruction (LTORG*+1) and before—but not including—the last two cards of the source program (DCW '.' and END START).

KWIC BLOCKS Operational Summary

Machine:

IBM 1401 with 8K, Advanced Programming, High-Low-Equal compare, and two tape units.

Input Schematic:

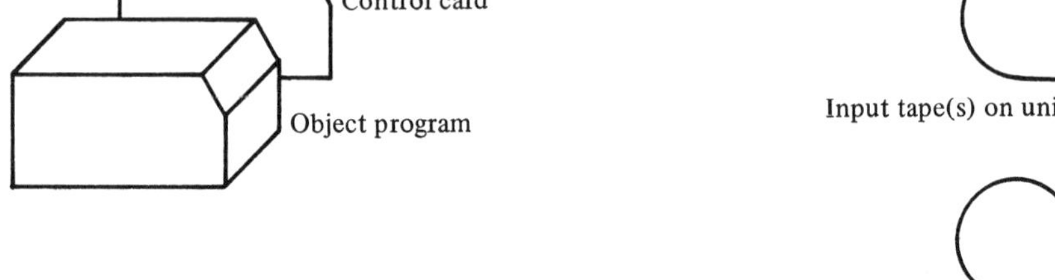

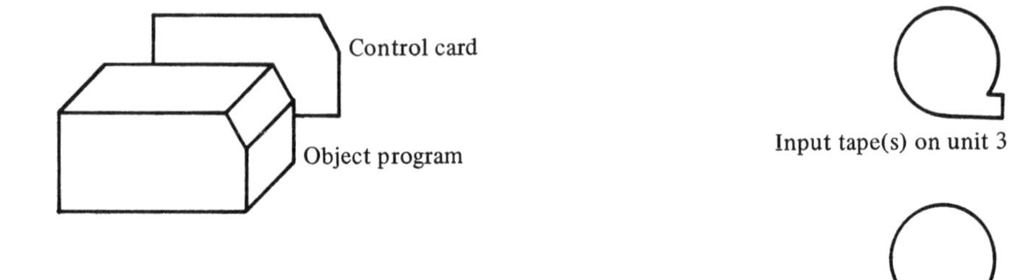

Machine-Operator Instructions:

1. Place card input in 1402 hopper.
2. Ready first and each successive input tape on unit 3 (ring out).
3. Ready first and each successive tape for output on unit 4.(ring in).
4. Ready 1403 for procedural and diagnostic messages only.
5. Press START RESET on 1401.
6. Press CHECK RESET and LOAD on 1402. Press START to process last two cards of input deck.
7. On procedures in case of defective input tape records, see § 26.2.
8. On procedures for readying successive input and output tape reels, see § § 14.6.1-14.6.2.

All sense switches are ignored.

CHAPTER 14

Kwic Blocks

INTRODUCTION

§14.1. Function

This program is designed to transcribe alphabetically sorted tape(s) in Format Six (§ 23.2) onto a tape or tapes in Format Seven (§ 23.3). In so doing, the program "blocks" or groups 45 consecutive input records into a single output record. (Each such blocked output record is thus a physical record comprised of 45 "logical" records).[1] This blocking procedure not only satisfies an input-format requirement of KWIC PRINT-STATISTICS (§ 15.1) but also reduces the amount of tape necessary to store the information to be processed by that program.

§14.2. System Considerations

Blocking may be done either before or after alphabetical sorting has been completed. Often, the investigator may have the sort program perform blocking, thus obviating use of KWIC BLOCKS. Blocked Format Seven is required by KWIC PRINT-STATISTICS.

INPUT AND OUTPUT SPECIFICATIONS

§14.3. Input

Input consists of the object program, a control card, and one or more tapes in Format Six. When processing of one input tape reel is completed, the next may be readied on unit 3 (§ 14.6.1).

[1] On the terms "logical record" and blocking," see § 9.1, footnote 2.

§14.4. Control Card

The control card apprises the program of the number of input tape reels to be processed. The format of the control card should be:

Card Columns	*Contents*
1-3	Number (001-999) of input tape reels to be processed.
4-80	Ignored.

§14.5. Output

Output consists of one or more tapes in Format Seven (§ 23.3) and of print-out of various messages (§ 14.6.3). If many input tape reels are to be processed, the number of output tape reels will, as a result of blocking, be considerably fewer. When the end of a tape on which output has been written is reached, another reel for output may be readied on unit 4 (§ 14.6.2).

An end-of-file mark will be written after the last physical record on each output tape.

TECHNICAL CONSIDERATIONS

§14.6. Language and Processing

The source program is written in 1401 Tape Autocoder. If defective records are encountered on an input tape, they are processed according to procedure one (§ 26.2).

§ *14.6.1. Processing Successive Input Tapes.* When the end-of-file mark (§ 23.2) on any input tape other than the last (as specified on the control card [§ 14.4]) is reached, the program unloads the tape just processed, prints out the message MOUNT NEW OUTPUT REEL ON UNIT 3. PRESS START, and then halts. After the next input tape reel has been readied on unit 3, processing resumes when START is pressed on the 1401.

§ *14.6.2. Readying Successive Tapes for Output.* When an output tape reel has been completely filled, the program writes an end-of-file mark on that reel, unloads it, prints out the message MOUNT NEW OUTPUT REEL ON UNIT 4. PRESS START, and then halts. Another reel of tape for output may then be readied on unit 4. Processing of the input tape still mounted on unit 2 will resume when START is pressed on the 1401.

§ *14.6.3. Program-Audit Messages.* When the end-of-file mark on the last input tape (as specified on the control card [§ 14.4]) is reached, the program prints out the number of processed input-tape reels with the message REELS READ, the number of processed input records with the message RECORDS READ, and the number of physical records generated on the output tape(s) with the message BLOCKS WRITTEN.

KWIC PRINT-STATISTICS Operational Summary

Machine:

IBM 1401 with Advanced Programming, High-Low-Equal compare, Multiply-Divide, two tape units, and 1403 Model 2 or 3.

Input Schematic:

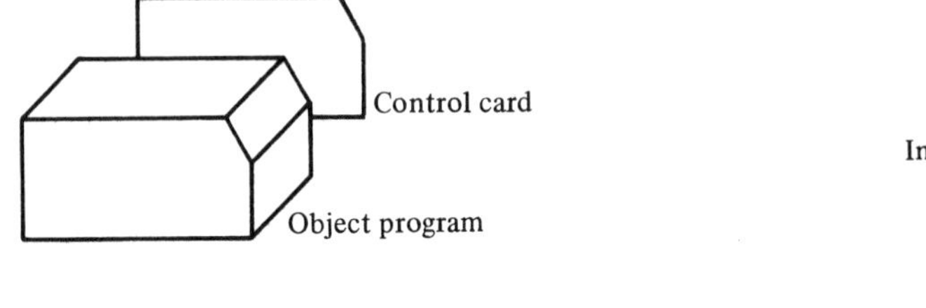

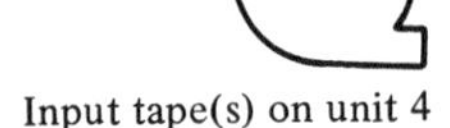

Input tape(s) on unit 4

Tape(s) for output on unit 5

Machine-Operator Instructions:

1. Place card input in 1402 read hopper.
2. Set sense switch B to terminate run (§ 15.8.3). All other sense switches are ignored.
3. Ready first and each successive input tape on unit 4 (ring out).
4. Ready first and each successive tape for output on unit 5 (ring in).
5. On 1403 ready continuous forms for desired number of copies of printed output (usual maximum four copies) and for diagnostic messages.
6. Press START RESET on 1401.
7. Press CHECK RESET and LOAD on 1402. Press START to process last two cards of input deck.
8. On procedures for readying successive input and output tape reels, see § § 15.8.1-15.8.2.

CHAPTER 15

Kwic Print-Statistics

INTRODUCTION

§ 15.1 Function

This program prints a key-word-in-context listing (Figure 15.A) from input tapes in Format Seven (§ 23.3) and also generates output tape(s) in Format Eight (§ 23.4). After each series of entries devoted to one and the same key word, the program prints a one-line statistical entry, consisting of four labeled scores that summarize the frequency of the key word and the number of document sources in which the key word occurred.[1] On the output tape, one record is written for each different key word and includes the word itself and the four summary scores.

§ 15.2. System Considerations

§ *15.2.1. Generation of Input Tape in Format Seven.* The input tape must be in a blocked format of 45 logical records per physical record. This blocking may be done by KWIC BLOCKS (§ 14.1) or by the program used for alphabetically sorting the tape created by KWIC RECORDS (§ 13.2.1).

§ *15.2.2. Processing of Output Tape in Format Eight.* The tape(s) in Format Eight generated by KWIC PRINT-STATISTICS can be sorted on any one of the four summary scores that comprise the record for each key word. For example, the investigator may want to list the key words in order of frequency starting with the most frequent word. In this case, the output information in Format Eight would be sorted according to descending raw frequency and a listing made of the results.

[1] This feature of the program is useful only if the input tape is alphabetically sorted on position 42 and subsequent positions (§ 13.2.1) of each logical record.

```
      CUT HIM UP FOR US. ANC THE EAGLE BIT A HOLE IN THE SKIN ON THE RUMP. THE    8L1 OMAHA
   THIS SUMMER. I HAVE LEARNED QUITE A BIT ABOUT ETHIOPIA AND ITS PEOPLE BUT I    2K1 RAMALLO
    MY HUSBAND. I HAVE WORRIED QUITE A BIT ABOUT HIS ILLNESS. I JUST HOPE THIS    4B2 FRISBIE DETROIT SAMPLE
     MORE TO DRINK. I CAN TELL A LITTLE BIT ABOUT IT. THIS HERE GIRL, SHE WAS UP  5A2 HARTMAN DETROIT GANGS
      IN THE SHOP WINDCWS NOT FEELING A BIT ALONE IN THIS STRANGE TOWN WHEN A     0B1 CHILDREN S DREAMS
   VERY SOCN AT THE TOP I FOUND A LEVEL BIT AND THEN A LAST RIDGE OVERLOOKING     6A3 T E LAWRENCE
  THEY FINISH DANCING THEY ATE A LITTLE BIT AND WENT HOME. WELL THE MAN IS KIND   5G1 NAVAHO TATS
  GROUP GOES. IN DOING THIS, HE SEEMS A BIT ANTAGONISTIC, AND, WHETHER HE HAS     2H3 SHAPIRO SMALL GROUP
     OBJECT WHICH IS FILLING THE NEK AS BIT AS A MOUNTAIN THAT IS KHOLUMOLUMO.    8B1 BASUTO TALES
LIVE WITH IT.,, THE OLDER MAN SMILES A BIT AS HE REMEMBERS HIS OWN YOUTH, BUT     5D1 WILLIAMSON UNDERGRAD
 REDICULOUS SPEAKING ABCUT IT A LITTLE BIT ASHAMED I GUESS BUT I DONT KNOW AND    1F1 JAFFE CASE
  BUT I/8P FIGURE/9 IT MIGHT BE LITTLE BIT BETTER IF HE/1C GOT/3 OUT AND MET/3    1G4 MILLS
I KNOW ARE THE CNES INFLUENCED QUITE A BIT BY WHAT I SAY. -UH -HUH. AND I         1A1 FAM INTERACTION  FRISBIE
 A RESPONSIBLE PERSON + A LITTLE 20191 BIT COCKY + LOYAL TO MY FRIENDS + A PLAY   9C2 WHO AM I
    TO THEM. THE OTHER THREE MEN ARE A BIT CONCERNED WITH WHAT IS BEING TOLD      5F2 N ACH TAT
        ADDITIONS TO THE GROUP. I AM A BIT DISAPPOINTED THAT THERE IS NOT MORE    2K4 RAMALLO
    SURREALISTIC HE SEEMED HE LOOKED A BIT DISTORTED POSSIBLY WITH HIS EYES IN    2E3 PSILOCYBIN
  THE FOOD YCU ARE GIVING ME. I FEEL A BIT DOWN WITH A COUGH I SAID. YOU SEE AH   0A3 ZINACANTAN DREAMS
      OF ANY READER WHC MAY HAVE FELT A BIT FRAYED AROUND THE EDGES AT ONE TIME   7F1 CITIZEN S COUNCIL
   SLIPPING THRCUGH THE UNIVERSE WAS A BIT FRIGHTENING OR RATHER TENSION          2E3 PSILOCYBIN
 THE GRATING SOUNDS OF CX CARTS, ALL A BIT FRIGHTENING TO ONE WHO HAD JUST LEFT   2D3 PEACE CORPS
 COOKING AND CLEANING FOR US. I FEEL A BIT FUNNY ABOUT THIS AS I HAVE NEVER       2K4 RAMALLO
   THINGS BROUGHT OUT THIS WEEK WENT A BIT FURTHER IN FORMULATING THE OPINION     2F1 CLEVELAND DIALOGUES
     OF COURSE IT/1 (SPECULATION) IS A BIT FUTILE/1, BUT PERHAPS INTERESTING/1.   2C5 RADCLIFFE EGYPT
   GOOD. SOME OF THE AFRICAN FOOD IS A BIT HARD TO GET USED TO BUT THE MORE I     2K4 RAMALLO
    I AM UNHAPPY IT SEEMS. I LIKE IT A BIT HE SAID. WHY HE WAS ASKED. AH          0A2 ZINACANTAN DREAMS
  PLAYING WITH HIS DOG WHEN THE ANIMAL BIT HIM ON THE WRIST. THE CUT BLED         0B2 CHILDREN S DREAMS
  VERY CLOSE TO THE LITTLE BOY THE BOY BIT HIS (SAINT MICHAEL S) THUMB AND        0B1 CHILDREN S DREAMS
  ,,KIND SIR,, BCYS WHC WERE PERHAPS A BIT INTIMIDATED BY THE MERE PRESENCE OF    2D3 PEACE CORPS
   RIGHTNESS CF THIS. I BEGAN TO SEE A BIT INTO THE FUTURE. I UNDERSTOOD THAT I   2E2 PSILOCYBIN
MY HEALTH HAS BEEN WORRYING ME QUITE A BIT LATELY. I HAVE BEEN WANTING            4B3 FRISBIE DETROIT SAMPLE
    STATES A BIT MORE DCMESTIC HELP, A BIT LESS OF OTHER CONVENIENCES, BUT NOT    2D5 PEACE CORPS
   TOO MUCH ALREADY HE SAID. AH WAIT A BIT LET ME FINISH SPLITTING MY WOOD HE     8A1 ZINACANTAN FOLK
 NOT LOVE ME + A GOOF CFF AT TIMES + A BIT LOST + I AM. THE LAST TIME I SAW       9C4 WHO AM I
      WITH LIFE IN THE UNITED STATES A BIT MORE DOMESTIC HELP, A BIT LESS OF      2D5 PEACE CORPS
   ENOUGH SHE SAID I MUST ADD A LITTLE BIT MORE SO THAT THE BAG CAN BE FASTENED   8J1 KIKUYU
NEW/1 YORKERS/1, + HOWEVER, (CHANGE) A BIT MORE/1 BUSTLE/1 ONCE/4 IN/4 A          4D4 MASTERS NEW CASTLE
     SPRING WAS BEAUTIFUL IT WAS NOT A BIT MUDDY. ALL THE FECES CAME OFF MY       0A1 ZINACANTAN DREAMS
HOURS. I MUST SAY I FINC DOING THESE A BIT OF A NUISANCE SINCE I WRITE THE SAME   2K4 RAMALLO
 DO IF WE HAD BETTER FINANCES. IT IS A BIT OF A SMALL PROBLEM WITH THE CHILDREN   4B3 FRISBIE DETROIT SAMPLE
 I HAD THE TIME AT SCHOOL) ACTRESS + A BIT OF A SNOB + A LOVER OF SHAKESPEARE,    9D2 ALYMER SENT COMP
  HAVING READ THE PAPERS HAVE A LITTLE BIT OF ACQUAINTANCE WITH WHAT IS GOING     1A1 FAM INTERACTION  FRISBIE
   I DID OR THOUGHT MADE THE SLIGHTEST BIT OF DIFFERENCE. I WOULD HAVE GIVEN      2E2 PSILOCYBIN
  WE NEED THE CAR AND IT NEEDS QUITE A BIT OF FIXING. SICKNESS. I AM AFRAID I     4B1 FRISBIE DETROIT SAMPLE
     FOR THE MCST PART. WE DID HAVE A BIT OF FRUSTRATION WHEN WE HAD TO SIT       2K1 RAMALLO
```

FIGURE 15.4 Sample page of a KWIC index. For detailed explanation see §13.1, §13.6, and §15.6. Sample page does not show a statistical summary.

§ *15.2.3. Number of Sources Represented in the Listing.* Each line of the KWIC listing (Figure 15.A) is associated with the title card (§ 3.4) preceding the section of text in which the given occurrence of the key word for that line appeared. KWIC PRINT-STATISTICS examines the character obtained from column 3 of the title card and counts how many different characters have appeared in that position of all lines for each key word. This count is printed on the summary statistic line after the label NUMBER DIFFERENT SOURCES (§ 15.6).

Given this use of column 3 of title cards, the investigator may want to prepare these cards in such a way that the character in column 3 identifies the type of document but the rest of the title card—that is, through column 30 (§ 13.2.3)—gives the actual name of the document. All those documents of the same type (that is, having the same character in column 3) will be considered a single source. A source may in this way include a number of differently titled documents.

KWIC PRINT-STATISTICS can recognize a maximum of 40 different characters in column 3 of title cards. If more than this maximum are used, the NUMBER DIFFERENT SOURCES printed by the program will be 40, no matter how many more in fact occur.

§ *15.2.4. Percentage Statistics.* In addition to printing raw frequencies, KWIC PRINT-STATISTICS also gives the number of key-word occurrences as a percentage of the total number of words in the sample, and the number of sources represented in the listing as a percentage of the total number of sources in the sample (§ 15.4). The total number of words in the text is printed by KWIC RECORDS (§ 13.8). The number of different sources represented by different characters in column 3 of title cards is presumably known by the investigator. However, the investigator's choice is not limited to these particular divisors, since any numbers may be specified on the control card.

INPUT AND OUTPUT SPECIFICATIONS

§ 15.3. Input

Input consists of the object program, a control card, and one or more tapes in Format Seven (§ 15.2.1). When the processing of one input tape reel is completed, another may be readied on tape unit 4 (§ 15.8.1).

§15.4. Control Card

The control card apprises the program of the number of input reels that are to be processed and the numbers that are to be used as divisors in the calculation of percentage statistics (§ 15.2.4). The numbers in each of the three fields should be punched with leading zeros.

Card Columns	*Contents*
1-3	Number (001-999) of input-tape reels to be processed.
4-10	Divisor (0000001-9999999) for computing frequency of key-word occurrence as a percentage of the number of words in the text.
15-16	Divisor (01-40) for computing frequency of the number of sources appearing in key-word listing as a percentage of the total number of sources appearing in the text sample.
17-80	Ignored by the program.

§15.5. Output

Output consists of an alphabetic key-word-in-context listing and the tape in Format Eight. Because of sorting procedures, isolated punctuation marks are listed first and numbers are listed last.

§15.6. Key-Word-in-Context Listing and Statistical Summaries

Each line in the KWIC listing (Figure 15.A) is 132 positions long and is composed of:

1. Key word (beginning in print position 42) with surrounding text (in print positions 1-41 and from the end of the key word to print position 82).
2. As many as 19 sentence-identification characters (in print positions 83-102).
3. The contents of columns 2-30 of the title card (in print positions 104-132).

A space in the listing and a statistical summary occur after all instances of a given key word have been printed. Each of the various inflected forms of a word is considered a separate key word, but a word that is immediately followed by a punctuation mark or subscript (§ §3.10; 3.12) is listed with other occurrences of that same word.

Each statistical entry contains four scores that summarize the frequency and distribution (in the sample text deck processed by KWIC

RECORDS [§13.1]) of the occurrence of the preceding key word. The scores are labeled, positioned, and to be interpreted as follows:

Print Positions	*Contents (Label)*	*Print Positions*	*Contents (Score)*
8-24	NUMBER OCCURRENCES	26-31	*Frequency raw score*—that is, the number of key-word entries for the preceding key word (and thus the number of times that word occurred in the text).
32-47	PERCENT OF TOTAL	52-57	*Frequency index score*—that is, the frequency raw score as a percentage of all key-word entries in the index (the divisor specified in columns 4-10 of the control card [§15.4]).
59-82	NUMBER DIFFERENT SOURCES	84-86	*Distribution raw score*—that is, the number of different documents in which the preceding key word occurred (column 3 of title cards).
89-95	PERCENT	97-102	*Distribution index score*—that is, the distribution raw score as a percentage of the total number of documents in which all key words in the index originated (the divisor specified in in positions 15-16 of the control card [§15.4]).

§15.7. Output: Tape(s) in Format Eight

On the output tape in Format Eight is written one record for each different key word printed in the index. Each such record contains a given key word and the frequency and distribution scores printed in the index's statistical entry for that word (§15.6). For details of Format Eight, see Appendix One (§23.4).

If many input tapes are to be processed, a single reel of tape may not suffice for output.

§ 15.8. Language and Processing

The source program is written in 1401 Tape Autocoder. If defective records are encountered on the input tape, they are processed according to procedure one (§ 26.2).

§ *15.8.1. Processing Successive Input Tapes.* When the end-of-file mark (§ 23.3) on any input tape reel other than the last (as specified on the control card [§ 15.4]) is reached, the program rewinds and unloads the tape, and halts. The next input tape reel may then be readied on unit 4, and pressing START will cause the program to begin processing new tape.

§ *15.8.2. Readying Successive Tapes for Output.* When the end of a tape on which output has been written is reached, the program writes an end-of-file mark on the tape, unloads it, and halts. Another reel of tape for output may then be readied on unit 5, and pressing START will cause the program to resume processing the input tape on unit 4.

§ *15.8.3. Terminating the Run (Sense Switch B).* Sense switch B may be set *up* at any time in order to terminate the run. If sense switch B is set up during processing of an input tape, the run terminates when the program reaches the end-of-file mark (§ 23.3) on that tape. If sense switch B is set up during a programmed halt (§ § 15.8.1-15.8.2), the run terminates at that time. In either case, before finally halting, the program will write an end-of-file on the output tape if the latter had not already been unloaded (§ 15.8.2) and will unload whichever of the tapes on units 4 and 5 had not already been unloaded.

CROSS-SORT RECORDS Operational Summary

Machine:

IBM 1401 with 8K, Advanced Programming. High-Low-Equal compare, and at least one tape drive if tape output is requested.

Input Schematic:

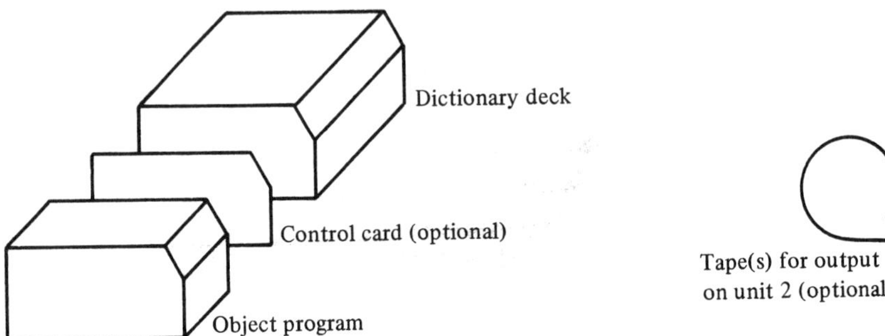

Machine-Operator Instructions:

1. Place card input in 1402 hopper; ready 1402 punch if punched output is requested (§ 16.8).
2. Set sense switches on 1401.
   A: Always up (§ 16.9).
   B, C, D, E, F, G: Ignored.
3. Ready tape on unit 2 (ring in), if tape output is requested (§ 16.6).
4. Press START RESET on 1401.
5. Press CHECK RESET and LOAD on 1402. Press START to process last two cards of input deck.
6. On procedures for readying successive output tape reels, see § 16.10.

CHAPTER 16

Cross-Sort Records[1]

INTRODUCTION

§16.1. Function

This program consecutively examines each card in a dictionary deck (§ 2.4; Figure 2.A), and, as illustrated in Table 16.A, generates one logical record for each tag or instance of the operator N that is specified in the instruction associated with each entry (§ § 2.8-2.12). Each record will contain the entry itself and that field (§ 16.7.3) of the instruction which contained the given tag.

In generating an output tape, the program blocks 20 logical records per physical record.[2] However, a control card option (§ 16.5) permits either a lower blocking factor to be specified or punched card output to be generated instead of tape output.

§16.2. System Considerations

An output tape generated by CROSS-SORTS RECORDS (§ 16.7) should be sorted on positions 78-79[3] (§ 16.7.5) and 1-20 (§ 16.7.1) by a standard tape-sorting program.[4] The contents of the tape produced by this sorting operation can then be printed by CROSS-SORT LIST (§ 17.1) in the format illustrated in Figure 17.A.

[1] Stone, Philip J., Dexter C. Dunphy, Marshall S. Smith, Daniel M. Ogilvie, with associates, *The General Inquirer: A Computer Approach to Content Analysis* (Cambridge, Mass.: The M. I. T. Press, 1966), p. 91.

[2] See §9.1, footnote 2.

[3] Or on positions 78-80 if syntax markers as well as tags are to be sorted.

[4] Recommended is Sort 7 for the IBM 1401, on which see §2.15, footnote 21.

Alternatively, CROSS-SORT RECORDS can be run in its card output mode (§ 16.5, column 2). The resultant card output (§ 16.8) can be sorted on columns 78-79[5] by a sorting machine.

INPUT AND OUTPUT SPECIFICATIONS

§16.3. Input

Input consists of the object program, a dictionary deck, and, at the investigator's option, a single control card.

§16.4. Dictionary Deck

A dictionary deck as described in § § 2.4-2.5 and illustrated in Figure 2.A, constitutes the primary input to the program. However, all required special entries (§ 2.6), and any regular entry (§ 2.8) longer than 39 characters, should be removed from the deck before the latter is submitted for processing by CROSS-SORT RECORDS.

No special measures need to be taken in the case of an instruction continued from the card on which its entry appears onto one or more additional cards (§ 2.5.2), provided that not more than 20 continuation cards are used for a single entry. Also, the program ignores blank cards, as well as columns 73-80 of all cards in the dictionary deck (§ 2.5.3).

The number of cards in the input dictionary deck is recorded at the end of the program run (§ 16.11).

§16.5. Control Card (Optional)

A single control card may be used at the investigator's option in order either to specify an output-tape blocking factor lower than 20 (§ 16.7), or to request punched card output (§ 16.8) instead of tape output. If used, the control card should conform to the following format:

Card Columns	*Contents*
1	[period]
2	Either the character T if the purpose of the control card is to specify an output-tape blocking factor lower than 20; or the character C if the purpose of the control card is to request card output instead of tape output
3	Blank.

[5] Or on positions 78-80. See footnote 3.

Card Columns	Contents
4-5	If T in column 2, the desired blocking factor (01-19); if C in column 2, blank.
6-80	Ignored by program.

If no control card is submitted, a special message is printed out (§ 16.6).

§ 16.6. Output

Aside from various diagnostic messages (§ § 16.10-16.12), the sole output of the program is either tape(s) or punched cards containing records (as illustrated in Table 16.A) of input dictionary cards.

If no control card had been submitted (§ 16.5), the message CTL CARD MISSING STANDARD ASSUMPTIONS MADE will be printed out before the program begins to read the input dictionary deck. The "assumptions" referred to in this message are that output is to be written on a tape which has for this purpose been readied on unit 2 and that 20 logical records are to be written per physical record.

If a control card was submitted (§ 16.5), no special message is printed out but the program generates (as requested on the control card) either tape output with a blocking factor lower than 20 or card output *instead of* tape output.

§ 16.7. Tape Output

This tape will consist of a series of 80-position logical records, one such record for *each* tag or instance of the operator N in the instruction for each entry in the input dictionary deck (§ 16.4). Twenty logical records will be blocked as a single physical record[6] unless a control card is submitted to request a lower blocking factor (§ 16.11).

Each 80 position logical record will consist of the five fields (a-e) illustrated in Table 16.A and described in § § 16.7.1-16.7.5.

If the tape on which output records are being written becomes full to capacity, the program halts with an explanatory message (§ 16.10) in order to allow a fresh output tape to be readied.

§ *16.7.1. Field A.* In field a of a record will be written a regular dictionary entry (§ 2.8) or an optional special entry (§ 2.7) derived from an input dictionary card (§ 16.4). The first character of the entry will

[6] Unused positions of the last physical record generated in a run will automatically be padded with the character 9.

appear in position 1 of field a, and the rest of the entry in consecutive positions immediately thereafter. If the entry is shorter than 15 characters, all positions after the last character of the entry and through position 15 will be blank.

Table 16.A. Examples of Records Generated by CROSS-SORT RECORD†

Field Positions	*A 1-15*	*B 16-20*	*C 21-72*	*D 73-76*	*E 77-80*
	HAT		=S,28,Ø,33,49		28S
	HAT		=S,28,Ø,33,49		33Ø
	HAT		=S,28,Ø,33,49		49Ø
	ARM		=9,S,52 *		09
	ARM		=9,S,52 *		52S
	ARM		=9,S,52,(W,2,TWIST,11) *		/11
	ARM		=9,S,52 *43 *		43S
	ARM		=9,S,52 *(T,4,67,71,V,72)		/71
	ARM		=9,S,52 *(T,4,67,71,V,72)		/72V

†The first three records in this table would be generated from assumed input dictionary card HAT=S,28Ø,33,49. The last six records would be generated from assumed card ARM=9, S,52,(W,2,TWIST,11),43,(T,4,67,71,V,72). Asterisk (*) within positions 22-72 indicates programmed omission of part of an instruction; slash (/) in position 77 indicates that the following tag had been specified in conditional expression. For full explanation see §§16.7-16.8.

The entry on a single input dictionary card will be written in field a of as many successive records as there were tags in the entire (input) instruction (§§2.9-2.12) for the entry. In other words, one record is created for each tag in the instruction.

§*16.7.2. Field B.* Field b of a record will invariably consist of five blank positions. These blanks will fall in positions 16-20 unless field a of the same record extended beyond position 15. In the latter case, field b will be the first five positions after the last character of the entry written in field a.

§*16.7.3. Field C.* Field c of a record will begin in the first position (normally position 21) after the end of field b and will invariably extend through position 72. In field c will be written no more than two instruction fields of the entry that appears in field a of the same record. An instruction field may be either any number of consecutive unparenthesized tags (with or without syntax markers) or a single parenthesized conditional expression. Thus, an unconditional instruction (§2.9) on an input dictionary card can yield only one instruction field, although this one definition field will be replicated in field c of as many records as there were tags in the instruction on the input dictionary card. In Table 16.A, for example, the three records generated from the unconditionally defined entry HAT are identical with respect to field c.

On the other hand, a conditional instruction (§ 2.10) can yield any number of fields, since there are no limitations on the number of conditional expressions (§ § 2.11-2.12) in such an instruction, as well as no restrictions on the position of unparenthesized tags in relation to conditional expressions (§ 2.10.2). Thus, as illustrated in Table 16.A, ARM=9,S,52,(W,2,TWIST,11),43,(T,4,67,71,V,72) yields four instruction fields, whereas the equivalent ARM=9,S,52,43,(W,2,TWIST,11), (T,4,67,71,V,72) would have yielded only three.

Field c of *every* output record that is generated from a single conditional instruction containing two or more instruction fields will begin with the first of those fields. But each field after the first will appear in field c of only as many different records as there are tags in the given field. For example, in Table 16.A, the initial instruction field 9,S,52 appears in field c of each of the six records generated from 9,S,52,(W,2,TWIST,11),43,(T,4,67,71,V,72). However, the second instruction field, the conditional expression (W,2,TWIST,11), appears in only one record, since the expression specifies only one tag for assignment in case the test succeeds. Note in Table 16.A that there are two rather than three records in which the last conditional expression (T,4,67,71,V,72) appears. This is because tag 67 is tag θ—that is, the tag to be searched for (§ 2.12)—whereas only tags 71 and 72 are τ tags—that is, tags specified for assignment.

Note further in Table 16.A that each point at which one or more fields of the entire input instruction have been omitted from field c of an output record is indicated by an asterisk (*).

In the first position of field c (normally position 21) will be written the equals sign that had divided the entry from its instruction on the input dictionary card (§ 16.4). However, if the one or two instruction fields that must be written in field c of the record exceed the available number of positions in that field (normally positions 22-72—that is, 51 positions), then the remaining characters will be written within position 22-72 of as many as 20 continuation records. In this case, position 21 of each continuation record will contain a serial number to indicate whether it is the second, third, fourth, or *n*th record devoted to the one or two instruction fields.

§*16.7.4. Field D.* Field d of every record will invariably comprise positions 73-76 and will invariably be blank throughout.

§*16.7.5. Field E.* Field e of a record will invariably comprise positions 77-80, and a two-digit tag (01-99) will invariably be written in positions 78-79. The tag written in positions 78-79 will be one of those that appeared in field c of the same record, and will be followed by the syntax marker, if any, which modifies (precedes) it in the instruction. No tag specified in an input instruction will be written in field e of more than one record, unless the given tag happened to have been specified more than once in the instruction. In the latter case, one record will be created for each occurrence (in the entire instruction) of the given tag, and the given tag will be written in field e of each of the resulting records. The special operator N, if found in an input instruction (§ § 2.8.2; 2.10.4), will be treated exactly like a tag.

Position 77 will be blank if the tag in positions 78-79 derived either from an unconditional instruction (Table 16.A, all records generated for HAT) or from an unparenthesized portion of a conditional instruction (Table 16.A, first, second, and fourth records generated for ARM). But position 78 will contain a slash (/) if the tag in positions 78-79 is derived from a conditional expression (Table 16.A, third, fifth, and sixth records for ARM).

§16.8. Punched Output

If punched output is requested instead of tape output (§ 16.5, column 2), each dictionary record will be punched onto a single card. Each such card will consist of fields a-e, as described in § § 16.7.1-16.7.5 and illustrated in Table 16.A.

TECHNICAL CONSIDERATIONS

§16.9. Language and Processing

The program is written in 1401 Tape Autocoder. Sense switch A must be set up in order to enable the program to confirm that the last input card has been read.

In order to be able to distinguish between tag θ and tag(s) τ in a tag-test conditional expression (§ 2.12) on an input record, the program counts the number of commas it has encountered after a left parenthesis. No tag specified before the third comma after a left parenthesis can be written in field e of an output record (§ 16.7.5).

§ 16.10. Readying Successive Tapes for Output

When an output tape reel has been completely filled, the program writes an end-of-file mark on that reel, unloads and rewinds it, prints out the message MOUNT NEW TAPE, and then halts. Another reel of tape for output may then be readied on unit 2. Processing will resume when START is pressed on the 1401.

§ 16.11. Program-Audit Messages

When all input has been processed, the program prints out the following messages, each accompanied by an appropriate number:

CARDS INPUT	The number of cards encountered in the input dictionary deck (§ 16.4).
RECORDS WRITTEN	The total number of logical records either written on the output tape(s) (§ 16.7) or punched onto cards (§ 16.8).
BLOCKS WRITTEN	The total number of physical records on the output tape(s), if any. Cf. § 16.5.

§ 16.12. Processing of Defective Input Cards

If the program encounters an input dictionary card on which a blank precedes the equals sign (§ 2.5.1, column n+1), the instruction on that card is not processed. The image of the entire card will be printed out, followed by the message ERROR CARD. The next card in the input deck is then processed.

CROSS-SORT LIST Operational Summary

Machine:

IBM 1401 with 8K, Advanced Programming, High-Low-Equal compare, and at least one tape unit.

Input Schematic:

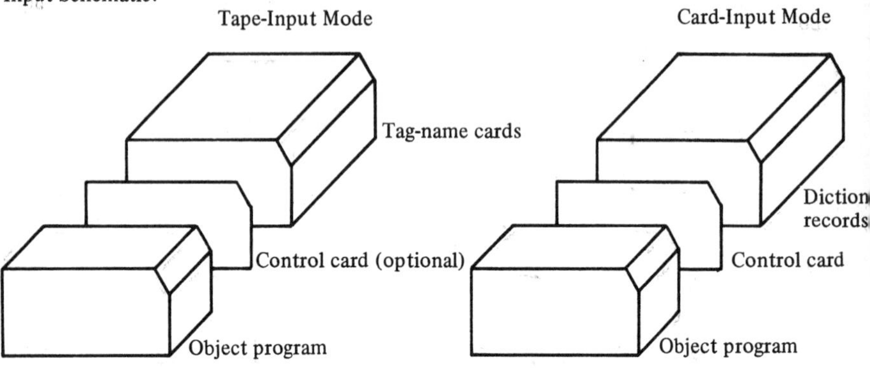

Input Dictionary-records tape(s) on unit 2

Input tag-name tape on unit 3

Machine-Operator Instructions:

Tape-Input Mode

1. Place card input in 1402 read hopper.
2. Set sense switches on 1401.
   A: Always up.
   B,C,D,E,F,G: Ignored.
3. Ready first and each successive input tape on unit 2 (ring out).
4. On 1403 ready continuous forms for desired number of copies of printed output (usual maximum four copies) and for procedural and diagnostic messages.
5. Press START RESET on 1401.
6. Press CHECK RESET and LOAD on 1402. Press START to process last two cards of input deck.
7. On procedures for readying successive input tapes, see § 17.10.
8. For procedures in case of defective input tape records, see § 26.2.

Card-Input Mode

1. Place card input in 1402 read hopper.
2. Set sense switches on 1401.
   A: Always up.
   B, C, D, E, F, G: Ignored.
3. Ready input tape on unit 3 (ring out).
4. On 1403 ready continuous forms for desired r ber of copies of printed output (usual maximu four copies) and for procedural and diagnostic messages.
6. Press CHECK RESET and LOAD on 1402. Pr START to process last two cards of input dec
7. For procedures in case of defective input tape records, see § 17.12.

CHAPTER 17

Cross-Sort List

INTRODUCTION

§ 17.1. Function

This program prints the dictionary records that CROSS-SORT RECORDS (§ 16.1), in processing a dictionary deck, had generated on either tape(s) (§ 16.7) or cards (§ 16.8). However, before being listed by this program, the dictionary records should have been sorted on either positions 78-79 (§ 16.7.5) or 78-80 (§ 16.2, note 3), and also on positions 1-20 (§ 16.7.1). The purpose of this sorting operation is to group together all entries in the respective instructions of which one and the same tag had been specified. Moreover, the sorting operation arranges in alphabetic order the entries defined, wholly or in part, by a particular tag. In printing this sorted input (Figure 17.A), CROSS-SORT LIST creates one alphabetically arranged section for each tag used in the dictionary and entitles each page of each section with the name of the content analysis category identified by the given tag. A separate section, entitled EXCLUDED WRD, is created for the special operator N (§ § 2.8.2; 2.10.4; 16.7.5). Also, the program calculates and prints at the end of each section of the listing the number of different entries defined by the given tag. A listing of this type displays the dictionary in "cross-sorted" format.

§ 17.2. System Considerations

This program accepts as input either type of output which CROSS-SORT RECORDS can generate—tape (§ 16.7) or cards (§ 16.8). There is no requirement that the records generated by that program be sorted before they are submitted as input to CROSS-SORT LIST. However, unless the intermediary tape- or card-sorting operation is performed,

```
CICTICNARY LIST BY TAG                                                    PAGE

TAG = 01   TITLE =   RACE

 AFRC-AMERICAN         =01
 BACKGROUNC            =02(T,5,01,C1) *
 BLACK                 =01 *
 BRCTHER               =06,C8 *(W,1,SOUL,C1)
 BROWN                 =C1 *
 CAUCASIAN             =C1
 CCLOR                 =C1
 CESCENT               =02(T,5,01,C1) *
 HERITAG               =C2(T,5,C1,C1) *
 INCIAN                =C1
 INCIAN-NEGRO          =01
 MCSLEM                =03(W,1,BLACK,03,26,01)
 MUSLIM                =03,26,01
 NEGRC                 =01
 NIGGER                =C1,46 *
 NIGGER                =01,46 *(T,3,56,01,58,56)
 ORIENTAL              =01
 RAC                   =C1 *
 SKIN                  =30 *(W,2,BROWN,C1) *
 SKIN                  =30 *(W,2,LIGHT,C1)
 SKIN                  =30(W,2,BLACK,01) *
 SKIN                  =30 *(W,2,DARK,01) *
 SKIN                  =30 *(W,2,WHITE,01) *
 TAN                   =01 *
 WHITE                 =C1(W,3,PASS,C1)
 WHITE                 =C1 *

NUMBER OF UNIQUE DICTIONARY ENTRIES/TAG =     20
```

FIGURE 17.A. Sample of cross-sorted dictionary listing. For detailed explanation see §17.1 with §16.7 and Table 16.A.

the listing generated by CROSS-SORT LIST will not be in the cross-sorted format described (§ 17.1).

The display of a dictionary in cross-sorted format makes explicit the structure of each content analysis category in the dictionary, since the cross-sorted listing groups together all entries defined by any one tag. The cross-sorted listing facilitates checking both entries and instructions for inconsistencies, omissions, redundancies, and the like.

INPUT AND OUTPUT SPECIFICATIONS

§17.3. Input

The program can be run in either of two input modes, depending on whether the presorted (§ § 16.2; 17.2) dictionary records are submitted on tape (§ 17.3.1) or cards (§ 17.3.2).

§ *17.3.1. Tape-Input Mode.* In this mode, input consists of the object program, a set of tag-name cards, and one or more dictionary-record tapes. However, if either more than one tape is submitted, or the tape input is not blocked 20 logical records per physical record, a control card will also have to be submitted.

§ *17.3.2. Card-Input Mode.* In this mode, input consists of the object program, a control card, the tape transcription of a set of tag-name cards, and a set of dictionary-record cards.

§17.4. Preparation of Dictionary Input

The input, as generated by CROSS-SORT RECORDS (§ § 16.7-16.8), should have been sorted on positions 78-79 (or positions 78-80 if syntax markers are also to be sorted) and 1-20 before it is processed by this program (§ § 16.2; 17.2). Dictionary input may be submitted either on one or more tapes or on cards but not on both. On processing of successive input tapes, see § 17.10.

§17.5. Tag-Name Records

From this input are derived the names of the tags used in the dictionary. The name for a given tag will be printed at the top of each page of the section of the output listing devoted to that tag (§ 17.8; Figure 17.A).

Tag names should be submitted on cards (§ 24.2) if dictionary input (§ 17.4) is submitted on tape but on tape if the dictionary input is on cards. An input tag-name tape should be unblocked but need not be sorted.

On defective tag-name input, see § § 17.11-17.12.

§ 17.6. Control Card (Optional)

A single card should be submitted if any one of the following input conditions is not true: (a) dictionary records (§ 17.4) are submitted on tape; (b) only one dictionary-records tape is submitted; (c) the dictionary-records tape(s) is blocked 20 logical records per physical record (§ 16.5, columns 4-5). If all three of these conditions are true, no control card should be submitted, and just before processing the input dictionary tape the program will print out the message CTL CARD MISSING STANDARD ASSUMPTIONS MADE.

If used, the control card should conform to the following format:

Card Columns	*Contents*
1	. [period]
2	Either the character T if dictionary records (§ 17.4) are submitted on tape(s), or the character C if dictionary records are submitted on cards.
3-5	If T in column 2, the blocking factor (001-020) of the submitted dictionary-records tape(s); or, if C in column 2, blank.
6	Blank.
7-8	If T in column 2, the number (01-99) of dictionary-records tapes to be submitted; or, if C in column 2, blank.
9-80	Ignored by program.

§ 17.7. Output

Output will consist of a cross-sorted display of the dictionary submitted as input to CROSS-SORT RECORDS (§ 16.1), and various procedural and diagnostic messages (§ § 17.10-17.12).

§ 17.8. Cross-Sorted Dictionary Listing

One section of the listing will be devoted to each tag in the dictionary, and sections will be printed in numeric order (01-99). Within the section for any one tag will be printed records (Table 16.A) of all entries defined, wholly or in part, by that tag. (However, field a of continuation records [§ 16.7.3] will automatically be suppressed.) See the sample output in Figure 17.A. Each section will begin at the top of a new page; at the top of every page of the section devoted to any one tag will be printed the name of that tag. At the end of each section will be printed the summary message NUMBER OF UNIQUE DICTIONARY WORDS/TAG=, followed by the number of different entries defined, wholly or in part, by the tag for the preceding section.

Before the section for the first tag, the program will print a separate section, entitled EXCLUDED WRD, for any instructions in which the special operator N appears (§ § 2.8.2; 2.10.4; 16.7.5). This section of the listing will be organized exactly like the section for any tag.

TECHNICAL CONSIDERATIONS

§ 17.9. Language and Processing

The program is written in 1401 Tape Autocoder. Sense switch A must always be set up in order to enable the program to confirm that the last input card has been read.

If defective records are encountered on an input dictionary-records tape (§ 17.4), they are processed according to procedure one (§ 26.2). Compare § 17.12.

§ 17.10. Processing Successive Input Tapes

When the end-of-file mark on any dictionary-records input tape other than the last (as specified on the control card § 17.6, columns 7-8) is reached, the program rewinds and unloads the tape and prints out the message END OF REEL. MOUNT ANOTHER, and then halts. The next input tape may then be readied on unit 2, and pressing START will cause the program to process the new tape.

§ 17.11. Unidentified Tags

If the name of a tag is omitted from an input tag-name record (§ 17.5), the title of the section of the output listing (§ 17.8) for the unidentified tag will specify the correct number of the tag followed by blanks. If there is no input tag-name record whatsoever for a tag found in an input data record (§ 17.4), the title of the output section for the unidentified tag will specify the correct number of the tag followed by the message NO TAG NAME. In neither case will processing be interrupted.

§17.12. Processing of Defective Tag-Name Tape

If the program encounters on an input tag-name tape (§ 17.5) a record that contains one or more characters with incorrect parity, the message BAD TITLE RECORD PROCESSED is printed out. The program is not interrupted, but the title of every page in the section for the tag whose name had been specified in the defective tag-name record may be garbled.

However, the condition described in § 17.11 may also occur if the parity error happens to fall within positions 1-2 of a defective tape record.

APPENDIX ONE

TAPE FORMATS

CHAPTER 18

Format One

§18.1. System Considerations

A tape written in the format described in this chapter is generated by TAGGING as the primary output of a tagging operation (§4.2), and can be both listed and transcribed into tape Format Two by TEXT-TAG LIST (§§5.1; 19.1).

The organization of the tagged text on a tape in Format One in a series of document files (§1.9) is determined by the insertion of either end-document cards (§3.5) into the text or of *AUTODOC control cards (§4.29) into TAGGING's general input deck. The document-file organization of a tape in Format One in turn determines the organization of information on tapes in Formats Two and Three (§§19.1-20.1).

§18.2. Contents

On this tape will be written one sentence record (§§18.3; 1.8; Figure 1.C) for each text sentence except those that are longer than 810 characters (§4.32.5, no. 19) and those into which one or more attributive numeric subscripts (§3.12.3) had been inserted when the text was edited. If the text of a sentence is longer than 810 characters, it will be divided among as many separate records as necessary. For each sentence with attributive subscripts, two sentence records are created. This tape may also contain title records and end-of-file marks (§§18.4-18.5) and should invariably end with a terminal file (§18.6).

§18.3. Sentence Records

One sentence record is created for each series of input text words keypunched between one sentence or clause delimiter and the next

(§ 3.11; Table 3.A). The order of sentence records depends on that of the sentences in the text input processed by TAGGING. Each sentence record may be of variable length and format as will be described. However, the maximum length of a sentence record is 1698 positions (§ 5.10).

Positions	*Contents*
1-3	Number of words, as counted by TAGGING, in the text sentence to be written in positions n+2 to x of this record. Parenthesized proper noun or pronoun descriptors (§ 3.9) and unprocessed comments (§ 3.13) are not counted in this total.
4-6	Serial number, as determined by TAGGING, of the text sentence to be written in positions n+2 to x of this record. This serial number specifies the ordinal position of the sentence in the series of sentences which constitutes the present document file (§ 18.5).
7 to n (maximum length 70 positions)	Sentence- or document-identification code of as many as 70 characters, if such a code is stored in the code buffer when the end of the sentence is read (§ § 3.6; 3.8).
n+1	Blank.
n+2 to x (maximum length 810 positions)	Text sentence literally and with editorial insertions as keypunched after the first blank column on one or more text cards (§ 3.3.1), except for the following deletions: all but the first of two or more consecutive blanks (§ 3.3), any hyphen that was the last character on a text card (§ 3.3.2), and all alphabetic and numeric subscripts and the slash or pair of slashes dividing a text word from its subscript(s) (§ § 3.10; 3.12). However, deletion of subscripts and slashes can be suppressed if TAGGING's *UNEDITED option (§ 4.25) is exercised.
x+1	= [equals sign]

Positions	*Contents*
x+2 to end of record (maximum length 810 positions)	String of tags assigned to words or idioms in the sentence written in positions n+2 to x of this record. To each tag in this string is appended one of the four syntax markers–S, V, Ø, or U–as determined by the priorities enumerated in § 2.9. The order of the tags corresponds to the order of the words in the text sentence to which they had been assigned. Thus, any tags assigned as a result of a sentence-summary test (§ § 4.5; 27.1) would be written at the end of the string.

For each text sentence into which one or more attributive numeric subscripts had been inserted when the text was edited (§ 3.12.3), TAGGING writes two consecutive sentence records (a and b) of variable length and format as follows:

Record a

Positions	*Contents*
1-3	Number of words, as counted by TAGGING, to be written in positions n+2 to x of this record.
4-6	Sentence serial number (also to be written in positions 4-6 of record b).
7 to n	Sentence- or document-identification code, if any (also to be written in positions 7 to n of record b).
n+1	Blank.
n+2 to x	Words of text to which an attributive subscript had been applied. The first word will be preceded by a left parenthesis, the last followed by a right parenthesis.
x+1	= [equals sign]
x+2 to end of record a	String of tags assigned to the words written in positions n+2 to x of this record. To each tag will be appended the syntax marker controlled by the attributive numeric subscript applied to the now tagged words.

Record b

Positions	*Contents*
1-3	Number of words, as counted by TAGGING, to be written in positions n+2 to x of this record *minus* the number written in positions 1-3 of record a.
4-6	Sentence serial number of sentence to be written in positions n+2 to x of this record.
7 to n	Sentence- or document-identification code, if any, of sentence to be written in positions n+2 to x of this record.
n+1	Blank.
n+2 to x	Text of the entire sentence.
x+1	= [equals sign]
x+2 to end of record b	String of tags assigned to words or idioms written in positions n+2 to x of this record, except for the tags beginning in position x+2 of record a. In other words, this string will consist of tags assigned only to words to which a nonattributive subscript (§ 3.12.2) had been applied during text editing and to words to which no numeric subscript had been applied.

§ 18.4. Title Records

An 84-position title record is written on the tape in Format One whenever the program encounters a title card (§ 3.4) in the input text. Each title record will be the image of a title card.

§ 18.5. End-of-File Marks

Whenever the program encounters an end-document card (§ 3.5) in the input text or an *AUTODOC limit (§ 4.24), an end-of-file mark is written on the tape in Format One. These end-of-file marks thus define each group of sentence (and title) records that constitute a document file (§ 1.9) for subsequent General Inquirer processing.

§ 18.6. Terminal File

When the program encounters either the *FINISHED control card (§ 4.26) at the end of the input deck or an end-of-file mark on the A2 input tape (§ 4.8), a terminal file is written after the end-of-file mark (§ 18.5) that follows the last processed document file. The terminal file consists of a single record which contains an asterisk (*) in position 1 and which will be immediately followed by an end-of-file mark.

CHAPTER 19

Format Two

§19.1. System Considerations

A tape written in the format described in this chapter can be generated by TEXT-TAG LIST (§ 5.1) and RETRIEVAL (§ 7.1) and can be used as input to TAG TALLY (§ 6.1) and RETRIEVAL.

§19.2. Contents when Generated by TEXT-TAG LIST

When generated by TEXT-TAG LIST from a tape in Format One (§ 18.1), a tape in Format Two (§ 5.9) will contain all sentence and title records, all end-of-file marks, and the terminal file that are written on the antecedent tape in Format One. Moreover, the information will be written in the same order as on the antecedent tape. However, TEXT-TAG LIST reformats the input records by inserting 99 additional positions before the first position of each record. These 99 positions will be blank in title records and in the terminal file, but in sentence records will contain code characters that summarize the first occurrence of each tag in each syntax position that had been written in the tag string of the sentence record in Format One. See § 1.8.5 with Figure 1.C and § 19.5.

§19.3. Contents when Generated by RETRIEVAL

When generated by RETRIEVAL (from a tape which is itself in Format Two), a tape in Format Two will contain all input sentence records satisfying retrieval questions that had been accompanied by a tape output instruction (§ § 7.5.4; 7.13). Moreover, any terminal file on an input tape will be transcribed onto the output tape. However, sense switch settings (§ 7.13) control whether title records and end-of-file marks found on the input tape(s) will be transcribed onto the output tape.

§ 19.4. Sentence Records

Sentence records are of variable format as tabulated here, and of no more than 1800 characters in length (§ 5.10). Except for the insertion of 99 initial positions and the omission of first tag occurrences in the tag string, a sentence record will, with respect to format and data, be identical with a record on the antecedent (or ultimately antecedent) tape in Format One (§ 18.3).

Positions	*Contents*
1-99	Code characters and blanks (§ 19.5).
100 to x+100	Same as in positions 1 to x+1 in the sentence record on the antecedent tape in Format One (§ 18.3).
x+101 to end of record	Tag string beginning in positions x+2 of the sentence record on the antecedent tape in Format One (§ 18.3) except for the omission of first occurrences of each tag in each syntax position, as described in § 19.5.

§ 19.5. Positions 1-99 of Sentence Records

Positions 1-99 of sentence records correspond, respectively, to tags 1-99. A blank in any one of these positions indicates that the tag which corresponds in number to that position did not appear in the tag string in Format One. But if one of the fifteen code characters to be tabulated here appears in any of these positions, it indicates that the tag occurred at least once in a particular syntax position. The code character tells whether the occurrence was marked with an S, V, Ø, or U, or with some combination of two or three of these syntax markers, or with all four of them. For example, if the code character G is written in position 88 of a given TEXT-TAG LIST sentence record, tag 88 must have appeared in the tag string of the antecedent TAGGING record with at least one S, one Ø, and one U marker (but without a V marker).

Furthermore, TEXT-TAG LIST omits from its own tag string (§ 19.4, positions x+101 to end of record) all first occurrences whose presence is identified by a code character in positions 1-99. Thus, in the example just given, 88 will be removed from the tag string three times. However, if 88S happened to have appeared twice in the tag string of the antecedent TAGGING record, the occurrence of the second 88S will not be implied by code character G and the second 88S will therefore be written as such in the tag string of the Format Two record.

The code characters which can appear in positions 1-99 of TEXT-TAG LIST sentence records are as follows:

Code Character	*Tag Occurring with Syntax Marker(s):*				*Code Character*	*Tag Occurring with Syntax Marker(s):*			
A	S				I	V			
B	S	V			J	V		Ø	
C	S		Ø		K	V			U
D	S			U	L	V		Ø	U
E	S	V	Ø		M			Ø	
F	S	V		U	N			Ø	U
G	S		Ø	U	O				U
H	S	V	Ø	U					

§ 19.6. Title Records

Whenever title records occur on a tape in Format One (§ 18.4), they will be transcribed onto the tape in Format Two. In content and format, each transcribed title record will be identical with its antecedent on the tape in Format One, except that 99 blank positions will be inserted before the dollar sign ($). But see § 19.3.

§ 19.7. End-of-File Marks

Whenever end-of-file marks occur on a tape in Format One (§ 18.5), they are transcribed onto the tape in Format Two. But see § 19.3.

§ 19.8. Terminal File

When reached, the terminal file of a tape in Format One (§ 18.6) will be transcribed onto the tape in Format Two, but 99 blank positions will be inserted before the asterisk (*) in the sole record of this file. An end-of-file mark will be written after the asterisk record of the terminal file.

CHAPTER 20

Format Three

§20.1. System Considerations

A tape written in the format described in this chapter can only be generated by TAG TALLY (§ 6.1) from a tape in Format Two (§ 19.1) and can serve as input only to SUMMARY PUNCH (§8.1) and TRANSPOSE (§9.1).

§20.2. Contents

On this tape will be written sets of six consecutive records—one set for each input document file for which sense switch D had been set up (§ 6.10). In each set of six records, the first will contain some identifying information; the second through sixth will contain ten scores (§ 6.2)—four subtotal raw scores and one raw score total, four subtotal index scores and one index score total—for every tag that appears in a tag string of any sentence record (§ 19.4) in one input document file. In short, each set of six records contains the same scores as would a tag tally table for the given document (Figure 6.A). As in the case of scores printed in these tables, the setting of sense switch G (§ 6.8) controls whether sentence-count or word-count scores will be written in every set of six records on this TAG TALLY output tape.

The only end-of-file mark on the tape is written after the last set of six records. There are no title records (§ 19.6) on this tape.

§20.3. Format of the First Record

The first record in each six-record set has the following format:

Positions	*Contents*
1-6	Total number of sentences in document if sense switch G was set up (§ 6.8); or total

Positions	Contents
1-6 (cont.)	number of words in document if sense switch G was set down.
7	Blank.
8-77	Document-identification code (§ 3.6) of the document for which tag-assignment scores are recorded in the second through sixth records (§ 20.4) of this six-record set.

§ 20.4. Format of Second Through Sixth Records

Each of the second through fifth records in every six-record set contains twenty 34-position fields. The twenty 34-position fields in the second record correspond to tags 01-20; the twenty in the third record to tags 21-40; the twenty in the fourth record to tags 41-60; the twenty in the fifth record to tags 61-80. The sixth record contains only nineteen 34-position fields, which correspond to tags 81-99.

The format of every 34-position field in the second through sixth records of every six-record set is as follows:

Positions	Contents
1-2	Tag (01-99).
3-5	Raw score subtotal for this tag with syntax marker S.
6-8	Raw score subtotal for this tag with syntax marker V.
9-11	Raw score subtotal for this tag with syntax marker Ø.
12-14	Raw score subtotal for this tag with syntax marker U.
15-18	Total raw score for this tag.
19-21	Index score subtotal for this tag with syntax marker S.
22-24	Index score subtotal for this tag with syntax marker V.
25-27	Index score subtotal for this tag with syntax marker Ø.
28-30	Index score subtotal for this tag with syntax marker U.
31-34	Total index score for this tag.

CHAPTER 21

Format Four

§21.1. System Considerations

A tape written in the format described in this chapter can only be generated by TRANSPOSE (§ 9.1) from a tape in Format Three (§ 20.1) and can serve as input only to GRAPH (§ 10.1), SORTED TRANSPOSE (§ 11.1), and MEANS-DEVIATION (§ 12.1).

§21.2. Contents

This tape consists of a header record containing control-card specifications (§ 9.4), and a series of logical records containing for all tags the scores of the type specified on the control card (§ 9.4, columns 7-8). The header record is a physical record. Logical records are divided into physical records of fixed length (§ 21.5). The only end-of-file mark on the tape follows the last logical record.

Each logical record contains for a single tag one score from each six-record set (§ 20.2) on the antecedent tape in Format Three. Each score in a logical record therefore applies to a different document. Within every logical record, the score for a given document occurs in the order in which the six-record set for that document was encountered on the antecedent tape in Format Three.

Each score in a logical record is immediately followed by the total number of sentences or words in the document to which the score applies. This total is transcribed from the first record (§ 20.3, positions 1-6) in that particular six-record set on the antecedent tape from which the given score was also transcribed. The total is in each case immediately followed by the document-identification code (§ 3.6) of the document to which the given score applies. All codes in all logical records on the tape will consist of as many of the characters that are recorded in positions 8-77 of a first record (§ 20.3) on the Format

Three tape as are specified by the character X in corresponding columns of the TRANSPOSE control card (§9.4, columns 11-80).

There will be as many logical records on the tape as the number of tags specified on the control card (§9.4, columns 1-3). The logical records will be in ascending (though not necessarily consecutive) tag order (01-99). There will be as many scores in each record as the number of documents specified on the control card (§9.4, columns 4-6).

§21.3. Format of Header Record

The header record will be a physical record containing much the same information as had been keypunched on the control card (§9.4). The header record will have the same number of positions as every other physical record on the tape (§21.5).

The format of the header record is:

Positions	*Contents*
1-3	Number of processed tags (§9.4, columns 1-3).
4-6	Number of processed documents (§9.4, columns 4-6).
7-9	Six plus the number of characters to be written in all document-identification codes on the tape—that is, six plus the number of columns on the control card in which the character X was keypunched (§9.4, columns 11-80).
10	The character R if all scores on the tape are raw scores; the character I if all scores on the tape are index scores (§9.4, column 7).
11	S, V, Ø, U, or T as in the control-card specification (§9.4, column 8) of the type of raw or index score to be transcribed onto the tape.
12-27	TRANSPOSE OUTPUT
28 to end of record	Enough blank positions to make the header record equal in length to every other physical record on the tape (§21.5).

§21.4. Format of Logical Records

Each logical record begins with the tag (*a*) to which all scores written in the record apply. After the tag follow *n* three-entry groups, where *n* is the number of processed input documents as specified in the header record (§ 21.3, positions 4-6). The three entries in each group are:

b. A three-character subtotal score for tag *a* if position 11 of the header record (§ 21.3) contains S, V, Ø, or U; or a four-character total score for tag *a* if position 11 of the header record contains T. All scores in all logical records will be of the single type specified on the control card (§ 9.4, columns 7-8).

c. A six-character total of the number of sentences or words in the document specified in entry *d* (cf. § 20.3, positions 1-6).

d. The document-identification code of the document to which the score for tag *a* in entry *b* of this group applies (cf. § 20.3, positions 8-77, and § 9.4, columns 11-80). The number of characters in all codes in all logical records is specified in the header record (§ 21.3, positions 7-9).

Thus, the over-all format of each logical record on a single tape may be summarized as:

$$a\,(bcd)_1\,(bcd)_2\,(bcd)_3\,\ldots\,(bcd)_n$$

§ 21.5. Division of Logical Records into Physical Records

Logical records are automatically divided into physical records of up to 400 characters each. Breaks in logical records will be between entries *b* or *c* or between entry *d* of one three-entry group and entry *b* of the next. The last physical record in any logical record will have a dollar sign ($) as its last character; any other physical record (except the header record) will have an asterisk (*) as its last character.

CHAPTER 22

Format Five

§22.1. System Considerations

A tape written in the format described in this chapter can be generated only by SORTED TRANSPOSE (§ 11.1) from a tape in Format Three (§ 21.1) and can serve as input only to GRAPH (§ 10.1) and MEANS-DEVIATIONS (§ 12.1).

§22.2. Contents

This tape consists of a single header record followed by one logical record for each tag. The logical records are identical in content and format with those on the antecedent tape in Format Four (§ 21.2). However, tag scores are written within each logical record in the sorted order specified on control cards (§ § 11.5-11.6).

§22.3. Header Record

The header record will be identical in format and content with the header record of the antecedent tape in Format Four (§ 21.3) except in two ways: first, in positions 12-27 the words SORTED TRANSPOSE will be written; second, the record will be 130 positions in length with positions 28-130 blank.

§22.4. Format of Logical Records

Logical records will be identical in format and content with those on the antecedent tape in Format Four, as described in § 21.4. However, the *n* three-entry groups of which each logical record is composed will be written in the sorted order specified on control cards (§ § 11.5-11.6).

For example, if the sequence of groups in each logical record of the tape in Format Four began:

$$a\,(bcd)_1\,(bcd)_2\,(bcd)_3\,(bcd)_4\,(bcd)_5\,(bcd)_6\,\ldots$$

the sequence in each logical record of the tape in Format Five might begin:

$$a\,(bcd)_4\,(bcd)_6\,(bcd)_3\,(bcd)_5\,(bcd)_2\,(bcd)_1\,\ldots$$

as dictated by the contents of entry *d* (the document-identification code in each group) and by the SORTED-TRANSPOSE control-card specifications (§ § 11.5-11.6).

§22.5. Division of Logical Records into Physical Records

Logical records will automatically be divided into physical records of equal length according to the rules specified in § 21.5.

CHAPTER 23

Formats Six, Seven, and Eight

§23.1. System Considerations

A tape in Format Six can be generated by KWIC RECORDS (§ 13.1) and then processed by a standard sort program or by KWIC BLOCKS (§ 14.1). A tape in Format Seven can be generated by KWICK BLOCKS or by a standard sort program and then processed by KWIC PRINT-STATISTICS (§ 15.1). A physical record in Format Six is transcribed as a logical record in Format Seven; 45 such logical records constitute a single physical record in Format Seven. Format Eight bears no similarity to Formats Six and Seven.

§23.2. Format Six

A tape in Format Six consists of a series of 132-position physical records, each in the format described here. An end-of-file mark follows the last record of every tape generated in a single KWIC RECORDS run (§ 13.7).

Positions	*Contents*
1-2	Blank.
3-41	Text, if any, that immediately preceded the key word that begins in position 42. The text in this field will always begin with a whole word.
42-81	Key word and the text, if any, that immediately followed it. The text in this field will always conclude with a whole word.
82	Blank.
83-102	No more than 19 characters of the sentence-identification code (§ § 3.8; 13.9) of the sentence in which the last word within posi-

Positions	Contents
	tions 42-81 occurred, provided the code for that sentence was keypunched on the very card from which that last word was transcribed. If this restriction is not met, positions 83-102 will be blank.
103	Blank.
104-132	Image of columns 2-30 of the title card (§ § 3.4; 13.2.3) for the document in which the key word that begins in position 42 occurred.

§ 23.3. Format Seven

A tape in Format Seven consists of a series of physical records, each of which is comprised of 45 logical records. Each logical record will be 132 characters in length and will contain the same information in the same format as does a physical record on the antecedent tape in Format Six (§ 23.2). An end-of-file mark follows the last physical record of every tape generated in a single KWIC BLOCKS run (§ 14.6.2). If the last physical record produced in a given run contains only n logical records, where n is less than 45, the padding character Z will be written in the final (132) (45-n) positions of that physical record.

§ 23.4. Format Eight

A tape in Format Eight contains one 72-position physical record for each different key word on the tape(s) in Format Seven (§ 23.3) processed by KWIC PRINT-STATISTICS. Each record contains a different key word and the four scores for that word's frequency and distribution printed in that word's statistical entry in the index (§ 15.6). An end-of-file mark follows the last record of every tape generated in a single KWIC PRINT-STATISTICS run (§ 15.8.2). The format of each 72-position record is:

Positions	Contents
1-50	Key word to which the four scores in this record refer.
51-56	Frequency raw score.
57-61	Frequency index score (see § 15.2.4).
62-64	Distribution raw score (see § 15.2.3).
65-69	Distribution index score (see § 15.2.4).
70-72	Blank.

APPENDIX TWO

CARD FORMATS

CHAPTER 24

Tag-Name Cards

§24.1. Contents and System Considerations

Each tag-name card contains a tag and its name. Sets of tag-name cards form part of the input deck for programs that generate listings in which tags are to be labeled by their respective names. These programs are TEXT-TAG LIST (§ 5.4), GRAPH (§ 10.7), MEANS-DEVIATIONS (§ 12.6), and CROSS-SORT LIST (§ 17.5).

For TEXT-TAG LIST, MEANS-DEVIATIONS, and CROSS-SORT LIST, the set of tag-name cards need only consist of as many cards as the number of different tags which may be encountered in the input data. These cards may be arranged in any order. However, for GRAPH, the cards should be in ascending sequence by tag number, and dummy (blank) cards should be inserted for intermediate unused numbers.

§24.2 Format

The format of tag-name cards is as follows:

Card Columns	*Contents*
1-2	Tag (if one digit, supply leading zero).
3	Blank.
4-15	Name of the tag in columns 1-2.
16-80	Ignored.

CHAPTER 25

Summary Cards

§25.1. Contents and System Considerations

For each document on an input tape in Format Two (§19.2), TAG TALLY can, at the investigator's option (§6.11), produce a set of seven summary cards containing total *index* scores based on either a sentence or word count, as specified by the setting of sense switch G (§6.8). For each document on an input tape in Format Three (§20.2), SUMMARY PUNCH can produce one set of seven summary cards for each type of *raw* score specified by the settings of sense switches B-F (§8.5). The scores punched by SUMMARY PUNCH during a given run will be either sentence-count or word-count raw scores, depending on the setting of sense switch G during the TAG TALLY run in which the input tape in Format Three had been generated (§8.2).

The summary cards punched by TAG TALLY and SUMMARY PUNCH are identical in format, except for the seventh card in each seven-card set (§25.4). The first card in each set of seven contains identifying information only; the six remaining cards contain the tag scores.

§25.2. Format of Card One

The format of the first summary card in each set of seven for a given document is as follows:

Card Columns	*Contents*
1-9	First nine characters of the document-identification code (§3.6) of the document to which the tag scores to be punched in cards two through seven of this set apply. See columns 11-79 of this card.

Card Columns	*Contents*
10	Sequence number of this card (=1) in the set of seven for the document specified in columns 1-9.
11-79	The entire document-identification code (§3.6) of the document to which the tag scores to be punched in cards two through seven of this set apply. See columns 1-9 of this card.
80	Score indicator—that is, the type of scores punched in the second through seventh cards in the set—according to the following key. Note that a blank in column 80 indicates TAG TALLY output (§6.11) but any (numeric) punch indicates SUMMARY PUNCH output (§8.4). Blank=Total index scores. 1=Raw score subtotals for tags assigned with syntax marker S. 2=Raw score subtotals for tags assigned with syntax marker V. 3=Raw score subtotals for tags assigned with syntax marker Ø. 4=Raw score subtotals for tags assigned with syntax marker U. 5=Total raw scores.

§25.3. Format of Cards Two through Six

Each of the second through sixth summary cards in the set of seven for a given document can contain scores for seventeen tags punched in the following format:

Card Columns	*Contents*
1-9	Same document-identification-code characters as in columns 1-9 of card one of this set (§25.2).
10	Sequence number of this card (=2,3,4,5, or 6) in the set of seven for the document specified in columns 1-9.
11-78	Seventeen four-column fields, each field con-

Card Columns	*Contents*
	taining the type of score specified in column 80 for a single tag assigned to sentences in the document specified in columns 1-9. Every score is right-adjusted within its field and preceded by leading zeros, if necessary. The series of tags for which the scores are punched on a given card depends on the sequence number in column 10 of that card according to the following key:

If column 10= { 2, 3, 4, 5, 6 } columns 11-78 contain the scores for { tags 01-17, tags 18-34, tags 35-51, tags 52-68, tags 69-85 }

79	Blank.
80	Same score indicator as in column 80 of card one of this set (§ 25.2).

§25.4. Format of Card Seven

The seventh and last summary card in the set for a given document differs in format from the second through sixth cards (§ 25.3) in that it specifies the total number of words or sentences in the document identified in columns 1-9 and can itself contain scores for only fourteen tags. There is a slight difference between the format of a seventh card as generated by TAG TALLY (§ 25.4.1) and that of a seventh card as generated by SUMMARY PUNCH (§ 25.4.2).

§ *25.4.1. Format of Card Seven when Generated by TAG TALLY.* When generated by TAG TALLY, card seven will have the following format:

Card Columns	*Contents*
1-9	Same document-identification-code characters as in columns 1-9 of card one of this set (§ 25.2).
10	Sequence number of this card (=7) in the set of seven for the document specified in columns 1-9.
11-66	Fourteen four-column fields containing the type of score specified in column 80 for

Card Columns	*Contents*
	tags 86-99, as assigned to sentences in the document specified in columns 1-9. Every score is right-adjusted within its field and preceded by leading zeros, if necessary.
67-71	Total number of sentences in the document identified in columns 1-9, if the scores punched in cards two through seven of this set were computed on the basis of a sentence count (§6.2); otherwise, blank.
73-77	Total number of words in the document identified in columns 1-9, if the scores punched in cards two through seven of this set were computed on the basis of a word count (§6.2); otherwise, blank.
79	Blank.
80	Same score indicator as in column 80 of card one of this set (§25.2).

§*25.4.2. Format of Card Seven when Generated by SUMMARY PUNCH.* When generated by SUMMARY PUNCH, columns 1-66 and columns 79-80 of card seven will be as described in §25.4.1, but columns 67-78 will be as follows:

Card Columns	*Contents*
67-72	Blank.
73-78	Total number of words or sentences in the document identified in columns 1-9, depending on the number written in positions 1-6 of the first record for that document on the input tape (§20.3).

APPENDIX THREE

PROCESSING OF DEFECTIVE RECORDS ON INPUT TAPES

CHAPTER 26

Processing of Defective Records on Input Tapes

§26.1. System Considerations

Data stored on a magnetic tape that has become dirty or creased, or from which the oxide coating has been worn thin, will usually prove illegible when the tape is used as input to a computer program. In very rare cases, machine malfunction during the writing of data upon an output tape can, when the tape is used as input to another program, also produce the same result. A defect of this type, whatever its origin, is usually localized in a small portion of the tape and thus affects relatively small amounts of data.

The eleven General Inquirer programs for the IBM 1401 which read input from magnetic tape follow standardized procedures for processing defective records[1] that are encountered on an input tape. There are three different procedures (§ §26.2-26.4), each one applying to a different group of programs. The three procedures share, insofar as practicable, certain general features. First, under all three procedures a program will make 30 attempts to correct the defect by backspacing the input tape and rereading the defective area. (Such multiple backspacing-rereading will sometimes remove dust or straighten a crease.) Second, if these attempts to correct the defect fail, those programs which follow procedure one or three (§ §26.2; 26.4) will either automatically or at the investigator's option attempt to use data in the defective record for processing. Third, under all procedures, printed messages apprise the

[1] Technically, a defective record is one which contains one or more characters with incorrect parity. This condition is sometimes termed a "redundancy error."

investigator of the location both of every defective input record and, if appropriate, of any output data derived from a defective input record. Always noted at the end of a run is the total number of defective input records encountered.

§26.2. Procedure One

Procedure one is followed by these programs:

RETRIEVAL (§§19.1-19.8)
SUMMARY PUNCH (§§20.1-20.4)
TRANSPOSE (§§20.1-20.4)
SORTED TRANSPOSE (§§21.1-21.5)
KWIC BLOCKS (§§23.1-23.2)

The sections just cited are those in which formats of the pertinent *input* tapes are described in detail.

When one of these programs encounters on an input tape a defective record which cannot be corrected by multiple backspacing-rereading (§26.1), an image of the first 132 positions of that record is printed out by the 1403 printer on a separate page. The message BAD RECORD–PRESS START TO BYPASS is printed out immediately after the image of the bad record, but the program then halts. If START is pressed on the 1401, the program resumes and the defective record will be ignored. But if START RESET and START are pressed, the program will attempt to use all data written in the defective record. Also, the message BAD INPUT RECORDS ENCOUNTERED = will be printed out just before the run is terminated. The equals sign will be followed by the total number of defective records encountered during the run.

§26.3. Procedure Two

Procedure two is followed by TEXT-TAG LIST and TAG TALLY, the input tape formats of which are described in §§18.1-18.6 and §§19.1-19.8, respectively.

When one of these programs encounters on an input tape a defective record which cannot be corrected by multiple backspacing-rereading (§26.1), the entire defective record is printed out but otherwise ignored by the program, and processing continues without interruption. Also, the message, BAD INPUT RECORDS NOT PROCESSED = will be printed out just before the run is terminated. The equal sign will be followed by the total number of defective records encountered during the run.

§26.4. Procedure Three

Procedure three is followed by these programs:

GRAPH (§§21.1-22.5 or §§22.1-22.5)
MEANS-DEVIATIONS (§§21.1-21.5 or §§22.1-22.5)
KWIC LIST (§23.3)
CROSS-SORT LIST (§§16.7-16.7.5)

The sections just cited are those in which formats of the pertinent input tapes are described in detail.

When one of these programs encounters on an input tape a defective physical record that cannot be corrected by multiple backspacing-rereading (§26.1), the program attempts to display all data in, or derived from, that record in its usual print format (Figures 10.A; 12.A; 15.A; 17.A). However, every printed line derived from any part of the defective physical record will be labeled BAD RECORD near the right margin of the page. Any line so labeled may contain incorrect information. Also, the message TOTAL BAD TAPE RECORDS PROCESSED = will be printed out just before the run is terminated. The equals sign will be followed by the total number of bad physical records encountered during the run.

APPENDIX FOUR

SENTENCE-SUMMARY PROCEDURES

CHAPTER 27

Sentence-Summary Procedures

§27.1. Introduction

After looking up the last word of a sentence, TAGGING (§4.2) is ready to write the text of the sentence, the tags assigned to it, and various other information in an output tape record in Format One (§§1.8; 18.3). At just this instant, before the sentence record is written, the investigator may wish to have the tags or the sentence-identification code tested and, on the basis of the test results, make additions or changes to the tag string or write a special message on the Program-Audit tape. Such optional, final steps of the tagging operation are referred to (§4.5) as "sentence-summary procedures."

TAGGING's sentence-summary capabilities are based on nine generalized test and command functions (§§27.3-27.11). These generalized functions, which are part of the program itself, can be used by the investigator when formulating specific sentence-summary rules in accordance with his own research concerns. The investigator's rules must be implemented in a standard programming language, such as FORTRAN, MAD, or BALGOL. Thus, unlike the rest of the General Inquirer system, the sentence-summary procedures require of the investigator some programming knowledge. While this knowledge is easily acquired, the novice may want to obtain the assistance of an experienced programmer in order to check his rules.

The steps necessary to incorporate a set of sentence-summary rules into the main TAGGING program are described at the end of this appendix (§§27.12-27.13).

§27.2. Scanning of the Tag String

TAGGING has a mechanism for scanning the string of assigned tags for specified tag occurrences. The scanning, which is used in most of the tag functions (§ §27.3-27.8) usually proceeds from left to right—that is, from those tags assigned first to those assigned last. The tags may be scanned as many times as necessary. The program uses a "pointer" to keep track of the current position in the scan.

TEST AND COMMAND FUNCTIONS

§27.3. OCCUR1 (Tag, Syncode)

This test function resets the pointer to the first tag in the string, and then searches down the string for the tag specified in the tag argument. The tag argument must be a two-digit integer (01-99). The "syncode" argument must be a single digit which specifies syntax restrictions (§ §2.9; 3.12.1) according to the following key:

1=Syntax marker must be U.
2=Syntax marker must be S.
3=Syntax marker must be V.
4=Syntax marker must be Ø.
0=No syntax marker restriction.

The OCCUR1 function advances the pointer down the list of tags until that combination of tag and appended syntax marker is found that satisfies the two arguments specified by the investigator. If such a combination is found, the pointer stops at that tag, and the IBM 7094 accumulator register ("AC") is set to 1. But if the end of the tag string for a sentence is reached without the test being satisfied, the pointer is left at the end of the string and the accumulator register is set to plus zero.

§27.4. PUT (Tag, Syncode)

This command function causes a tag to be added to the end of the current string of assigned tags. This tag will be included when the sentence and its tags are written on tape, and it will be printed by TEXT-TAG LIST (§5.7) at the end of the tag string for the sentence. The number (01-99) of the tag is specified in the first argument. The syncode argument must be a 1, 2, 3, or 4, with these numbers controlling the same syntax markers as in an OCCUR1 test (§27.3). A zero (0), if used as a PUT syncode, will be treated as a one (1)—that is, as referring to the unclassified marker U.

The functions OCCURI and PUT, taken together, allow for checking and noting of co-occurrences in the string of tag assignments. Suppose, for example, we wanted to add tag 93U to any sentence that already contained tag 34 (with any syntax marker) and tag 72 (with any marker). Using FORTRAN IV, we would then write the statement:

```
IF (OCCUR1 (34,0) .AND.OCCUR1 (72,0)) CALL PUT (93,1)
```

The same statement could be written in MAD as:

```
WHENEVER OCCUR1. (34,0) .AND. OCCUR1. (72,0), PUT. (93,1)
```

The differences between these two statements are simply a matter of language conventions. Both allow the two tags to occur in any order, with any number of tags intervening between them.

§27.5. OCCUR2 (Tag, Syncode)

This test function is the same as OCCUR1 (§ 27.3), except that the pointer is not reset to the beginning of the tag string. If the pointer had stopped at a certain tag as a result of a previous OCCUR function, the OCCUR2 search would begin with the next tag and would then continue down the string. Thus, an OCCUR2 test is for a tag and appended syntax marker anywhere in the remaining part of the sentence. The tag and syncode arguments for OCCUR2 are exactly the same as for OCCUR1.

Assume, for example, that we were interested in sentences that have tag 07 in the syntax position of subject—tag 07S—followed by tag 37 in a verb position—tag 37V. The rule to find such sentences would be written in FORTRAN IV as:

```
IF (OCCUR1 (07,2) .AND. OCCUR2 (37,3)) CALL PUT—
```

A match would be made only if the tags occurred in this order, not if they were in reverse order. If the pointer reached the end of the tag string before both test functions were satisfied, the accumulator would not be set to 1, and the call to the function PUT would not be made.

§27.6. OCCUR3 (Tag, Syncode, Range)

This test function is the same as OCCUR2 (§ 27.5), except that an additional argument, "range," limits the distance that will be scanned before the test is considered to have failed. The range argument is specified as a number of text words rather than a number of tags. Just before beginning an OCCUR3 search, the program determines which word had been assigned the tag at which the pointer is currently located; then, in executing the OCCUR3 search, the program notes whenever it has scanned the last tag that had been assigned to that and subsequent words. The test fails and the scan stops if the tag and syntax marker specified in the first two arguments (tag, syncode) have not been found when the pointer reaches either the last tag assigned to the nth following word (where n is the specified range argument) or the end of the entire tag string. (When a test fails for either of these reasons, the accumulator is set to plus zero.) If the range argument is zero (0), the search will not advance beyond the last tag of the word to which the last tag found had been assigned. If the range argument is one (1), the search can continue through all tags assigned to the next word. If the specified tag and appended syntax marker are found within the specified range, the pointer stops at the matching tag, and the accumulator is set to 1.

On the basis of the example given in §27.5, the use of OCCUR3 would allow us to specify that tags 07S and 37V must occur not only in that order but within three words of text. In FORTRAN IV the rule would be written:

```
IF (OCCUR1 (07,2) .AND. OCCUR3 (37,3,3)) CALL PUT—
```

§27.7. SKIP (Distance)

This command function moves the pointer the number of text words specified by the distance argument. If the argument is plus or unsigned, the pointer will be moved down the string. If the argument has a minus sign, the pointer will be moved back up the string. An argument of -0 will set the pointer back to the beginning of the current text word, so that the next tag searched will be the first tag assigned to that word. An argument of +0 moves the pointer to the end of the current word, so that a search would begin with the first tag of the next word. ("Skipping" ahead to the next word is a useful way of ignoring co-occurrences that result from including more than one tag in a dictionary instruction [§§2.9-2.12].) An argument of -5 would bring the pointer back five words; an argument of +5 (or 5) would move the pointer ahead five words. The pointer can be moved to words before the first tag that had been assigned to a sentence, and to words after the last tag in the string. To move the pointer to the beginning of the sentence, use SKIP (-1000); and to move the pointer as far ahead as possible, use SKIP (1000).

§27.8. REPLAC (Tag, Syncode)

This command function causes the tag and appended syntax marker specified by the arguments to replace those currently marked by the pointer. The arguments for REPLAC are the same as those for PUT (§27.4). If the syncode argument is zero (0), the syntax of the last tag will be erased rather than replaced. For example, the statement: IF (OCCUR1 (24,3) .AND. OCCUR2 (24,3)) CALL REPLAC (76,3) would cause tag 76V to replace the second occurrence in a sentence of tag 24V.

§27.9. SETAT: Scanning Attributive Tags

When attributive subscripts had been inserted into the text during editing (§3.12.3), all tags assigned to the sentence from the first word with an attributive subscript to the last such word are specially marked. Compare §18.3. Normally, these "attributive" tags, as well as all other tags, are searched and affected by any of the test or command functions described in §§27.3-27.8. But by means of the command function SETAT (2), the investigator can cause any subsequent test or command to be executed *only* upon the attributive tags. Similarly, the command SETAT (1) causes a search *only* of the "nonattributive" tags. *Both* kinds of tags will be searched if the command SETAT (0)–or no command whatsoever–is given. Note that the sequence of attributive and nonattributive tags will be the same as the sequence of the words to which they were assigned. Execution of PUT (§27.4) always results in the addition of a normal, nonattributive tag. Execution of REPLACE (§27.8) always causes either an attributive tag to be replaced by another attributive tag, or a nonattributive tag to be replaced by a nonattributive tag.

§27.10. PARAM

§*27.10.1. Testing Program Counts.* The function PARAM can be used to test any of nine counts which TAGGING automatically maintains as a run progresses. When so used, this function takes a one-digit argument, which specifies the count to be tested. The arguments are as follows:

1=Total number of documents so far processed in this run (see §4.32.2.f).

2=Total number of sentences so far processed in this run (see §4.32.2,f).

3=Total number of words so far processed in this run (see §4.32.2,f).
4=Total number of sentences so far processed in this document (see §4.24).
5=Total number of words so far processed in this document (see §4.24).
6=Number of attributive words in the current sentence (see §3.12.3).
7=Number of tags assigned to the current sentence (see §4.32.5, no. 19).
8=Number of words in the current sentence (see §4.32.5, no. 19).
9=Ordinal position in sentence of the word whose tags are currently being tested.

Thus, if a test were only to be executed upon a sentence containing more than ten words, a rule written in MAD might begin:

```
WHENEVER PARAM. (8) .GE. 10 .AND. OCCUR1. (42,3) .AND. OCCUR2. (53,4) . . .
```

§*27.10.2. Testing Sentence-Identification Codes.* The PARAM function can also be used to test the contents of a specified column of the sentence identification code (§3.8). In this case, the arguments 11-80 refer, respectively, to columns 1-70 of the identification field. For example, in FORTRAN IV:

```
IF (PARAM (14) .EQ. 7)—
```

would test whether the fourth column of the identification field contained a 7. (If the identification field for the current sentence had less than four columns, the last character of that field would be obtained.)

§27.11. OCWRIT: Writing Messages on the Program-Audit Tape

The command function OCWRIT permits the investigator to specify a message to be recorded on the Program-Audit tape (§4.33). OCWRIT may be used any number of times, but each OCWRIT message must be no longer than 126 characters.

Treatment of the OCWRIT function depends on the language in which the sentence-summary rules are programmed. In general, all actual literal messages that may later be recorded on the Program-Audit tape must be specified, storage space for them must be set up, and variable names must be assigned to each message. (These procedures require DIMENSION and DATA statements in FORTRAN IV and VECTOR VALUES statements in MAD.) Each OCWRIT function within the subroutine would take two arguments: first, the variable name of the specific literal message to be recorded on tape at that point; second, the number of characters in that message divided by six, rounded up, if necessary, to the next whole number.

Figure 27.A illustrates a FORTRAN IV sentence-summary subroutine in which OCWRIT functions are used to refer to messages that are labeled STMS and STM2 and had been set up in initial DIMENSION and DATA statements.

```
$IBFTC STSUD    FULIST,NUDD,DECK,M94,XR7
C TEST DECK SENTENCE SUMMARY --- RUN UNDER IBSYS (FORTRAN IV)
      SUBROUTINE STSUM
      EXTERNAL OCCUR1,OCCUR2,CCCUR3,PARAM
      LOGICAL OCCUR1,UCCUR2,OCCUR3
      INTEGER PARAM
      DIMENSION STMS(3), STM2(4)
       DATA STMS/18HMAIN PATTERN FOUND/,STM2/23HATTRIBUTE PATTERN FOUND/
      IF (OCCUR1(12,3) .OR. OCCUR1(13,3)) CALL PUT(16,0)
      IF (UCCUR2(52,2)) CALL REPLAC(53,0)
      IF (PARAM(6) .GE. 0) GO TO 2
    1 IF (OCCUR1(27,0) .AND. OCCUR3(29,1,3)) GO TO 4
      GU TU 3
    2 CALL SETAT(2)
      IF(OCCUR1(23,0) .AND. .NOT. OCCUR1(22,0)) CALL OCWRIT(STM2,4)
      CALL SETAT(1)
      GO TO 1
    4 CALL SKIP(-0)
      IF (OCCUR3(50,1,0)) CALL OCWRIT(STMS,3)
    3 RETURN
      END
```

FIGURE 27.A. Sentence summary subroutine written in FORTRAN IV. On language-dependent statements see §27.12.

TECHNICAL CONSIDERATIONS

§27.12. Compilation of Sentence-Summary Rules and Programming Document Summaries

The investigator's set of sentence-summary rules must be written in a computer language that compiles into relocatable binary and allows external functions. The rules should be written as a subroutine and can be compiled separately from the assembling of TAGGING itself (§4.43). In this way, sentence-summary rules can be recompiled quickly without having to reassemble the entire TAGGING program. If the rules are written in FORTRAN II, TAGGING should be assembled and run as a FAP program under FMS, and the five linkage instructions at the beginning of TAGGING should be modified accordingly. If the rules are in FORTRAN IV, TAGGING should be assembled and run as a MAP program under IBSYS, with no changes in the TAGGING source program.

An entire subroutine in FORTRAN IV is illustrated in Figure 27.A. Note that the subroutine must be called STSUM (§4.44). Only the functions OCCUR1, OCCUR2, OCCUR3, and PARAM must be identified as externals, since the other functions are called as subroutines. In some languages, OCCUR1, OCCUR2, and OCCUR3 must also be identified as logicals. Appropriate JOB cards and subroutine beginning and return cards must be placed on either side of the rules to form a complete subroutine. Language-dependent subroutine statements similar to those illustrated in Figure 27.A are also necessary if the sentence-summary rules are programmed in MAD, BALGOL, or some other language.

The programmer may implement a flagging strategy to save the results of tests upon previous sentences. This would permit document summaries to be generated at the end of each text document. Document-summary messages could be recorded by means of the OCWRIT function (§27.11).

§27.13. Removing and Replacing Dummy Sentence-Summary Subroutine

If the investigator implements sentence-summary procedures, the dummy sentence-summary subroutine at the beginning of the main TAGGING subprogram (§4.44) should be removed. This dummy subroutine is the first 13 cards of the source deck (labeled STSUD in columns 71-76) or the first two binary cards of the object deck. The dummy subroutine should be replaced if the investigator removes his own subroutine.